Leaps of Faith

Leaps of Faith

Sermons from the Edge

ROBERT J. DEAN

Foreword by Fleming Rutledge

RESOURCE *Publications* · Eugene, Oregon

LEAPS OF FAITH
Sermons from the Edge

Resource Publications
An Imprint of Wipf and Stock Publishers
199 W. 8th Ave., Suite 3
Eugene, OR 97401

www.wipfandstock.com

PAPERBACK ISBN: 978-1-5326-0412-6
HARDCOVER ISBN: 978-1-5326-0414-0
EBOOK ISBN: 978-1-5326-0413-3

Manufactured in the U.S.A.   FEBRUARY 1, 2017

For Anastasia and Nathanael

Contents

Foreword

Eight years ago, when I was teaching homiletics at Wycliffe College in Toronto, I had several particularly gifted students. We didn't have as much time for practice preaching as I would have liked, and there were a lot of students in my classes, so it took a while before we got to hear from them all. It was a memorable moment when a student whom I did not yet know arose to preach a sermon with the unforgettable title, "My Daddy Was a Pimp." I immediately recognized Robert Dean as one of those whom the Spirit raises up from time to time to be a genuinely *biblical* preacher.

It is more than a little perplexing that biblical preaching is so hard to find these days. Not only is it hard to find in the pulpit, it is hard to find congregations that expect it. It is as though no one even remembers what biblical preaching sounds like.

Now, what is meant by "biblical preaching"? Is the problem that to-day's sermons do not have biblical texts? Or do they fail because they are not peppered with declarations about what "the Bible says"? Or is the problem that they don't end with Billy-Graham-style altar calls? What is a "biblical sermon" anyway, and how does a biblical sermon function in our increasingly secular North American society, where so few today can even name the four Gospels?

The first thing to note is that many if not most sermons, especially in congregations that use a lectionary, *do* have a biblical text. The preacher will read the text and extrapolate from there. But this is not necessarily biblical preaching. More often than not, sermons today are collections of thoughts and illustrations, not always artfully deployed, assembled from various sources including the preacher's own experiences and the surrounding culture, and also from homiletical websites which tempt the preacher to cut and paste someone else's material. Such sermons are not biblical in the sense meant here. (Reader, I have heard thousands of these sermons from all over North America, Sunday after Sunday, for many decades.) A truly biblical sermon is likely to be wrested out of the preacher's gut, because the voice of God addresses us in ways that we do not expect, ways that challenge us in the deepest parts of our being. This action of the Word of God is what Robert Dean refers to in his title *Leaps of Faith*.

In some circles, preaching is still defined as "prophetic," just as it was in the late 60s and early 70s. This is not the same thing as a biblical sermon, because it differs from those of the ancient Hebrew prophets. They were pressed into service much against their wills. They did not volunteer for the job, and they suffered in it. Today's so-called prophetic sermons tend to be repetitions of what we might hear from secular activists, so often sure of being in the right while others are wrong. (I know; I was one of these subtly self-congratulatory "prophets" for many years.) The true prophet understands that the judgment he pronounces against society includes himself first of all.

A biblical sermon is one which dramatizes the startling power of the living Word of God. It is not an assemblage of assorted reflections, but a drama of the shocking irruption of the incarnate God into the mess we have made of his beloved world. A biblical sermon summons everyone *including the preacher* to a radical reorientation of values, not according to some vague notion of "inclusivity" to be determined by the right-thinking persons among us, but by the appearance of a Voice and a Power from another realm altogether. As the *numero uno* prophet and herald John the Baptist announces, "already the axe is laid to the root of the tree."

When you read Robert Dean's sermons, this is the sort of voice you will hear. It is a more friendly voice than that of John the Baptist, and often very funny, but it is bold in the same way. He understands his vocation to be always in the service of the God who surprises and unsettles us. His illustrations from ordinary life and popular culture, which always seem to be unmistakably his own—never borrowed—are there not in order to help us to see "the spiritual in the material," or "the extraordinary in the ordinary." Something very much greater and more specific than generic religiosity are at work in these sermons. The illustrations are there as disclosures of the active agency of the God who has made himself known to us as the God of Abraham, Isaac, and Jacob—the God and Father of the Lord Jesus Christ. The contemporary references are adroit and even "cool," but they are not there to hold our attention, or to entertain us, or to show off the preacher's knowledge of what's new. They are there to give us a shock of insight, a flash of revelation—God in action in the details of everyday life. Dean offers anecdotes and allusions with the ease of ordinary contemporary speech, but as he does so, the everyday examples are overtaken by another Voice, whether it be the trumpet call of I Corinthians 15 or the "still small voice" that spoke to Elijah. Thus the preacher seeks to be used as a vessel for the world-shattering, world-remaking Word of God.

The effort that Dean puts into crafting his sermons is very obvious. That's not the same thing as saying they are tedious—far from it, for he wears his learning lightly. But congregations appreciate it when they know their pastor works hard to interpret the Scripture. Sermons like this, heard on a regular basis, form a matrix in which everything that goes on in a local church is enabled to grow and develop. Combined with small Bible study groups during the week, this kind of deeply biblical preaching leads to congregational formation that is far deeper and more grounded than any kind of institutional program or process can produce. The Bible, being the very Word of God, has power for the creation of a new people, organically connected to the true Vine and to one another in a bond that cannot be destroyed, since it originates in the Word who is the Second Person of the blessed Trinity. The local congregation is the context in which Dean speaks, in his introduction, of "canon, church, and creation." The received canon of Scripture is meant, not for the supposedly autonomous individual, but for the people of God in fellowship with one another—for the ultimate benefit of the larger world beyond the church.

Robert Dean has written to me about the links that the preacher seeks to make between canon, church, and creation:

> Many of the connections come as surprises to me. It's a recur-
> ring experience as I'm wrestling with a text in the days leading
> up to the sermon wondering how it's all going to come together
> that I'll unexpectedly come across some story or detail, or some-
> thing will happen, etc. that connects in some type of profound
> and unforeseen way with the text. I don't think I'm making these
> connections, they are already there, and I receive them as gifts.

That's an apt description of the way in which the Word of God is being interpreted by the Spirit even as the preacher prepares. The links between the preacher, the Word, and those who will hear are being made by a tran- scendent power beyond the preacher's control. Only the Spirit knows whose ears will be opened. The sermon text, in the final analysis, simply escapes from the preacher and goes on its appointed way independent of any human agency.

A truly biblical sermon will always involve risk, even danger. Some- one's life may depend on this, John Wesley said of preaching a sermon, and Whitefield said that his vocation was "a dying man preaching to dying men."

Every sermon should be preached with that sort of commitment, that sort of boldness, that sort of last-ditch urgency. Robert Dean has shown himself willing to take such risks.

It is particularly valuable for preachers to read the sermons of other preachers. The sermons collected in this book have, to be sure, the particular individual voice of their author, and it would be a mistake for someone else to try to slip directly into that voice. Beginning preachers need to try out various ways of narrating the Great Story afresh until they find their own way. But reading sermons like these can call preachers, new and experienced alike, to a more intense engagement with Scripture, an engagement that can in turn result in a far more vivifying experience for their congregations. I hope that many preachers, as well as others who appreciate a sermon, will use this collection to strengthen their own commitment to the *ministerium Verbi divini*, the ministry of the divine Word of God.

Fleming Rutledge
October 2016

Acknowledgments

It is often said that it takes a village to raise a child. Transcribing this saying into a homiletical key, one could say it takes the whole company of the faithful to make a preacher. I am certainly no exception to the rule. The very existence of this collection of sermons is a testimony to the many gifts I have received through the hands and hearts of God's people.

Obviously, none of the sermons appearing in this book would have been possible apart from the congregations in which they were preached. I am grateful to the many congregations that have welcomed me into their pulpit. A cross-section of these congregations is represented in the pages of this book, but there are also many more that have entrusted me with the solemn responsibility and immense privilege of proclaiming the Word of God. I am thankful for their trust and hospitality.

It seems appropriate, however, to single out two congregations in particular. Upon returning from an overseas mission trip as a university student, I preached my first sermon at my home congregation of Byron United Church in London, Ontario. While no literary or theological masterpiece, the sermon did informally set in motion an organic process of discernment which solidified my sense of calling to the ministry of the Word. To this day, although I have been separated from the congregation by many miles and years, they continue to take a warm and encouraging interest in my ministry. For almost eight years, I served as a pastor at Good Shepherd Community Church in Scarborough. It was the people of Good Shepherd who ordained me to the ministry of Word and Sacrament, and, more than that, taught me to be a preacher and a pastor. They patiently endured a bevy of outlandish sermon titles and various experiments with style and genre as I attempted to find my voice. For the first half of my time at Good Shepherd I profited greatly from the mentorship of Paul Johansen. From Paul I learned the importance of exegeting not only the text, but also the congregation for the purpose of drawing the congregation's attention to the gracious work of the Holy Spirit in its midst.

My formation as a preacher is greatly indebted to the theological education I received, first, at Tyndale Seminary in Toronto and, following that, at Wycliffe College, a member institution of the Toronto School of Theology at the University of Toronto. Fred Penney graciously endured some of my earliest attempts to preach in his "Introduction to Preaching" course. John Rottman and Paul Wilson liberated me from methodological constraints by helping me to see that the Gospel is the proper subject of every sermon. While I have greatly benefited from the wisdom of these homileticians, if, as I argue in the Introduction, the area where canon, church, and creation overlap is the native habitat of preachers, then I must also give thanks for all of the teachers—theologians, biblical scholars, ethicists, apologists, and pastors—who have had a hand in my theological education. In particular, Victor Shepherd's passionate theology lectures presented a compelling example of theology in service of proclamation. At Wycliffe, I had the opportunity to write a doctoral dissertation on the theologies of Dietrich Bonhoeffer and Stanley Hauerwas. The importance of preaching for both Bonhoeffer and Hauerwas is frequently overlooked, but the interested reader will notice their influence, and that of their teacher, Karl Barth, throughout these sermons. My *Docktorvater*, Joseph Mangina, not only modelled what it means to be a theologian in service of the church, but also introduced me to the sermons of Fleming Rutledge. In her work, I discovered an eloquent witness to the loquacious Lord who encounters us in the Gospel. I had the privilege of studying with Fleming Rutledge when she was a visiting professor at Wycliffe in 2008. I am honored and deeply grateful that she was willing to provide the Foreword to this volume.

I owe some of my most fundamental rhetorical sensibilities to my parents, Tom and Ruth Dean, who are quite capable public-speakers in their own right. Under their influence I developed a love of reading, an intuitive grasp of dramatic narrative, and a recognition of the importance of speaking "slowly, clearly, and distinctly," all of which have served me well.

Over the course of preparing these sermons for publication I have come to discover that it is a great gift to be able to count a librarian among your friends. Armen Svadjian, a librarian at Tyndale Seminary, provided invaluable assistance in tracking down references which had seemingly disappeared in the mists of the time that had elapsed since some of these sermons were originally preached. Rachel Yousef and Robyn Elliott, two of my ablest theology students at Tyndale Seminary, and Barb Constable, a trusted colleague in ministry for many years at Good Shepherd, helped to prepare the manuscript for publication. Their careful reading, penetrating questions, and thoughtful suggestions have resulted in a stronger book. I am also thankful for those who read sections of the book and offered their comments and encouragement at earlier stages, including: Paul Johansen, David Schuchardt, Marian Nacpil, Glen Soderholm, Arthur Boers, Irene Devereaux, and Rebecca Idestrom. I am grateful to Wipf and Stock for being willing to take a chance on publishing a collection of sermons by a relatively young and unknown pastor-theologian from Canada. Finally, my wife Melissa remains my indefatigable cheerleader, grammatical con-science, and faithful partner in life's journey. This book is dedicated to our children Anastasia and Nathanael, who have just recently begun to notice the peculiarity of my calling as a pastor-theologian and are now asking the question, "What exactly does Daddy do?"

Introduction

"Leap of faith!" The deep bass of my father's voice resonated through the stairwell. For a five-year-old, five steps up from the bottom of the stairs might as well have been the summit of Everest. Yet there I was looking down at my dad as he stood on the landing at the bottom of the stairs, arms extended, proclaiming: "Leap of faith!" Perhaps the thick orange shag carpet would serve to cushion my fall and translate sure and certain doom into something less dramatic—like a mere handful of broken bones—should my father fail to catch me. Once again, his voice rang out, "Leap of faith!"

The steps the preacher must climb to enter the pulpit on a Sunday morning are in some ways strikingly similar to the steps that featured so prominently in my childhood game. In both contexts, the steps serve to bring to the fore that these are daring ventures characterized by the radical vulnerability of placing one's success and future in the hands of another. The great Swiss theologian Karl Barth was one who rightly recognized that there is hardly a more formidable challenge than the one placed before the preacher who is commissioned week after week with the task of speaking of God. Barth famously declared, "*As ministers we ought to speak of God. We are human, however, and so cannot speak of God. We ought therefore to recognize both our obligation and our inability and by that very recognition give God the glory.*"[1] The preacher in his or her speaking must, therefore, follow after God's own self-revelation in the hope that God himself will claim the preacher's words as his very own and, in so doing, make the sermon work. Talk about a leap of faith!

The documentary *Comedian* follows Jerry Seinfeld as he attempts to reinvent his stand-up act following the conclusion of his hit television series *Seinfeld*. At one point, Seinfeld describes the experience of being on stage

---

1. Barth, *Word of God*, 186 [italics original].

as being equivalent to standing before a room full of people in boxer shorts clothed only with a joke. Seinfeld's description of being a stand-up comic could easily stand in as a description of the experience of preaching. However, the preacher is clothed with the best "joke" of all—the Gospel! Sadly, we preachers struggle to trust the first-rate material we've been given. In the face of our fears of being found naked, it is perhaps not surprising that preachers would lose their nerve. Like the little child, who in response to his father's invitation to jump, slowly inches down one step at a time toward his father's outstretched arms, we preachers employ various means (such as apologetics, appeals to experience, rhetorical techniques, homiletical methods, etc.) in the attempt to avoid the risky leap of faith.[2] The result of such manoeuvring is the safety of a sermon that works regardless of whether God shows up.

Preachers who run the risk of appearing naked in the pulpit discover that to be clothed only in the Gospel is to be resplendently apparelled. Those who take the leap of faith discover connections they could never have imagined because the living God goes ever before us. Christians have employed various terms and phrases in the attempt to highlight these connections. One of these terms—canon—communicates that the text placed before the preacher is not a disparate collection of historical relics, but a unified witness to God's self-revelation to Israel and the church in the person of Jesus Christ. Another of these terms—church—tells us that what happens on a Sunday morning is not the voluntary assembly of a group of like-minded individuals, but the eschatological gathering of God's people who are being knit together in the body of the Messiah Jesus through the work of the Holy Spirit. A third term—creation—reminds us that the world cannot be reduced to the random forces and events of bare nature, but is storied by the purposes of the triune God, in whom it has its beginning, its continuing existence, and its end. The fecund region of overlap of canon, church, and creation is the natural habitat of the preacher. Actually, it is the natural habitat of all Christians, but it is the preacher who has the special privilege of naming and bringing to light for the community the various connections through which Christ constitutes our lives.

Preaching in such a manner should similarly summon listeners to their own leap of faith. Such a Gospel shaped re-narration of reality will open vistas to a new world. This world may appear absurd according to the prevailing standards of modern rationality, but those who make the leap of faith will discover that this strange new world is eminently habitable. The

---

2. The problem is not with any of these things *per se*, but rather lies in our failure as preachers to discipline our use of them in accordance with the logic and reality of the Gospel.

Christian faith is not irrational, rather it hangs together according to its own inherent rationality centered in the cross and resurrection of Jesus Christ. For this reason, Barth could criticize the great liberal theologians of the nineteenth century for failing to realize that "respectable dogmatics could be good apologetics."[3] Following Barth's line of argumentation, the sermons which follow are unabashedly theological. This does not mean, however, that they are necessarily dry or boring. In fact, theological speech that is dry or boring is speech that has lost sight of its proper subject, the inexhaustibly lively Lord of the Gospel. I hope this collection of sermons, in some small way, contributes to "the recovery of the sermon as the context for theological reflection."[4] In light of this aspiration, I have attempted to document my sources and acknowledge my intellectual debts by employing footnotes that identify some of my interlocutors. These notes may not be of interest to all readers, but they will hopefully present those who are interested with the opportunity to further pursue the theological conversation.

If preaching is to be truly reclaimed as a theological enterprise, it will involve the recognition that the sermon is an event which calls both the preacher and the congregation to risk taking a leap of faith. However, a truly theological understanding of preaching will press further to the recognition that these leaps of faith are predicated upon the leap of faith undertaken by Jesus Christ. He is the presence of the covenant-keeping God in the flesh, who through his faithfulness has reconciled humanity to God. It is my hope that these sermons would be unintelligible if this God does not exist.[5]

While it is my intention to allow the sermons to speak for themselves, a few words of orientation to the collection that follows could prove to be helpful. Each of the sermons was preached at a distinct time to a particular congregation, as indicated in the headings found at the beginning of each sermon. The sermons are therefore necessarily and unapologetically characterized by a certain degree of particularity. Where it seemed to me that the reader could benefit from additional insight into the context in which the sermon was delivered, I have provided such information in a footnote. The contextual nature of these sermons, however, does not need to stand as a roadblock to their comprehension. An analogous situation (and please note it is only an analogy) can be found in the letters of the apostle Paul that were written at a particular time and addressed to a particular people yet

3. Barth, *Humanity of God*, 20.

4. Hauerwas, *Cross-Shattered Church*, 12.

5. The grammar of this sentence reflects the saying of Cardinal Suhard popularized by Dorothy Day: "To be a witness does not consist in engaging in propaganda or even in stirring people up, but in being a living mystery; it means to live in such a way that one's life would not make sense if God did not exist." Coles, *Dorothy Day*, 160.

continue to speak to the church today. It is my hope that these sermons will be able to communicate through, rather than in spite of, their contextual character.

The sermons have been grouped into four sections. Admittedly these groupings are somewhat arbitrary. There are other ways the sermons could have been grouped and the reader is certainly free to read them in a different order according to their own interests. This is not to say there is no rationale for the divisions. The first part of the book, "Preaching in Extraordinary Time," largely consists of sermons preached during the season of the Christian calendar commonly referred to as "ordinary time." However, as the title suggests, when it comes to the ministry of the Word, there is no such thing as "ordinary" time. This title also allows me to include some sermons that were preached during other times of the Christian year, but are not obviously seasonal.

The second part of the book, "Preaching through the Christian Year," consists of sermons that are definitively situated within the church's annual pilgrimage with Jesus from Advent through Pentecost. While these sermons were preached to congregations that acknowledge the Christian year (or at the least the particular feast day on which the sermon was delivered), many of these congregations were not bound to any particular lectionary. As a result, readers from lectionary-based worshipping traditions will be confronted, in some cases, by the juxtaposition of Scripture passages and feast days that they may not have previously encountered.

While preaching is always occasional, the third section of the book, "Occasional Preaching," brings together sermons from a variety of occasions in which pastors are frequently called upon to preach. Some of these sermons find their home in the regular gathering of the worshipping congregation. Others are somewhat removed from Sunday morning, yet nonetheless are connected with important events in the life of the local congregation that are significant contexts for exercising one's vocation as a preacher.

The final section, "Preaching to Preachers," consists of two sermons that were delivered in the context of my role as a theology professor in the MDiv In-Ministry program at Tyndale Seminary in Toronto. The In-Ministry program is designed to give pastors who are serving in congregational contexts the opportunity to concurrently pursue theological education. These sermons are perhaps a little more demanding than those that have come before, geared as they are to preachers in a seminary context. It is also in these sermons where my theological understanding of the task of preaching comes most explicitly to the fore. For this reason, these two sermons could be read as a fitting epilogue to the book.

For the convenience of the reader, the location of Scriptural citations has been included in brackets within the text of the sermons. Scriptural citations are drawn from the NIV unless indicated otherwise, simply because this was the Bible translation utilized in most of the contexts where the sermons were originally preached. The sermons appear largely as they were preached, although there have been some minor editorial changes to reflect their new location on the written page. In this editing, I have strived to maintain a balance between observing the common grammatical conventions that make for pleasant reading and preserving a sense of the liveliness of texts written for oral performance. The heading for each sermon includes the Scripture readings associated with that particular sermon. The passage that features most prominently in the sermon is listed first. I would encourage readers to read the listed Scripture passages before engaging with the sermon. It may even prove fruitful to return to the passages a second time after reading the sermon.

May these sermons be for you, as they have been for me in preparing and preaching them, an instrument in the Spirit's hand in drawing you more deeply into the mystery of the fathomless depths of the Father's love for us in Christ through the leap of faith.

Part I

Preaching in Extraordinary Time

1

"My Daddy was a Pimp!" and Other Skeletons from the Closet

Good Shepherd Community Church

Scarborough, Ontario

Sunday, March 19, 2006

Genesis 12:10–20

"THE SAFEST PLACE TO be is in the center of God's will." I've heard that expression countless times from the pulpit and in conversation with well-meaning Christians. Yet the presence of a famine in the land at the beginning of our passage throws this pious platitude into question. After all, the passage follows closely upon the heels of the calling of Abram. At that time the LORD spoke to Abram saying, "Go from your country, your people and your father's household to the land I will show you. I will make you into a great nation and I will bless you; I will make your name great, and you will be a blessing. I will bless those who bless you, and whoever curses you I will curse; and all peoples on earth will be blessed through you" (Gen 12:1–3). In response to God's call, Abram packed up and left, but now in the very place of God's calling, Abram encounters famine. This famine sets the stage for two overarching questions around which the drama in our passage revolves: "Will God keep his outlandish promises?" and "Will the sojourning Abram and Sarai trust God to keep his word?"[1]

Abram and Sarai's response to the famine quickly provides us with the answer to the latter question. In the face of the threat of a food shortage, they quickly set aside the promise of God and sought security through their

---

1. These questions are a restatement of those raised by Brueggemann in *Genesis*, 125–26.

3

own devices by leaving the land of promise and traveling to Egypt. Standing on the border of the vast and powerful Egyptian empire, having left the land of promise behind, Abram and Sarai are left to ponder the question, "How do we ensure our survival within a potentially hostile culture?" For a people whose future rests upon the promises of God, it is the wrong question to be asking. Ensuring the survival of the chosen people is God's problem. The question that God's people should be asking is not "How do we ensure our survival?" but rather, "How do we faithfully respond to our calling in the midst of our current context?" But as we've seen, Abram has already left the Promised Land. He has already begun to travel down the road of unbelief and he has now been captured by fear.

It is at this moment that Abram opens his mouth to utter his first recorded words in Scripture: "Look. [Sarai.] We both know that you're a beautiful woman. When the Egyptians see you they're going to say, 'Aha! That's his wife!' and they'll kill me. But they'll let you live. Do me a favor: tell them you're my sister. Because of you, they'll welcome me and let me live" (Gen 12:11–13, MSG).[2] It's hard to say exactly how Abram was expecting his plan to function, but it probably hit a bit of a snag when Pharaoh, the ruler and most powerful man in all of Egypt, took Sarai into his harem. In exchange for taking Sarai into his harem, Pharaoh gave to Abram luxurious gifts and riches including servants, cattle, sheep, donkeys, and camels. If a contemporary filmmaker were to portray the scene he would probably show Abram cruising the streets in a shiny convertible, with gold chains around his neck, and a large feather sticking out of his purple suede hat. After all, that's how pimps are often depicted in television shows and movies, and anyone who peddles his wife in exchange for material goods can be considered nothing less than just that—a pimp!

Now when the Egyptians saw Abram's large herds and flocks, his camel train, and the many servants attending him, they might have thought that he was doing quite well for himself. However, those of us who have followed the story from the beginning know that Abram has placed the promises he has received in extreme jeopardy. As Abram sits in his tent surrounded by his numerous possessions, the promise hangs by not even a thread. Abram is far removed from the land of promise and the woman who is to be the mother of his children sleeps in another man's bed.

The church—the body of people that has been called out from the world to witness to the present and coming kingdom of God through their life together—has historically not fared much better than Abram in clinging

---

2. Ian Scott, a friend and Toronto-area pastor, has helped me to see the importance of carefully attending to the first words uttered by biblical figures.

to the promises of God. Sadly, the church has a less than sterling track record of standing on the promises of God, which includes numerous attempts throughout the ages to preserve its own future when resources were scarce or the surrounding culture menaced. When the Holy Roman Empire was threatened by the rise of Islam in the Middle Ages, rather than trusting in God's promises, the church sought to secure its borders and its future by taking up the sword—the Crusades began and the blood of the slaughtered cries out to this day. More recently in the middle of the last century the church in Germany, in an attempt to preserve its influence, entered into an unholy alliance with the state and quietly stood by as millions of Jews were sent to the gas chambers and the Nazi war machine spread its wings out across Europe. In South Africa, entire denominations made up of the ruling white population turned a blind-eye to the evils of apartheid. In our own time, it appears that the church in North America, out of concern for its continuing survival, may be in the process of selling itself out to our consumer-driven individualistic culture, marketing itself as one more service that exists to meet the entertainment and spiritual needs of today's discriminating shoppers.[3] The result of this trend is a generation of Christians who rather than being formed in the ways of following Jesus, jump from church to church seeking to find their next spiritual high and emotional fix. Ultimately, such a people are rendered incapable of embodying the reality of the kingdom when that reality stands in contrast to the agenda of a culture and country shaped by imperial self-promotion.

We see in each of these circumstances, much like the story of Abram himself, that whenever God's people are captivated by survival strategies or by the desire to preserve their place of influence or power, the people who were called to be a blessing end up becoming a curse. Compared to some of the examples that I just mentioned from the history of the church, the outbreak of what was possibly a sexually transmitted disease in Pharaoh's household ends up seeming relatively minor. Yet there was Abram, the one called to be a blessing to the nations, instead bringing a curse down upon one of those very nations through his faithlessness.

Now we cannot talk about Abram's failure to trust in God's promises and merely point to other congregations out there in the world and throughout history as examples of such failure. We must also point to ourselves. If we are going to claim for ourselves the calling of Abram and his initial faithful departure from the first part of Genesis chapter twelve, then we also have to be prepared to see ourselves in Abram's sojourn into Egypt.

3. For an insightful theological analysis of the church marketing movement see Kenneson and Street, *Selling Out the Church*.

The first part of Genesis 12, containing the call of Abram and God's promises of blessing, was the Old Testament reading at the first worship service in the history of Good Shepherd Community Church. On that Sunday, some twenty-five years ago, the sermon was entitled "Great Expectations" and the expectations for Good Shepherd certainly were great. In the months leading up to that first service, various newspapers and magazines ran articles which boldly pronounced a remarkable vision for Good Shepherd. There was talk of plans to construct a one thousand-seat sanctuary equipped with the latest in audio and video technology for the purpose of producing a weekly television broadcast. Good Shepherd was to be the site of a first-of-its-kind school of theology for lay people and was to function as a hub in North Toronto for training, equipping, and sending out local church leaders. From the articles I came across, it sounded like Good Shepherd was going to be a mega-church before there even was such a thing.

Would those who made such bold predictions some twenty-five years ago even recognize Good Shepherd Community Church as it exists today? Would they be disappointed by our motley crew of just over one hundred that is gathered here this morning? What would they think if they heard that we weren't even the largest congregation that met for worship on this property?[4]

What happened? Why didn't the vision materialize? Even though we're twenty-five years removed from the framing of that epic vision, we're still too close to come to a definite conclusion. From where we stand, we can't say with certainty whether the vision was compromised by a failure somewhere along the line on the part of the congregation and its leadership, or whether the lofty goals were even really part of the calling that God had laid upon this community. Of course, we also have to remember that these developments in the early history of Good Shepherd Community Church all unfolded within the context of an ugly dispute and ultimately a split with the denomination.[5] There are skeletons in our closet. Unbelief, compromise,

---

4. In the early-1990s, Good Shepherd entered into a condominium agreement (the first of its kind in Canada) with Milliken Chinese Community Church which allowed for the construction of new facilities and the sharing of property. As Asian immigrants began to arrive in increasing numbers in Scarborough in the late 1990s and into the new millennium, the size and scope of Milliken's ministry quickly surpassed that of Good Shepherd.

5. Good Shepherd Community Church was the result of a church plant by West Ellesmere United Church. The local land developer who made the parcel of land available on which the church building would be built established some conditions surrounding the transfer of the property that were not amenable to the United Church of Canada. The church planters, however, were convinced of their call and moved forward without the approval of the denomination.

and brokenness are a very real part of Good Shepherd's story, but then why should we expect our corporate life together to be any different from the experiences of our individual lives? Yes, there are skeletons in our closets and some of them may still be swaying on their hooks, having only been hung recently behind the closet door.

Fortunately for us the fulfillment of the promise does not rest in our hands—if we are faithless, God will remain faithful (2 Tim 2:13). In the story of Abram's sojourn down into Egypt, we see that God remained faithful to his promise even when Abram had not. When Abram had seemingly closed the door on his calling, God entered the story and opened the door to new life; God intervened, restoring Sarai to her husband and leading them both back into the Promised Land.

It's all rather scandalous, that God would intervene in such a way that the lying pimp would leave Egypt not only with his wife, but as an enormously wealthy man. In fact it's not just *rather* scandalous, it's *incredibly* scandalous, but it's grace through and through. Grace is scandalous. It catches us by surprise. It's hard for us to wrap our heads around. It's so scandalous that one biblical commentator who wrote a book on Genesis didn't even get it. Instead, he wrote, "In spite of Abram's failure of faith, God extends him grace and plunders the real criminal, Pharaoh, who we may presume would have killed Abraham to gratify his lust."[6] Grace is so shocking to this commentator that although he uses the word, he actually ends up denying its presence. He has to read his own meaning into the text, importing motives and filling in the blanks, to get around the fact that God has dealt graciously with the real scoundrel—Abram, the lying pimp. The commentator is so mired within the world of karma, where everyone always gets what they deserve, that he is unable to recognize the radical intrusion of grace.

In a recently published collection of autobiographical interviews, Bono, the unlikely prophet and lead-singer of the band U2, comments upon the distinction between grace and karma. Bono is quoted as saying:

> You see at the center of all religions is the idea of Karma. You know, what you put out comes back to you: an eye for an eye, a tooth for a tooth, or in physics—in physical laws—every action is met by an equal or an opposite one. It's clear to me that Karma is at the very heart of the Universe. I'm absolutely sure of it. And yet, along comes this idea called Grace to upend all that "As you

---

6. I have adapted a sentence about all three of the wife-sister episodes in Genesis to fit the context of the sermon. The original sentence reads, "In spite of the patriarchs' failure of faith, God extends them grace and plunders the real criminal, who we may presume would have killed Abraham to gratify his lust." Waltke, *Genesis*, 214.

reap, so will you sow" stuff. Grace defies reason and logic. Love interrupts, if you like, the consequences of your actions, which in my case is very good news indeed, because I've done a lot of stupid stuff . . . I'd be in big trouble if Karma was going to finally be my judge . . . It doesn't excuse my mistakes, but I'm holding out for Grace. I'm holding out that Jesus took my sins onto the Cross, because I know who I am, and I hope I don't have to depend on my own religiosity . . . It's not our own good works that get us through the gates of Heaven.[7]

If you prefer someone with somewhat of a more distinguished theological pedigree, consider the great Reformer Martin Luther, who wrote, "The love of God does not find, but creates, that which is pleasing to it."[8] This bears repeating, "The love of God does not find, but creates, that which is pleasing to it." In other words, God doesn't offer his love to people as a result of some redeeming quality they possess. It is not that God saw something in Abram. God didn't choose Abram because he was the most faithful or the most righteous person living at that time. Rather Abram became the father of the people of God because God first chose him and then formed him in faith over the course of his wanderings.

Throughout the course of their history, the people of Israel were reminded time and time again in their practices of worship, through the words of the prophets, and through the preserving and passing on of stories such as the one we've heard this morning, that they were not chosen because they were in some way special or superior to the nations surrounding them. Rather, Israel was special because it was chosen.[9] Through Jesus Christ we too have been engrafted into Israel and made children of Abraham. Through the work of the one who was confronted by famine in the wilderness and who refused to turn stones into bread, insisting, "Man shall not live on bread alone, but on every word that comes from the mouth of God" (Matt 4:4), we have been granted a share in God's people and in the promises made to Abraham. Through the faithfulness of the one who when his life was threatened by the powers of his day, set his face toward Jerusalem and did not forsake the cross, trusting in the promises of God even unto death, we have been given a share in the very life of God and the privilege of sharing that life with the world.

---

7. Assayas, *Bono*, 203–4.

8. Martin Luther, "Heidelberg Disputation," in *Luther's Basic Theological Writings*, 32.

9. This comes across clearly, for example, in Deuteronomy 7:7–8.

As a result we can affirm that these stories of God's gracious dealings with Israel are also our stories. We can affirm that Abraham is our father and, without shame, make the scandalous, yet grace-filled declaration that "our daddy was a pimp!" Recognizing that "our daddy was a pimp" reminds us of our humble origins and should help us to preserve space for the other, to welcome those who are different from us into our midst. Remembering Father Abraham's foibles in Egypt, reminds us that there is no one whose personal history places them outside of the realm of God's call and redeeming love. Declaring that "our daddy was a pimp," reminds us of the gracious God who chooses to include in his work of salvation: pimps like Abram, liars like Jacob, hookers like Rahab, adulterers like David, cowards like Peter, religious terrorists like Paul, and a strange group of people with all sorts of annoying quirks and darker vices like you and like me. It's a reminder that God does not give up on his people, as often as they might give up on him. It's a reminder that after twenty-five years of struggling and sometimes failing to be the people God has called us to be in this place, that God has not abandoned the people of Good Shepherd and that he continues to invite us, the rag-tag group that we are, to share in the fellowship of the Spirit and bear witness to the love of Christ that will not let us go.

A friend of mine recounted to me a conversation he had with a Christian worker involved in international missions. This missionary admitted he was growing tired of various well-meaning Christians he encountered in his travels asking him how his children were, or, more specifically, if they were walking with the Lord. It's an important question, but one that is difficult, if not impossible to answer definitively, for only God knows the heart. But what this servant of the Lord rightly noted is that although we may not be able to accurately assess the progress our loved ones are making on their spiritual journey, we can affirm the primary and more fundamental reality that wherever they are, God is walking with them. For even when we are faithless, God remains faithful. Nothing can separate us from the love of God in Jesus Christ. Not famine, nor powers, nor death, nor life, not the skeletons in our closet, or even our continuing struggle with sin and unbelief. Now that's amazing grace!

2

A Long and Winding Word

Knox Presbyterian Church
Toronto, Ontario
Sunday, November 14, 2010
Psalm 119:97–112

THIS MORNING I HAVE been charged with the daunting task of covering the whole of Psalm 119 in a single sermon. The path which runs through Psalm 119 is a long and winding road. In fact, we could say that Psalm 119 is a long and winding word. At 176 verses, it is by far the longest of the Psalms. It stands as the longest chapter in the entire Bible. The Church Father St. Augustine once remarked that what Psalm 119 really needs is not "an expositor, but only a reader and a listener."[1] So with Augustine's advice in mind, what I'm going to attempt to provide this morning is not so much an exposition of this massive psalm, as a ground-clearing exercise which will hopefully enable us to be better readers and listeners of this word. Such a ground-clearing is necessary, for in Psalm 119 we are confronted with several formidable obstacles that must be acknowledged and addressed if we are to become faithful readers and doers of this word.

The first of these roadblocks is the problem of form. As a piece of literature Psalm 119 is vastly different from the forms of writing we are familiar with. To our modern ears, it often seems dry, repetitive, and agonizingly monotonous. After all, how many times and in how many different ways does one need to hear how wonderful the law of the LORD is and how important it is to walk in his ways? However, the Great Psalm, as it is sometimes called, is actually incredibly creative and "endlessly inventive"—just not in a way

---

1. Augustine, *Psalms*, 560, quoted in Goldingay, *Psalms*, 378.

that we are equipped to appreciate.[2] Psalm 119 is something Old Testament scholars call an acrostic poem. In an acrostic each line of the poem begins with a different letter of the alphabet, which serves as a helpful memory device. In the case of Psalm 119, each of the eight lines within a stanza begins with the same letter. So, for example, verses one to eight begin with the first letter of the Hebrew alphabet, "*Aleph*," verses nine to sixteen begin with the second letter, "*Beth*," and so forth. Unfortunately, the acrostic structure of the poem is inevitably lost in translation. Not only are there eight lines per stanza, there are also eight key words that together occur 177 times over the course of the 176 verses of the psalm.[3] The NIV translates these eight words as: law, statutes, precepts, commandments, laws, decrees, word, and promise. The number eight surfaces once again when it is observed that Psalm 119 is one of eight acrostic poems in the Psalter. Interestingly, when one adds together the number of lines in the other seven acrostic psalms the result is 176, exactly the same number of lines as there are in Psalm 119.[4]

It should be becoming apparent that in Psalm 119, we are not confronted by a randomly recurring collection of sayings, but rather by a magnificent edifice arising like a great cathedral in the midst of the village of the Psalter. It is a work characterized by exquisite attention to detail; perhaps more akin to the elegance of a complex solution arrived at by a physicist or mathematician, than to what we normally associate with poetry. This is a work of profound thoughtfulness and intentionality. Like the composer of a majestic fugue, the psalmist returns again and again to his theme in ever new and refreshing ways, not a single note is wasted or out of place.

Of course, this is often lost on us. One commentator goes so far as to say that it takes the psalmist 176 verses to say what he has already said in the first verse: "Blessed are those whose ways are blameless, who walk according to the law of the LORD."[5] But that is just the point. One must immerse oneself in the Torah of the LORD, in God's Word, in God's Law, his teaching and instruction.[6] In the Gospel we are called to life, not given a cliché. Don't get me wrong, the Gospel itself is simple, but it is not simplistic. For the subject of the Gospel, the triune God who has acted for us and our salvation, is inexhaustible. What we are presented with in the Gospel is not a word to be possessed, but a living Word who is the very presence of the living God. The Christian faith cannot be reduced to a series of catchy slogans, step-by-step

2. Freedman, *Psalm 119*, 87.

3. Ibid., 26.

4. Ibid., 3.

5. Weiser, *Psalms*, 740, referenced in Freedman, *Psalm 119*, 89.

6. Freedman, *Psalm 119*, 89.

programs, or pious clichés, because the Christian faith is not a set of ideas to be mastered, but an immersion into the eternal life of love shared between the Father, Son, and Holy Spirit.

Psalm 119 is an invitation to enter into that life. Notice in verse one hundred, that when the psalmist claims he has more understanding than the elders it is not because he knows more about God's precepts, but rather it is because he obeys them. As good Presbyterians, I expect that right about now the words of John Calvin are probably dancing through many of your minds: "all right knowledge of God is born of obedience."[7] The elders in the psalm who know the word but do not live it are like someone who has visited the City of Toronto's website and downloaded the map of Toronto's parks and trails, but then becomes so enamoured with the intersecting lines and colours that he spends all his time sitting in front of his computer monitor staring at the map and never actually goes hiking on the trail.

The psalmist is one who recognizes that the life of faith to which we are called is a journey which encompasses every dimension of life from A to Z. Journey language features quite prominently in the psalm. In the short section of the psalm that we read together this morning we heard such things as, "I have kept my feet from every evil path" (v. 101), "I have not departed from your laws" (v. 102), "Your word is a lamp for my feet, a light on my path" (v. 105), "I will follow" (v. 106), and "I have not strayed" (v. 110). This is an important word for those of us within an evangelical tradition that often seems to be preoccupied with beginnings. Reflecting upon this, his favourite psalm, the great German pastor, theologian and martyr Dietrich Bonhoeffer observed that as Christians, we are freed from the anxiety of having to create and constantly re-create our own beginnings, for God has made the beginning for us and sets us upon the path whose goal God will also bring to fruition.[8] Bonhoeffer can say this because he knows that Christ is the Alpha, the Omega, and also the Way. This imagery of the life of faith as a journey with God is reflected in the self-understanding of the earliest Christians in the book of Acts who described themselves as followers of "the Way." Eugene Peterson has wonderfully captured this reality in the title of one of his books by describing the life of Christian discipleship as *A Long Obedience in the Same Direction*.[9]

This is where we encounter the second major roadblock that threatens our ability to read and listen to this psalm. If we are honest with ourselves,

---

7. Calvin, *Institutes*, 1.6.2.

8. Bonhoeffer, *Theological Education Underground*, 497.

9. Ironically Peterson's title, as he himself openly acknowledges, is taken from a quotation by Friedrich Nietzsche.

we will have to admit that we are not particularly fond of the language of obedience. In fact, the recurring emphasis in the psalm upon the law and the commandments, the statutes and the precepts, and the decrees of the LORD makes us rather uncomfortable. We are not quite sure what to do with all of this law talk. As children of modernity, we are taught to look upon any external demands that are placed upon us as being restrictive, burdensome, and oppressive. We find ourselves immersed in a culture where freedom has been enshrined as the greatest good. However, it is a bit misleading to speak of freedom as our culture's greatest good because there is actually no agreement at all as to what freedom is for. Instead, the only thing that unites us is our desire to be free from anything that might limit our options or hinder our ability to fashion our lives according to our own whims and preferences.

Our difficulties with the law do not end there. As descendants of the Protestant Reformation we have inherited a legacy of reading the Old Testament and thinking about the Jewish people that has been inextricably shaped by the arguments of the sixteenth century. The unfortunate result is that whenever we come across a reference to the Jewish people and the law in the Old Testament, we presume that what the Bible is talking about are people who are attempting to merit their salvation through performing religious rites and works. This is a complete misunderstanding of the intention and place of the law in the life of Israel. The law was *never* intended to provide a means for people to accumulate good works in order to earn their salvation. Rather, it was a gift of God for the people on whose behalf God had already decisively acted. This is particularly clear in the book of Exodus, where, after having delivered the Israelites from slavery in Egypt and having brought them safely to Mount Sinai, the LORD instructs Moses to say to the people: "You yourselves have seen what I did to Egypt, and how I carried you on eagles' wings and brought you to myself. Now if you obey me fully and keep my covenant, then out of all nations you will be my treasured possession. Although the whole earth is mine, you will be for me a kingdom of priests and a holy nation" (19:4–6). Here we see that the gift of the law is the invitation for the covenant people of God to become who they already are in God's sight. As they live into their inheritance in the LORD their life together will bear witness to the reality of God and they will be a kingdom of priests who reflect the glory of the LORD to the nations. The people of Israel have been freed *from* slavery in Egypt so that they may be free *for* the worship and service of the living God.

This exodus language and imagery is taken up in various ways throughout the New Testament to describe the redeeming work of Christ through which God calls into existence a new people for the praise of his glory. The apostle Peter writes to the church, "But you are a chosen people, a royal priesthood, a holy nation, God's special possession, that you may declare the praises of him who called you out of darkness into his wonderful light" (1 Pet 2:9). The apostle Paul uses similar language in his letters to describe how we who are Gentiles have been made to share in the promises made to Israel. Paul tells us that through Christ we have been liberated from slavery to the idolatrous powers which seek to rule our hearts and our world, so that we may serve the true and living God (1 Thess 1:9). From a biblical perspective freedom is always both freedom *from* something—the power of Sin, Death and the Devil—for the sake of freedom *for* something—the love and service of the triune God. That is why the apostle Paul, at the beginning of his great letter to the Romans can describe his mission as being one of calling "all the Gentiles to the *obedience* that comes from faith" (Rom 1:5).

Yet the obedience that comes from faith is not burdensome or oppressive, rather it is walking in the freedom for which we have been created. Jesus invites his disciples into the freedom of this obedience calling out, "Take my yoke upon you and learn from me, for I am gentle and humble in heart, and you will find rest for your souls. For my yoke is easy and my burden is light" (Matt 11:29). Bonhoeffer, reflecting upon this morning's psalm, exclaims, "It is grace to know God's commands. They release us from self-made plans and conflicts. They make our steps certain and our way joyful."[10] To live in accordance with the law of the Lord is to live in accordance with the deep reality of all that God has created. It is to live in accordance with the way things really are. It is for all of these reasons that the psalmist is able to receive the law with such exclamations as: "Oh, how I love your law!" (Ps 119:97); "How sweet are your words to my taste, sweeter than honey to my mouth!" (Ps 119:103); and "Your statutes are my heritage forever; they are the joy of my heart" (Ps 119:111).

The same outlook is found in "The Collect for Peace," a prayer which Anglicans throughout the world recite together every day as part of their service of Morning Prayer. It goes like this: "O God, who art the author of peace and lover of concord, in knowledge of whom standeth our eternal life, whose service is perfect freedom; Defend us thy humble servants in all assaults of our enemies; that we, surely trusting in thy defence, may not fear the power of any adversaries, through the might of Jesus Christ our Lord. Amen."[11]

Beyond the wonderful turn of phrase, "O God . . . whose service is perfect freedom," there is another similarity between the prayer and Psalm 119, which brings us to our third roadblock to living this long and winding word.

---

10. Bonhoeffer, *Prayerbook*, 164.

11. Church of England, "Morning Prayer."

Both "The Collect for Peace" and Psalm 119 are quite open in acknowledging that those who seek to walk in the way of the Lord will encounter opposition and adversity. In fact, Psalm 119 can actually be classified as a psalm of lament.[12] Over half the verses in the psalm are petitions asking the Lord to show mercy, to be compassionate, and to enact his salvation. A large proportion of these petitions arise on account of the fact that the psalmist finds himself surrounded by enemies.

The life of faith is a blessed life, but it is not easy one. The narrow road that leads to life is lined with snares set by the wicked (Matt 7:13; Ps 119:110). Clarence Jordan was a man who understood the afflictions that accompany the narrow way of discipleship.[13] Seized by the Gospel, Jordan, along with several others, set out in 1942 to form a communal farm in rural Georgia where black and white people would work together, learning about productive farming while simultaneously seeking to develop a community life based on the teachings and life of Jesus. They existed in anonymity for a while, but eventually word got out about what they were doing and the storm clouds began to gather. They were accused, among other things, of being communists and "race-mixers." Their business was boycotted. No one would handle their accounts. They were harassed in the courts. Klu Klux Klan caravans began visiting their property. There were cross burnings, vandalism, shootings, buildings burnt to the ground, and bombings. It was in this context that Clarence approached his brother Robert Jordan, later a state senator and justice of the Georgia Supreme Court, asking him to legally represent Koinonia Farm. Here's how the conversation unfolded, with Robert responding to Clarence's request for legal representation. "Clarence, I can't do that. You know my political aspirations. Why, if I represented you I might lose my job, my house, everything I've got."

Clarence quietly replied, "We might lose everything too, Bob."

"But, it's different for you," Robert countered.

"Why is it different? I remember, it seems to me, that you and I joined the church the same Sunday, as boys. I expect when we came forward the preacher asked me about the same question he did you. He asked me, 'Do you accept Jesus as your Lord and Savior?' and I said, 'Yes.' What did you say, Robert?"

"I follow Jesus, Clarence, up to a point."

"Could that point by any chance be—the cross?"

---

12. Freedman, *Psalm 119*, 93.

13. For the details of Clarence Jordan's life and the particular story which follows, I am indebted to McClendon, *Biography as Theology*, 89–113.

"That's right, Clarence. I follow him to the cross, but not *on* the cross. I`m not getting myself crucified."

Clarence stood silently for a moment, staring at the ground, before looking up and responding to his brother, "Then I don't believe that you're a disciple. You're an admirer of Jesus, but not a disciple of his. I think you ought to go back to the church you belong to, and tell them you're an admirer not a disciple."

In exasperation Robert responded, "Oh come on now, if everyone who felt like I do did that, we wouldn't have a church, would we?"

"The question," Clarence said, "is, 'Do you have a church?'"

As a pastor and theologian, I am continually haunted by this question. It is one that resonates with the deep challenge presented to us in Psalm 119. For the roadblocks that we encounter in our attempt to read and live this long and winding word are not actually intrinsic to the psalm itself, but rather are obstacles that arise within us. It is not so much the case that there are intellectual difficulties with the text of the psalm that must be overcome, as it is that the psalm reveals the poverty of our own souls and the barricades to the grace of God that we have erected within our own hearts. As we are encountered by this word we come to recognize that we prefer a life of superficiality, autonomy, and ease to walking in the way of the Lord. That is why the first and last word about living the Word must be the Living Word. It is Jesus Christ who is the Alpha and the Omega and it is only in him that we are able to pray this psalm as he prays it for us and with us.[14] He is the one who has remained faithful until the end, dying surrounded by his enemies with the words of the Psalms upon his lips: "My God, my God, why have you forsaken me?" (22:1; Matt 27:46) and "Into your hands I commit my spirit" (31:5; Luke 23:46). With his blood he has sealed the final verse that we read together this morning, "My heart is set on keeping your decrees to the very end" (Ps 119:112). If we are to pray this psalm, to live this word, it will only be in him. In the words of your congregation's namesake, John Knox, Christ alone "'is our mouth, by whom we speak of God; he is our eyes, by whom we see God, and also our right hand, by whom we offer anything to the Father'; who, unless he make intercession, neither we, neither any of the saints, may have any society or fellowship with God."[15]

The good news of the Gospel is that Christ does make intercession for us. Joined to him, through the power of the Holy Spirit we are restored

14. Bonhoeffer, *Prayerbook* , 157.

15. Knox, "A Declaration What True Prayer Is," in *Works of John Knox*, 3:97, quoted in Purves, *Reconstructing Pastoral Theology*, 43. The first part of the quotation is attributed by Knox to Ambrose and the whole quotation has been translated into contemporary English by Purves.

to fellowship with the Father. He sets our feet upon a rock and makes our footsteps firm (Ps 40:2). He goes before us as our guide, he accompanies us as our companion, and he himself is the way on which we travel. His faithfulness makes possible lives that radiate with the reflection of his glory.

I recently had the opportunity to celebrate one such life when I attended the funeral for a member of the church in which I was raised in my hometown of London, Ontario. Keith Brown was almost 90 years old when he passed away. As a younger man, he had served for several years with his wife, Jean, as a missionary in Angola before returning to Canada where he served as an ordained minister for many years. However, I did not know him in either of those contexts. My only experience with him was within the congregation in London which he and his wife had made their church home after he had retired. I knew him as a quiet, gentle man, who didn't draw attention to himself. I never heard him preach, or saw him lead worship, but I knew that Keith and Jean were profound people of prayer. The defining moment of the funeral occurred when three of his grandchildren, two young women and one young man, got up together to eulogize their grandfather. Alternating among themselves, the three grandchildren spoke eloquently; their words the obvious product of deep and faithful reflection. They skilfully avoided the pitfalls of pious clichés which always threaten to plague eulogies and instead spoke in the most natural way of the calm and constant presence of their grandfather. They shared how he would make time to attend their concerts and games, how he loved his wife, and of the tender expressions of care he demonstrated both for her and for them. They spoke of his Bible as a cherished inheritance and described the underlining and notes which filled the margins of the pages that had been worn thin from years of study. It was quite a moving experience hearing them speak, not only because the portrait they painted of their grandfather was deeply consistent with what I had experienced of this man of faith, but also because it was apparent how much they had been influenced and impacted by their grandfather's walk with the Lord. The most powerful and beautiful words were saved for the very end of the eulogy when one of the granddaughters concluded by saying, "Thank you grandpa, for you have shown me that the life of faith, a life of walking in the way of the Lord, is worth it."

It is true that Psalm 119 does not need an expositor, but only a reader and a listener. But it is also true that by the grace of God, the reader and listener of the Word becomes a living exposition of the Word for others. Praise the Lord for such living expositions of his Word as Dietrich Bonhoeffer, Clarence Jordan, and Keith and Jean Brown. May we too by the grace of God, be counted among the blessed, whose ways are blameless, who walk according to the law of the Lord.

3

A Prodigal and His Son

Martin Grove Baptist Church

Etobicoke, Ontario

Sunday, October 18, 2015

Luke 15:11–24; Isaiah 61

THE SCRIPTURE PASSAGE WE have just heard, popularly referred to as the parable of the prodigal son, is perhaps the most beloved and well known of Jesus' parables. For centuries, Christian commentators have referred to this parable as the *Evangelium in Evangelio*—"the Gospel within the Gospel."[1] The great British Baptist preacher Charles Spurgeon fittingly made the parable of the prodigal son the subject of his landmark one thousandth-sermon.[2] The popularity and influence of the parable extends well beyond the walls of the church. Shakespeare alludes to the parable more than any other and almost every major English and American fiction writer and dramatist makes reference to it.[3] In light of this, I find it somewhat surprising that an adaptation of the story has not yet appeared on the big screen. I wonder how the movers and shakers in Hollywood would portray the parable, if they got the chance. I think they would probably set the story in the present day with the father ably played by Sean Connery. Not the James Bond-era Sean Connery, but Sean Connery as he is today. Connery would be the head of a mid-sized steel company located on the eastern seaboard of the United States. Chris Pine, who plays Captain Kirk in the new

---

1. Bailey, *Poet and Peasant*, 158, quoting Arndt, *Luke*, 350.

2. Spurgeon, "Number One Thousand; Or, 'Bread Enough to Spare,'" in *Spurgeon's Sermons*, 17:395–407.

3. Jeffrey, *Luke*, 193.

Star Trek series of movies, would play the younger son. Although the boy is slightly misguided, it is clear that deep down he has a heart of gold. With stars in his eyes, the younger son cashes in the college trust fund that had been set up for him by his father and jumps in his dad's Rolls Royce and heads west to find himself. The son makes a few wrong turns and ultimately hits rock bottom when he finds himself lying face-down in a gutter in Las Vegas after a wild night of gambling, drinking, and drugs. With no money left and Daddy's Rolls the casualty of manipulative friends with expensive vices, the son finally comes to his senses and begins the long trip back across the continent to his father's home. With Simon and Garfunkel's "Homeward Bound" serving as the soundtrack, the son commences his arduous journey—hitchhiking, riding the rails, and simply walking across the country on his way back home. In the climactic scene of the film, the son enters his father's lavish executive suite at the company headquarters. As the father looks sternly on, the son falls before him weeping, admitting his failure as a son. After a moment of silence, broken only by the sniffling of the son, the camera pans to the stern-faced Sean Connery, who utters the momentous pronouncement, "Welcome back to the family, son!" At this point the two embrace and the tears freely flow. The younger son ends up going back to college and after graduating works his way up the corporate ladder, introducing new manufacturing practices that take the company to the next level. Eventually the son follows in his father's footsteps as head of the corporation. It would make for great cinema! There is only one problem—it doesn't line up at all with the parable as Jesus told it.

First of all, there is nothing redeeming about the prodigal. He is not a slightly misguided child with a heart of gold. Rather, he is a scoundrel whose motives are entirely driven by selfish desires. At the beginning of the parable he goes to his father and asks him to execute his will while he is still alive. In effect he is saying, "Drop dead, Dad!"[4] The wounds inflicted by such a statement would have been magnified by the disgrace that would have fallen upon the family when word got out about what the son had done. Then the son takes his portion of the estate and liquefies his assets, converting the property into hard currency. Now in those times, a family would hold a piece of land for hundreds of years and each subsequent generation would raise their families upon the land of their fathers. By selling off his portion of the estate the younger son is selfishly limiting the horizons of the rest of his family and bringing further shame and disgrace upon his father's house. Not only that, but with his pockets overflowing with dollar bills the son skips town, completing his self-initiated breakdown of the family unit.

4. Capon, *Kingdom, Grace, Judgement*, 294; Bailey, *Poet and Peasant*, 165.

There is a great spiritual irony at play here. In order to set out on his quest for independence and establish himself as his own person, the prodigal is completely reliant upon the generous gift of his father. In a similar way, in our flight from God the only thing that carries us are the very legs which God himself has given us. Even in our rebellion against God we remain reliant upon him for our very existence.

Jesus tells us that after the son had spent everything there was a severe famine in that whole country and he began to be in need. Commenting upon this passage, the great Scottish preacher Alexander McLaren observed, "There is always famine in the land of forgetfulness of God, and when the first gloss is off its enjoyments, and one's substance is spent, its pinch is felt."[5] Finding himself in desperate need, the son hired himself out to a wealthy landowner. The Greek text is actually more pointed. It literally reads that the son joined, or cleaved to, or glued himself to the citizen of that far country. It is the word that is normally used in the Greek translation of the Old Testament, known as the Septuagint, to exhort the people of Israel to cling or cleave to the LORD alone (eg. Deut 6:13, 10:20). Like the son who has sought to escape the sphere of his father's influence, but now finds himself joined by dire necessity to a pagan landowner, our misguided quest to be free from God ultimately results not in freedom, but in the basest of slavery.

At some point, we are told, the son came to his senses. But if we listen closely to the plan he devises, it becomes clear that it is the grumblings of an empty stomach fuelled by devious motivations and not the cries of a broken and contrite heart which lead him to return to his homeland.[6] We can almost imagine the prodigal sitting in the field sharing his plan with the pigs. "Look at you guys. Who would have thought it would have come to this? I'm probably the only Jew in the world who spends his days living among pigs. Don't snort at me like that! Those pods may not be the best, but at least you have something to eat. Back in my father's house even the servants had plenty to eat, and here I am without anything, dying of hunger. Wait a minute! Why don't I go back and work as an employee for my father's business? I'll be guaranteed to have enough food and I won't have to deal with such vile creatures as you. If I can just win another chance from my father, then maybe—just maybe—I can even work my way back into his favor. Why wouldn't he hire me? After all, I do have a lot to offer: I know the business, I know the property, and I know all of the other servants by name. All I need is one more chance. It won't be easy. I'll have to come up with something really good. How about, 'Father, I have sinned against heaven

---

5. Maclaren, "The Prodigal and His Father," in *Expositions*, 299.

6. Capon, *Kingdom, Grace, Judgement*, 295.

and against you. I am no longer worthy to be called your son; make me like one of your hired servants'" (Luke 15:18–19).

There is something about the prodigal's plan that strikes a chord in all of us. We love the stories where the down and out person who is given one more chance, rises up to seize the moment. Some years ago now I had the opportunity to see the movie *Seabiscuit* when it was released in the theatres. Its release, close to a decade ago, marked the beginning of what could be called "the equine renaissance" in contemporary film. It has been followed by numerous other horse movies like *Secretariat* and *War Horse*. Those of you who have seen it will recall that the movie centers around four main characters: the racehorse Seabiscuit, the former automotive mogul who became Seabiscuit's owner, the troubled jockey who formed a bond with the racehorse, and the trainer who was an outcast to society. Each of the characters were united by the fact that through poor choices, or perhaps simply through suffering "the slings and arrows of outrageous fortune," they all found themselves down and out.[7] However, fate brought them together and provided them with one more chance, and this unlikely crew succeeded in seizing the day. As Seabiscuit raced to the finish line to secure a victory not just for himself but for everyone who had ever been labeled a failure or a loser, the crowd in the movie theatre erupted in spontaneous applause. That was several years ago now, but I haven't seen a reaction like it since. We love these stories. Perhaps we think that if we are given one more chance, we too can put the mistakes of yesterday behind us and get our lives together once and for all. Even in the church we like to think that we can leave behind the sin that has plagued us, if we just try a little harder. All we need is a fresh start, just one more chance.

I hate to be the one to tell you this, but one more chance won't help us and it wouldn't have helped the prodigal. The prodigal is not merely sidetracked, he is lost. He is dropped from a helicopter in the middle of the Sahara desert without a compass, map, or bottle of water—lost! He is dead. Not merely sick in bed with the flu, but buried six feet under the earth—dead! The father recognizes the lostness and deadness of the son. A lostness and deadness that is not a result of whatever distant land activities the son may have been involved in (which the father may or may not have even known about), but a lostness and deadness springing from the son's alienation from the father. No more chances are going to help the son earn his way back into the family; he can't possibly do it. The only thing the son brings back with him are his tattered rags and the pig manure between his toes. That is why

7. Shakespeare, *Hamlet*, III.1.

the father, rather than giving the prodigal one more chance, puts an end to the business of earning one's way and makes things right himself.

It is the father who is truly the star of this story.[8] The title "The Parable of the Prodigal Son" is a misnomer. "The Amazing Love of the Father" or "The Parable of the Gracious Father" or even "Father Knows Best" would be much better titles for this story. Right from the start of the parable the father has shown grace to the younger son. When the younger son came to him wishing that he was dead, the father did not meet him with a swift backhand, as most fathers of the day would have done, but instead he obliged his painful request.[9] Rather than annihilating the rebelling son, the father chose to keep the wounds of alienation open each day with the hope that one day there would be reconciliation. While the son ran far from home searching for a freedom that would ultimately lead him into base slavery, the father was rising early each morning and ascending to the roof of his home, from where he could gaze over the entire surrounding countryside for any sight of his lost son.[10] It was as he continued this routine of rising and looking over the countryside that one day the father caught sight of what appeared to be his son far off in the distance. The father bounded down from the roof and, in a most unbecoming manner for a civilized and honorable wealthy landowner of his society, hiked up his robe with his hands so that he could run out to meet his son.[11] It was the father that found the son. He met him off in the distance and there in a display of unbridled joy fell upon him continuously hugging and kissing him.

"Can you believe what happened today?" the neighbors must have asked one another. "Can you believe what the old man did? He made a complete fool of himself. We thought he was a little nuts before when he let that little punk leave with his inheritance, but now he's proved that he's right out to lunch. Did you see how he ran through town with his robe hiked up like some little school child and then how he embraced that 'good-for-nothing' son, fawning over him like a mother over an infant? He didn't even make the boy grovel or beg and admit the disgrace that he had brought upon his family. He didn't strike him or spit on him. He didn't let him say a single word before he embraced him and started kissing him. What type of father is he?"

---

8. This is one of the central insights of Henri Nouwen's profound set of reflections upon Rembrandt's *The Return of the Prodigal Son* in his book which shares the same title.

9. Bailey, *Poet and Peasant*, 165.

10. Stephen C. Barton, "Parables on God's Love and Forgiveness (Luke 15:1–32)," in Longenecker, *Challenge of Jesus' Parables*, 211.

11. Bailey, *Poet and Peasant*, 181.

It was when the son truly beheld this amazing love of the father—this love that moved the father to take the suffering and shame that rightly belonged to the son upon himself—that the son's words of repentance became real. It was when the son was captured by this incomprehensible love that he was able to truly utter, "Father, I have sinned against heaven and against you, I am no longer worthy to be called your son." Full stop. That was it. That was all he could say. As his father held him in his warm embrace, the son realized that he could never work his way back into the family; the father had welcomed him back for free. The reconciliation and restoration to sonship was further confirmed by the prodigal display which followed. The father called for his best robe to be brought and placed on the young vagabond's shoulders, for sandals to be placed upon the young man's calloused feet, and for the family ring of authority to be placed on the finger of the welcomed-home son. There was only one thing left to do—celebrate! For the son who was lost had been found, the one who was dead, had been brought back to life. So the father ordered the slaughter of the fattened calf, a rare treat in first century Palestine that would feed the entire village, and the party began.

There are perhaps no bigger parties and spectacles in our time than the Olympic Games. Twenty-three years ago the eyes of England were focused on Barcelona, Spain, where Derek Redmond, a native of Great Britain, was among the favorites to win a medal in the four hundred-meter dash.[12] It had been a long and winding path leading up to the Games for the twenty-six-year-old Redmond. Injuries had plagued him for most of his career, even forcing him to withdraw from his race four years earlier at the Olympics in Seoul, South Korea, but now it appeared as if things were finally coming together. Heading into the Games, Derek had told his coach that he firmly believed an Olympic medal was within his grasp. In order to capture that medal, he would first have to advance through a difficult semi-final. It was a warm August evening in Barcelona as Redmond settled into the starting blocks for the biggest race of his life. The gun sounded and Redmond exploded off the line. He quickly began to make up the stagger on the competitors to his outside. On his inside the defending Olympic champion and the Cuban national champion were also moving well. The competitors raced down the back stretch toward their second and final turn on their way to the finish. Suddenly, the unthinkable happened. With a "*pop,*" excruciating pain surged through Derek's right leg and he fell to the track in a heap with a torn

12. I remember watching Redmond's race on the Canadian Broadcast Corporation's Olympic broadcast and even have a VHS video-recording which I was able to review while preparing this sermon. One recounting of the events can be found in Bondy, "British Runner is a Hero."

hamstring. From his crumpled position on the track, Derek was able to look up and see the seven other competitors fly by, racing for a spot in the final and taking with them his dream of Olympic glory.

Then to the disbelief of the sold-out crowd of sixty-five thousand, Derek Redmond got to his feet and on one leg, fighting back the tears, began to hop toward the finish line. One by one, the crowd rose to recognize the bravery of this young man. Pain shot through his leg with every step. Yet Derek Redmond was going to finish what he started. As he approached the final straight-away, in what by this point had become the slowest four hundred meters in the history of the Olympic Games, a large, thick-necked, barrel-chested man wearing a Nike t-shirt and shorts burst through security and raced toward Derek. The man attempted to take hold of Derek, but Derek gamely fought him off. Once again the man reached out toward Derek and this time Derek recognized the familiar voice of his father, Jim Redmond.

"You don't have to do this."

"I've got to finish," Derek replied to his dad.

Jim Redmond turned to his son, "Well then, we're going to finish this race together." Derek began to sob and tears began to stream down his face as he sagged into the strong, loving arms of his father. The elder Redmond fended off wave after wave of security guards and overzealous track officials who attempted to impede their progress. Then, to the roar of assembled throng, after what seemed like an eternity, father and son crossed the finish line together.

We too have a Father who comes to us with open arms, saying, "Let's finish this race together. I don't care where you've been or what you've done. I have forgiven you. You are my beloved daughter. You are my beloved son." In the figure of the father in the parable, we catch a glimpse of the prodigal love of God, who will stop at no length in order to bring his children home—even if that means going to hell and back. If you look carefully, you'll see that the wide open arms of the father are the same arms that were spread wide and nailed to the cross at Calvary. Such amazing love was not brought about by anything we've done. We didn't earn it by offering some Oscar caliber repentance performance, nor was it offered to us because God saw that we would somehow make good if we were given just one more chance. Rather, out of the abundance of the love shared for all eternity between the Father, the Son and the Holy Spirit, the Word became flesh and set out into the far country to seek and to save the lost.[13] Just as in the parable the father loves

13. "The Way of the Son of God into the Far Country" is the title and theme of a sub-section within Karl Barth's magisterial treatment of the doctrine of reconciliation in *Church Dogmatics*, IV.1:157–210.

the unlovable, in the same way, "while we were still sinners, Christ died for us" (Rom 5:8). There is no one who deserves God's mercy, yet there is no one to whom God does not extend his mercy. You see, God's in the business of finding the lost and raising the dead. The words of the prophet Isaiah have been fulfilled, "He has clothed us with garments of salvation and arrayed us in robes of his righteousness" (Isa 61:10).[14] So let us stop clinging to our filthy rags and enter into the party. It's time to celebrate!

14. I have emended the text to reflect the congregational context by including the first-person plural, rather than reproducing the original first-person singular.

4

A Prodigal and His Other Son

Martin Grove Baptist Church

Etobicoke, Ontario

Sunday, October 25, 2015

Luke 15:1–32; Jeremiah 31:3–14

It seems hard to believe that for twenty-seven seasons competitors have been racing around the world in the hit television series *The Amazing Race*. Their travels have taken them to distant and exotic lands where they have been charged with completing various tasks, solving challenging puzzles, and overcoming numerous obstacles. In the final episode of each season the top teams return home and race to the finish mat in the attempt to claim the grand prize. We even have our own Canadian version of the series, hosted by former Olympic star Jon Montgomery. However, the Canadian version appears rather austere compared to the lavish prodigality of the American series. The parable of the prodigal son actually played an influential role in an early season of the American *Amazing Race*, as competitors had to travel to the Hermitage museum in St. Petersburg, Russia to find Rembrandt's painting, *The Return of the Prodigal Son*. It was interesting to watch the various competitors attempt to track down the painting. Some knew right away what they were looking for, while others weren't so certain. You could almost see the wheels turning in one man's head as he reasoned to his partner: "The story of the prodigal son is from the Bible and . . . isn't Jesus the prodigal son . . . so what we need to find is a painting about Jesus coming back." The older brother of the prodigal probably would have got some sense of satisfaction out of seeing his younger brother misidentified on national television. Not only did the older son feel neglected by his father in the original telling of the story, but for the past two thousand years he has been largely overlooked by the church whenever the story is retold. It is the younger son who occupies center stage in paintings. It is the descriptive title of the younger "prodigal son" which has firmly established itself as part of the English language and the parable itself is frequently named after the younger "lost" or "prodigal" son. The second part of the parable, involving the older son, has more often than not been relegated to the sidelines of the Christian imagination. However, without consideration of the plight of the older son, we risk missing the true parabolic punch of Jesus' story as it has been recorded for us in the Gospel of Luke. Furthermore, as much as we might be tempted to romanticize the plight of the younger son and imagine ourselves letting loose in a far-away, exotic land, the sad reality is that if we have been in the church for any length of time, it is the older son that we are much more likely to resemble.

Before we move into this second part of the parable, it seems necessary to first move back a few verses to the beginning of Luke 15: "Now the tax collectors and sinners were all gathering around to hear Jesus. But the Pharisees and the teachers of the law muttered, 'This man welcomes sinners and eats with them'" (vv. 1–2). It seems as if Jesus' eating practices had become the occasion for dispute. The dispute does not center upon what Jesus is eating, or whether he would be better off eating ancient grains or going gluten-free. Rather, the controversy arises on account of the company that Jesus is keeping at his dinner table.

The concerns are raised by the Pharisees and Scribes, whose knowledge of the law, education, and political and religious connections, place them among the social, spiritual and moral elite. In the game of life, the Pharisees and the Scribes were clearly coming out ahead. One of the Pharisee's primary concerns was maintaining ritual purity at all meals. They saw each meal as a foreshadowing of God's final banquet at the end of time and therefore ate only with those who they deemed to be pure.[1]

Tax collectors and "sinners" would obviously be disqualified from such a meal. Tax collectors were Jewish men enlisted by the government to collect taxes from their fellow citizens on behalf of Rome. Because of their affiliation with the Romans, the tax collectors were often viewed as traitors by their own people. This dislike was compounded by the fact that many tax collectors were known to collect a little extra to line their own pockets. The term "sinners" was a derogatory term, used to describe anyone who had, according to the knowledge of the community, committed a transgression against the Mosaic Law. It may have also included those who

1. For a brief discussion situating Jesus' table fellowship with sinners within the context of first century Jewish understandings and practices surrounding table fellowship, see McKnight, *New Vision for Israel*, 41–49.

were disqualified from Temple worship because of any physical ailment or imperfection.[2] Tax collectors and "sinners" were the outcasts of first century Jewish society; they are perhaps best described as losers.

In the minds of the Pharisees there was no way that a respected teacher, even more so the Messiah, would eat with such outcasts and losers. Sharing table fellowship with someone indicated one's full acceptance of another; who one ate with represented one's status within the community.[3] You can almost hear the Pharisees observing Jesus' table fellowship practices and muttering to themselves, "Birds of a feather, flock together."

Jesus responds to the criticism of the Pharisees and Scribes with a series of three parables that address the issue of winning and losing head on.[4] In these parables, Jesus turns winning and losing on its head by taking the winning and losing paradigm to its logical extreme: living and dying. To begin with, Jesus tells the story of a lost sheep. Now any sheep that is lost on its own in the wilderness is a dead sheep. Then Jesus moves on to tell the story of a lost coin. A lost coin is of no monetary use and is therefore dead currency. Finally, Jesus moves on to the elaborate, final parable featuring the two sons. It begins with the younger son coming to his Father and saying, "Dad, I want my share of the will, drop dead!" The father kindly obliges and from a legal perspective drops dead. The younger son then meets his spiritual and moral death in a far country where he becomes the servant of a Gentile hog farmer. Due to the famine in the land it becomes apparent that the son's physical death is not far behind. Basically, this younger son is as good as dead. There is even a prized calf which drops dead so that there can be one giant blowout of a party. Then while all these dead characters are living it up, we meet the older son, who, although he is the only character in the parable that is still alive, appears to be the walking dead.

So what do we do with all this? Rather than wrestling with and entering into the mystery of the Gospel message, we often attempt to domesticate the parable. We cast the younger son as the hero, who has just gotten a little bit of dirt smeared on his white suit. We portray the older son as the villain, clothed in black, who slithers onto the stage to the jeers and catcalls of the audience. We reduce the mystery to simple principles to live by. We say, "Like the prodigal, you too must come home"; or, "Don't be a Pharisee."

---

2. Stephen C. Barton, "Parables on God's Love and Forgiveness (Luke 15:1–32)," in Longenecker, *Challenge of Jesus' Parables*, 202–3.

3. Bailey, *Poet and Peasant*, 143.

4. The winning/losing and living/dying motifs presented in this paragraph are indebted to the provocative exposition of these three Lucan parables in Capon, *Kingdom, Grace, Judgement*, 184–88, 293–301.

But if we saw the older son today, or the Pharisee who so clearly stands behind the character of the older son, I am not at all convinced that we would identify him as a villain. If the parable were told today the older son might very well be found within our very midst. There would be a regular seat that he would occupy each and every Sunday for worship and there wouldn't be a Sunday when the offering plate would be missing an envelope with his name on it. With his charming good looks and his lightning quick mind, it would be no surprise to find him at the top of the field in his industry. If you were to follow him around for a while you would see that he doesn't drink, he doesn't smoke, and he's never cheated on his wife or his taxes. His voice rings out for justice and fairness, and he warns against the dangers of appearing to condone the actions of a world that appears to be going to hell in a hand-basket. All in all, most would describe him as just a good, decent man. The world would look kindly upon this figure who has got the game of life all figured out and is well on his way to winning.

The older brother fits into the world's expectations that the solution to the human condition is found in living. Overcoming the difficulties that ail us is simply a matter of working harder and finding a way to win. Living is a message that we instantly gravitate toward. It was a temptation that the prodigal faced when he devised his plan to return to his father's house as a hired hand. He thought he could work his way back into the family. Where do you think the younger son got this idea, if it wasn't from observing his older brother's relationship with his dad? To our fallen human nature there is something inherently appealing about the message of living. Bookstores now often devote an entire section of the store to the topic of "living well," which includes works by such luminaries in the field as Martha Stewart and Dr. Phil McGraw. We are bombarded by messages about living well ranging from Lance Armstrong, who up until his fall from grace encouraged us to "live strong"; to Oprah Winfrey who aspires to help each and every one "live your best life"; to the prosperity preacher Joel Osteen who takes it one step further by promising to help anyone and everyone "live your best life now." But we don't need to turn on the television to encounter such messages; we only need to attend to the architecture and layout of our cities. Whereas at one time cathedrals stood at the center of the village and their spires could be seen from miles around, today the tallest buildings in our cities belong to the banks, and hospitals stand at the center of our universities. The former points to our society's faith that we will ultimately be justified through hard work, ingenuity and success, the latter to our hope that we might yet find a way to get out of this life alive.[5]

5. Stanley Hauerwas has emphasized the soteriological significance of hospitals (the

Yet this obsession with living well is not just found out there in the world; it has also infiltrated the church. Back when I was a seminary student I spent a summer working on the greens staff at a Toronto area golf course. One day, during a lunch break, I heard one of the older men describing how he had not had a drink for twenty years and how he had also quit smoking. After which he added the following commentary, "Now, if I just give up sex and start reading the Bible, I could be a saint." We may laugh at his naïve understanding of Christianity, but he must have gotten this understanding of the Christian life from observing someone. The temptation to transform a relationship with the God who comes to us into a religion where we climb the ladder toward heaven is a formidable one. Rather than wearing the best robe that the Father has given to us—the robe of Christ's righteousness—there is a strong temptation to mend together our own robe of self-righteousness.

The older son in our parable this morning, with his focus on living and winning, has lost sight of his relationship with his father. He has reduced a father-son relationship into a system of rules and commandments. This becomes evident in the speech and actions of the older son. In verse twenty-nine, the son states, "Look! All these years I've been slaving for you and never disobeyed your orders." The son understands his relationship with his father in terms of servant-master rather than father-son. He is working for pay, not out of love for his father. The older son is so caught up in the gods of performance, productivity and efficiency that he has lost sight of his relationship with his generous father. Where the younger son was a law-breaking sinner, the older son is a sinner within the law. While the younger son was lost in the far country, the older son is lost at home. This reality was already anticipated in the first two parables Jesus told to the Scribes and Pharisees. In the first, he spoke of a sheep that was lost in the wilderness. In the second, he told of a coin that was lost in the home. While the older son may be a good, moral, law-keeping fellow, he is alienated from his father. This becomes painfully clear in the latter part of the parable. The older son has no qualms about showing up his father in front of the entire village by refusing to enter into the party when social customs required him to come in and, at the very least, greet the guests.[6] He refuses to show his father proper respect by addressing him in the appropriate cultural manner by his title of father and he distances himself from his family by referring to his younger brother as "your son." On top of all that, he chastises his father for

---

cathedrals of modernity) for the American (and, I would also add, Canadian) attempt "to get out of life alive" (*War and the American Difference*, 19).

6. Bailey, *Poet and Peasant*, 194–95.

not allowing him to have a party with "his friends," implying that whoever his friends are they do not include his brother, his father, and the guests who are assembled at the party. Furthermore, by criticizing how his father has chosen to dispose of the property, the older son is, much like the younger son, saying, "I wish you were out of the picture. Dad, I wish you were dead!"

We can only imagine what the guests would have been saying among themselves, when for the second time in the same day the father demonstrated costly love in taking shame upon himself in order to win back a son. "It's a great spread the old guy has put out for us, but can you believe what we've seen today? Talk about a dysfunctional family. Obviously, this father hasn't read Rabbi Spock's book on parenting. First, when that "no good" son of his, who wasted his living and disgraced his father's name in a far-away land came home, he ran out to him with his robe hiked up like some school-child and started fawning over him like a mother over an infant. And now this older son! When this older son started to make a big scene outside and embarrass him in front of everybody, what did he do? Did he ignore him and carry on with the party? No! Did he go out there and beat him back into line? No! Instead he's out there pleading with him, like some shameful loser!"

Since the father has already died to the rules and expectations of the world, suffering shame and disgrace and being labeled a loser are of no concern to him. His only concern is bringing his son back into the fold. It's an amazing conversation that we're drawn into. The older son's indignation almost jumps off the page.

"Listen here, I've been my working my butt off for you for years now. In fact I don't think the family business would have survived, if I hadn't been here keeping it afloat. I follow all of the rules and not once have you ever given me anything to throw a party with. And then, when that little drunkard son of yours comes home, bringing nothing with him but the venereal diseases he picked up in that far country, you throw a giant party for him!"

After such an outburst, we expect punishment, a scathing rebuke; instead we're overwhelmed by grace. The self-righteous "better living" of the older son is met by the self-sacrificing love of the father.

"My child, you are always with me, and all of mine is yours. You could have thrown yourself a party anytime you wanted to. All of the livestock is at your disposal, and you have free access to my wardrobe. You're the one who insisted on making a job out of everything. And son, I do appreciate the effort you've put into the family business, but you've got it all wrong. You see we're not in the accounting business, son. We're in the business of finding the lost and raising the dead."

Jesus' parable stops at this point. We don't know how the story ends. We are not told if the older son repents and enters into the party to share in the father's joy or if he remains outside. Kenneth Bailey, a New Testament scholar and student of Middle Eastern culture, has written a play based on the parable of the prodigal son in which he supplies his own ending to the story.[7] In Bailey's dramatic staging of the parable, the older son, after rejecting the father's desperate pleading, turns his staff upon the father and bludgeons him to death. When considered within the context of Jesus' historical ministry, Bailey's presentation accurately depicts how the opposition to Jesus hardened in the time following his telling of the parable. Jesus' gracious invitation to enter into the joy of the kingdom was ultimately refused when Jesus was hung on the cross to die. I think there is something profoundly right about Bailey's insights—the religious elite of Jesus' day would not come into the party. However, it is important to recognize that the parable remains, in a very real sense, open-ended, because Jesus' story does not end with the crucifixion. The grave could not hold him. Although we would rather live our lives as if God does not exist, carefully constructing fortresses of solitude within which we can be insulated and protected from the claims of others, particularly the Divine Other, the crucified one keeps coming back, searching out younger and older sons alike. He goes out to find both those who are lost in the far country and those who are lost at home. He invites both to enter into the joy prepared for them from the foundation of the world.

The prophet Jeremiah was given a glimpse of the joy of the kingdom to be experienced in the Father's household. Jeremiah was instructed to proclaim to the beaten and beleaguered people of Israel, who had been trampled on and seen their best and brightest carried into exile in Babylon on account of their leaders' attempts to secure life on their own terms apart from God, a word of hope and consolation. Through the mouth of the prophet Jeremiah the LORD declared to his people, "I have loved you with an everlasting love; I have drawn you with unfailing kindness" (31:3). Like a shepherd, the LORD seeks out the lost sheep of Israel and gathers and tends his flock. As we heard earlier in the service, these shepherding images then give way to the sights and sounds of celebration. "Then young women will dance and be glad, young men and old as well," says the LORD. "I will turn their mourning into gladness; I will give them comfort and joy instead of sorrow" (Jer 31:13). Perhaps it should not surprise us then that Jesus spent so much time eating and drinking with the least, the last, and the lost that he was accused of being "a glutton and a drunkard, a friend of tax collectors

---

7. Bailey, *Cross and the Prodigal*, 75–131.

and sinners" (Luke 7:34). This eating and drinking was at the heart of his mission, for "the Son of Man to seek and save the lost" (Luke 19:10). It turns out there is such a thing as a free lunch. The party is now underway. The lost, now found, are dancing to the divine melody and the champagne of God's love is flowing freely. Who are we to linger outside in the shadows when the voice of the Good Shepherd calls, saying, "Come, for everything is now ready" (Luke 14:17)?

5

Holy Spirit-uality

Knox Presbyterian Church

Toronto, Ontario

Sunday, July 10, 2011

John 20:19–23; Ezekiel 37:1–14

"I'm not religious, but I am very spiritual." I bet you've heard that expression before. In fact, it's so common today that it could be considered a cliché. At least three in ten people in the United States identify themselves as "spiritual, not religious."[1] Here in Canada, statistical data has shown that while participation in organized religion continues to decrease, more people than ever claim to be "spiritual."[2] Spirituality is at an all-time high. It seems to be the new buzzword for the twenty-first century. From actors, to musicians, to celebrities, people are climbing over one another in their race to come out of the closet to confess their spirituality. So it probably won't surprise you when I tell you that the website of Oprah Winfrey—the high priestess of North American culture—at one point authoritatively declared itself to be, "your leading source for information about love, life, self, relationships, food, home, spirit and health."[3] While we dare not underestimate Oprah's influence, census data suggests that there are at least 20,000 people

1. Daniel Stone, "NEWSWEEK Poll."

2. For a newspaper article which points to the trend I have highlighted, but was published after this sermon was preached, see Carlson, "Organized religion on the decline?"

3. Oprah.com toned down its audacious tagline at some point between August 12, 2007 and September 7, 2007 to read "Get Health, Beauty, Recipes, Money, Decorating, and Relationship Advice on Oprah.com." The site has been revised at least once more since that time.

in Canada who have not bowed the knee to Oprah—as self-professed Jedis, their loyalty belongs to Yoda![4] Even our health care facilities and schools are getting into the act by recommending a holistic approach that includes recognizing the importance of spirituality.

What exactly is meant by the term spirituality is hard to say. Spirituality is a fairly nebulous term that remains relatively undefined. Perhaps that's why so many different people can be found under its umbrella. Generally speaking, those who speak of spirituality share a common conviction that there is more to life than meets the eye. Most proponents of spirituality contend that it involves some type of attempt to connect with something greater than oneself. Usually this takes the form of some sort of journey into the depths of one's being in an attempt to discover the truth of one's inner self.

Some have seen this spiking interest in spirituality as a positive development for Christians interested in spreading the good news of Jesus Christ. In some ways it is, as Christians agree that there is more to life than meets the eye and that we are all spiritual beings. On the other hand, though, Christianity isn't so much about a quest to find something as it is about being found. This morning's passage from John's Gospel tells us that the disciples had shut themselves up behind locked doors. But that didn't stop Jesus; locked doors couldn't keep out the risen Lord! Christian spirituality is brought to life by the risen Lord who finds his way through locked doors into the hardest of hearts. Often those who aren't even searching and sometimes even those who stand in an antagonistic relationship to the faith are among those who are found by Christ. For evidence of this, one has to look no further than the great twentieth-century Christian writer and apologist C.S. Lewis, who was fond of speaking about how the "hound of heaven" relentlessly pursued him during his years as an agnostic. Eventually he succumbed to the grace of God and, in the words of the title of his autobiography, was *Surprised by Joy*.

The journey of Christian spirituality begins with being found by the living God and sprouts and springs forth from there. The disciples' spiritual journey began on that Resurrection Sunday when they were sought out and found by the risen Lord. Within the context of the narrative, Jesus' "finding" of the disciples stands as the fulfillment of many of the promises that Jesus had given to the disciples throughout John's Gospel. During his final conversation with the disciples in the Upper Room before his death, Jesus had said, "Are you asking one another what I meant when I said, 'In a little while

4. The "Jedi order" has apparently been in decline in Canada. The most recent census results (2011) published in 2013 shows that the number of professing Jedi has decreased by more than half from its high of around 20,000 in the 2001 census. See Canadian Press, "Canada's Jedi Knights."

you will see me no more, and then after a little while you will see me?' Very truly I tell you, you will weep and mourn while the world rejoices. You will grieve, but your grief will turn to joy" (John 16:19–20). After going away from them and crossing the threshold of death, Jesus has now returned to his disciples and stands triumphantly before them. John tells us that "the disciples were overjoyed when they saw the Lord" (20:20). Earlier in that same farewell speech, Jesus had promised to give his disciples peace. Now he stands in their midst, risen from the grave, and the first words the disciples hear from his lips are "Peace be with you" (John 20:19). The climax of this pattern of fulfillment occurs in verse twenty-two when the risen Lord breathes upon the disciples, bestowing upon them the Holy Spirit, which he had repeatedly promised them over the course of his ministry.

This breathing of the Holy Spirit is a clear echo of the creation story in the book of Genesis where God breathed the breath of life into the nostrils of the man he had formed from the dust of the earth (2:7). It seems that John is intending for us to understand this outpouring of the Holy Spirit as a type of new creation. This interpretation is underscored by the fact that John reminds us at the beginning of this section of Scripture that it was still the first day of the week. The day of the resurrection marks the first day of the new creation and the birth of a new humanity. This creation of a new humanity had been promised throughout the Hebrew Scriptures almost from the very moment that those recipients of the first breath of life had introduced sin into the world through disobeying God's command and eating of the forbidden fruit in pursuit of their own egocentric spirituality. Through sin, death entered the world and human beings found themselves estranged from God and in enmity with God and one another. Something had to be done about this sin problem, so God began an offensive campaign against sin. At one point, the prophet Ezekiel, one of God's foot soldiers in the struggle, was taken to a valley of dry bones—bones as dry and as dead as his people Israel, who were languishing in exile on account of their sins. Ezekiel was commanded to prophesy over the bones. All of a sudden the hip bones were connecting to the thigh bones, the thigh bones were connecting to the leg bones, the leg bones were connecting to the ankle bones and, before he knew it, Ezekiel was surrounded by a vast army. But it was not until the breath of God came upon them that this army came to life in a glorious anticipation of the forgiveness of sins and the resurrection of the dead.[5] In the upper room, behind the locked doors on the evening of

5. The first part of the sentence is an allusion to the well-known spiritual, "Dem Bones" by James Weldon Johnson (1871–1938). Craig Keener includes a discussion on the historical connection between Gen 2:7, Ezek 37:9, the resurrection of the dead, and the pouring out of the Holy Spirit in *John*, 2:1204–6.

that first Easter, we see this vision coming to fruition as the Holy Spirit is breathed out upon the disciples, ushering in the age of a new humanity—a humanity recreated by the Holy Spirit in the image of God that has shone forth in Jesus Christ. Over the centuries God has added, through the Holy Spirit, a legion of saints to those first disciples, so that his people may, in all ages, serve as his strike force in the battle against sin. Those who remain loyal to the cause, wage their warfare by the same means that their Master and Commander has secured the ultimate victory. They are commissioned to triumph over sin by forgiving it.

Notice that in this morning's passage the gift of the Holy Spirit is sandwiched between two commands of Jesus: "As the Father has sent me, I am sending you," and afterwards, "If you forgive anyone's sins, their sins are forgiven; if you do not forgive them, they are not forgiven" (John 20:21, 23). The gift and reception of the Holy Spirit is intimately connected with the commissioning of the disciples and the forgiveness of sins. As one New Testament commentator has observed, "The point of receiving the holy spirit, it's clear, is not to give the disciples new 'spiritual experiences,' though to be sure they will have plenty. Nor is it to set them apart from ordinary people, a sort of holier-than-thou club—though to be sure they are called to live the rich, full life of devotion and dedication that is modelled on Jesus' own. The point is so that they can do, in and for the whole world, what Jesus had been doing in Israel."[6]

This is considerably different from the spirituality that is bandied about today by Oprah and others. Christian spirituality is not an egocentric journey inward into the depths of oneself. Rather, it is an eccentric existence which consists of living in Christ by faith and in our neighbours by love.[7] All of this is made possible by the Spirit of the living God who now dwells within us and propels us outwards toward God and neighbour. Christian spirituality then must begin and end with the person of the Holy Spirit. It must truly be a Spirit-uality. This is reflected in the language of Scripture. The word "spirituality" never appears in the Bible. The closest we come to it is found in the apostle Paul's use of the adjective "spiritual." However, Paul uses the word in such a way that it is always closely linked to the work and ministry of the Holy Spirit; so much so that whenever we come across

---

6. Wright, *John for Everyone*, 2:149.

7. The phrase "eccentric existence" is employed by David H. Kelsey as the title of his theological anthropology. The latter part of the sentence is essentially a summary of Luther's great insight from his tract, "The Freedom of a Christian," trans. W.W. Lambert in *Career of the Reformer*, 371.

the word "spiritual" in Paul's letters we would do better to read it as "Holy Spiritual."[8]

A true Christian Spirit-uality is neither ethereal nor otherworldly, for the work of the Holy Spirit is a sociology and that sociology is called church.[9] Church is the name given to that community of people that have been called out from the world for the sake of the world by Jesus Christ in the power of the Holy Spirit to witness through their life together to the present and coming kingdom of God. In other words, the Holy Spirit creates community. This is clearly on display in the often overlooked conclusion to the recounting of the events of the day of Pentecost in the book of Acts. It is hard not to be caught up in the dramatic events associated with the outpouring of the Holy Spirit on the day of Pentecost: the violent wind, the tongues of fire, the disciples speaking in tongues. But what is often overlooked is that this occurred for the sake of the formation of a new community whose life together is shaped by a particular set of practices, described as devotion "to the apostles' teaching and to the fellowship, to the breaking of bread, and to prayer" (Acts 2:42). Sandwiched between the disciples preaching in tongues and the description of the common life of the new community is the historical recollection that about 3,000 were baptized that day and added to the number of disciples. In a similar way, this morning, through the sacrament of baptism, we have welcomed Jessica and Angela into the new humanity of Christ's body. In doing so we pray that as they share in our common life of worship, fellowship, and prayer, they, along with us all, will be formed together in such a way that we are freed to inhabit the story of God's creation, reconciliation, and redemption of the world in Jesus Christ as a forgiven people empowered by the Holy Spirit to forgive.

It is no accident that life in the Spirit and the ministry of forgiveness are so closely connected in our passage this morning from the Gospel of John. However, there are a lot of misconceptions today surrounding what it means to forgive. For example, according to the renowned psychologist Dr. Phil McGraw, "Forgiveness is a choice you make to release yourself from anger, hatred, resentment."[10] Now, release from emotional baggage such as anger or resentment may be a consequence of forgiveness (and one that should not be overlooked), but it's not what forgiveness is all about. Dr. Phil is stuck in an egocentric model of spirituality, but since Spirit-uality always

8. Fee, *God's Empowering Presence*, 28–32.

9. This is one of the central themes of Dietrich Bonhoeffer's doctoral dissertation *Sanctorum Communio*. The actual wording of this sentence is indebted to Stanley Hauerwas's terse formulation in *Performing the Faith*, 19n9.

10. Cited in Volf, *Free of Charge*, 168. The url provided in the book for the quote is no longer active.

directs us outside of ourselves, we know that forgiveness is primarily for the sake of the other.

So forgiveness then is not merely an emotional or psychological game that is played within ourselves, but rather it is something that is social, directed toward another with the intention of freeing them from their burden of guilt and, ultimately, hopefully winning a brother or sister.[11] Another common misconception is that forgiveness is the same thing as looking the other way or ignoring wrongdoing. This probably arises not so much as a theoretical problem, but rather as a practical response on our part in an attempt to avoid the hard work of forgiving. We convince ourselves that in putting up with someone's miserable or destructive behaviour we are being forgiving. But turning a blind eye is not the same as forgiving. To forgive someone is not the same as saying, "You're alright. I'm alright. We're all alright." Forgiveness contains an implicit word of judgment.

Don't believe me? Then consider this. Suppose I was to extend forgiveness to someone for something they didn't do. Let's say for example that I say to Andrew, "Andrew, I forgive you for taking money off the collection plate when it was passed around earlier this morning." How is Andrew going to respond? Probably, he's going to be indignant and rightfully so, because the offer of forgiveness with its implicit word of judgment is received as an insult by an innocent person.

So there we see that a word of judgment is implicitly included within forgiveness; wrong does not go unaddressed, it is named for what it is. On the other hand, if it stopped there, it wouldn't be forgiveness, but mere condemnation. So forgiveness contains not only an implicit word of judgment, but it goes on to release that person from the burden of guilt and the punishment that the offender would rightfully bear.

Some of you are probably thinking to yourselves right now, "What about repentance? How does repentance fit in with forgiveness? Surely one must repent before forgiveness can be offered to them? Surely one must be sorry for what they have done before they deserve to be forgiven?" Repentance is important, but that line of thinking is a little off target—no one deserves to be forgiven. Forgiveness can only come as a gift, as grace. Sure, in our human relationships and dealings with one another, a repentant offender might help the offended one to offer forgiveness, but if we follow the divine model that is presented to us in the person of Jesus Christ we see that forgiveness comes before repentance.[12] As the apostle Paul puts it

11. The next few paragraphs have been significantly influenced by Volf's astute discussion of forgiveness in *Free of Charge*, 193–224.

12. A helpful article that I sometimes make available to theology students who are struggling with this concept is Wood, "God's Repentance-Enabling Forgiveness," 64–70.

in Romans, "God demonstrates his own love for us in this: While we were still sinners, Christ died for us" (5:8). Our repentance doesn't earn God's forgiveness; rather God's forgiveness leads us to repentance. Repentance is the proper way that we receive the word of judgment implicit within God's word of forgiveness. In a similar way, the proper way we receive the pardon and release of guilt inherent in God's forgiveness is with faith and gratitude. That's why you'll notice that when we, as Christians, gather for worship we take the time to both confess our sins and to thank and praise God, because without either our reception of God's forgiveness is incomplete.

As we've explored earlier, we, the church of Jesus Christ, have been commissioned to go into the world and enact a ministry of forgiveness patterned on the life, death, and resurrection of Jesus Christ; the one who died for us, while we were still sinners. But who can do that? Who can truly forgive their enemy? Who can extend blessing and mercy to the one who has wronged them? To the one who has burned down their home? To the one who has taken their child or childhood away from them? To the one who has stabbed them in the back? Only God can forgive like that. After all, "to err is human, to forgive divine."[13]

But that's just the point! Jesus didn't just appear to the disciples on that first Easter evening and say, "You've traveled with me for the past three years and together we've been through some good times and some bad. You've seen how I've lived my life, now it's time for you to pull up your socks and get out there and do your best to do likewise." Jesus didn't say that. Rather Jesus breathed on them and said to them, "Receive the Holy Spirit" (20:22). Receive the very life of God within you; the power of God at work in your life.

By the power of the Holy Spirit we are equipped to do what we could never do on our own. It is the Holy Spirit who fashions the beautiful life of giving and forgiving that is possible in Christ.[14] This beauty has been on display in the Amish community of West Nickel Mines, Pennsylvania.[15] You'll recall that West Nickel Mines was the site of a horrific school shooting, when on October 2, 2006, thirty-two-year-old Charles Roberts IV entered the single room schoolhouse and shot ten young girls, killing five of them and wounding the others. In the days that followed, the attention of the media and the gaze of the watching world were directed beyond the

13. Alexander Pope is commonly given credit for this particular formulation. See, for example, Rogers, *Alexander Pope Encyclopedia*, 281

14. Volf's "Postlude" to *Free of Charge* is an imagined conversation between the author and a skeptic about this "beautiful life" (225–34).

15. For two informed treatments of the West Nickel Mines shootings and the response of the Amish community, see Ruth, *Forgiveness*; and Kraybill, *Amish Grace*.

terrifying events of that grisly October morning to the incredible response of the Amish community. The blood was barely dry on the floor of the small one-room schoolhouse when the Amish parents incredibly sent words of forgiveness to the family of the one who had slain their children. It was more than a token gesture. It is reported that after the murders one Amish man visited Charles Roberts's parents and ended up holding Roberts's sobbing father in his arms comforting him for over an hour. At the funeral of the killer at least half of the people in attendance were Amish and they made a particular effort to greet his wife and three children. Subsequently, the Amish have helped to establish a charitable fund for the children the shooter left behind when he took his own life. In an open letter to the Amish community, Marie Roberts, the widow of the killer extended her thanks to her Amish neighbours for their forgiveness, grace, and mercy. In this letter she wrote: "Your love for our family has helped to provide the healing we so desperately need. Gifts you've given have touched our hearts in a way no words can describe. Your compassion has reached beyond our family, beyond our community, and is changing our world, and for this we sincerely thank you."[16]

God is changing our world by empowering through his Holy Spirit a people who live by the light of the resurrection within a dark and deadly world. Only the Spirit of the living God can move hardened human hearts like our own to extend forgiveness to those who have hurt us. To forgive truly is divine. And whenever or wherever such forgiveness is exercised we know that, whether it is acknowledged or not, the hand of God has been at work. But the promise that is given to the disciples of Jesus Christ is even more astounding than that, for the risen Lord says to his followers, "If you forgive anyone's sins, their sins are forgiven" (John 20:23). God himself is at work extending his forgiveness in and through us whenever we extend forgiveness to another. That's a pretty amazing thought! Throughout the course of church history, theologians have sometimes described a sacrament as a human activity which God works in and with, through and under. Protestants have traditionally considered there to be two sacraments: baptism and the Lord's Supper. Alongside the proclaimed word of God, these sacraments are the places where we can be assured of meeting God. But if we follow this definition of a sacrament—a human activity which God works in and with, through and under—then the promise that is extended in this passage from John's Gospel suggests that our extending forgiveness to another may be among the most sacramental activities of all.[17]

16. Associated Press, "Shooter's Wife Thanks Amish Community."
17. John Howard Yoder makes the case for understanding fraternal admonition, the

To forgive is truly divine, but for those who have received the gift of the Holy Spirit and are being recreated in the image of Jesus Christ, to forgive is also truly human. Forgiveness is at the heart of Spirit-uality because it is a gift from the heart of the one, who having conquered death, stands in our midst saying, "Peace be with you." May we hear his voice and be brought to life by his breath, for behold, he is making all things new.

---

open meeting, the diversification of gifts, baptism, and Eucharist as being "actions of God, in and with, through and under what men and women do" (*Body Politics*, 72–73).

6

Body Odor

Amberlea Presbyterian Church

Pickering, Ontario

Sunday, April 10, 2016

2 Corinthians 2:14—3:6; Numbers 28:1–15

For the past several months my family has been coming here to Amberlea on Thursday nights to participate in your "Messy Church" ministry. Our five-year-old daughter loves the hands-on activities and crafts that immerse her in the world of the Bible. We frequently find her singing the "Messy Church" songs at home. Our two-year-old son simply enjoys being at "Messy Church," even though he often ends up wandering around and doing his own thing. On top of that, as a parent, I have to admit that there's something appealing about not having to prepare another weeknight meal! Often as we are driving down Whites Road on a Thursday night, one of the kids will catch sight of your building here at Amberlea and yell out, "There it is! There's the Messy Church!" The first time this happened I tried to explain to them that Amberlea Presbyterian is not really a messy church, but that "Messy Church" is simply the name of the Thursday night family ministry. My careful distinction however was lost on my children and I've long since given up on trying to explain. For my family, you simply are the "Messy Church." This morning, I want to go a step further and suggest that not only are you the "Messy Church," but you are also a "Smelly Church." To support this outlandish contention we will need to take a closer look at our passage from 2 Corinthians. Hopefully by the end of the sermon, you'll agree that in calling you a smelly people, I have not actually insulted you, but rather pronounced a blessing over you rooted in the good news of the Gospel.

43

So let's turn our attention to our text from 2 Corinthians. While 1 Corinthians appears to have been written with the intention of reconciling members of the church in Corinth to one another, 2 Corinthians seems to be concerned with bringing about reconciliation between the church at Corinth and the apostle Paul himself.[1] It seems that questions had arisen in Corinth about the authority and status of Paul's apostolic ministry. To the Corinthians, Paul appeared to be inconsistent, perhaps even unreliable. Several times he had shared travel plans with them, but he had yet to return to Corinth as he had promised (1 Cor 16:5–9; 2 Cor 1:15—2:4).[2] The suspicions surrounding Paul seem to have been magnified by the arrival of traveling evangelists, poaching on Paul's territory. These teachers, whom Paul later sarcastically refers to as "super-apostles," seemed to align more closely with the Corinthians' own conception of what apostolic leadership was all about (2 Cor 11:5, 12:11). These "super-apostles" were smooth operators who came with five-star references. They were slick communicators who set about plying their trade in a town which prided itself on recognizing oratorical excellence. The rhetorical skill of these "super-apostles" allowed them to delight their listeners and to cozy up to wealthy benefactors who lined their pockets.[3] Paul, on the other hand, seemed to have very little going for him. He was not a particularly flashy speaker. In fact, some of the Corinthians were saying among themselves, "Paul's letters are brawny and potent, but in person he's a weakling and he mumbles when he talks" (2 Cor 10:10, MSG). Paul brought no letter of reference with him, he refused to sidle up to the powerful and accept handouts from the rich, and everywhere he went he seemed to be accompanied by afflictions and persecutions. In the eyes of some of the Corinthians, this was certainly not a successful or victorious leader, but rather one who reeked of the stench of death.

It is within this context that Paul launches into what one biblical commentator has called "the most profound discussion of apostolic ministry in the New Testament."[4] The passage we heard a few moments ago occurs at the very beginning of this discussion and includes several rich and fertile metaphors. We are going to focus primarily upon the metaphor Paul introduces at the end of verse fourteen and develops through verses fifteen and sixteen. Paul begins verse fourteen by saying, "But thanks be to God, who always leads us as captives in Christ's triumphal procession and uses us to spread the aroma of the knowledge of him everywhere." The image of

---

1. Witherington, *Conflict and Community*, 328.
2. Young and Ford, *Meaning and Truth*, 14.
3. Matera, *II Corinthians*, 20–24.
4. Ibid., 65.

a Roman triumphal procession is an evocative metaphor that Paul uses in several of his letters (1 Cor 4:9; Col 2:15). However, the image of a victory parade is not one that we who live in the Toronto-area can easily relate to! So for our purposes, I want to draw attention to how Paul expresses his understanding of his apostolic ministry through connecting how he is led here and there as a captive in God's great victory parade with his spreading of the fragrance of the knowledge of God and the aroma of Christ. At this point, when Paul speaks of the fragrance which he spreads, he may have in mind the burning incense that was waved or the spices that were sprinkled before the triumphal procession. Or, he may even have been thinking of the odor given off by the dirtied and bloodied captives themselves. However, there are also several important Scriptural allusions that Paul may have had in mind. The Wisdom of Sirach, a Jewish writing from the second century BC, which Paul would have been familiar with, described *wisdom* as a pleasing fragrance (Sir 24:13-15). The two words that Paul uses to speak of the fragrance and aroma are also frequently combined in the Greek translation of the Old Testament, which was the Bible of the early church, to describe the "pleasing aroma" created by the burning of sacrificial offerings.[5]

Our Old Testament reading this morning from the book of Numbers repeatedly emphasized how each offering it described was an aroma pleasing to the Lord (28:1, 6, 8, 13). At this point it might be helpful to take a step back and consider the nature of sacrifice from a biblical perspective. The Jews had a much different conception of sacrifice than the ancient peoples who surrounded them, yet I am afraid that for many Christians today their understanding of sacrifice more closely resembles that of the pagans than that of the Jews. For the pagans, sacrifice was a way of keeping an angry and unpredictable god off your back. It was something akin to an economic transaction—an "I'll scratch your back, you'll scratch mine" kind of arrangement. Sacrifice was the human attempt to keep the gods at bay or in-hand. This stands in profound contradiction to the biblical understanding of sacrifice. In the Old Testament, we see that the sacrificial system was a gift given by God to his people as a way for God's people to be reconciled to him and share in fellowship with him. The sacrificial system, then, was not an attempt by human beings to placate a capricious god, but rather it was the God-ordained means for God's people to share in communion with God. Not only were the people of God drawn into fellowship with God through the sacrificial offerings, they literally became a smelly people. Think of all of the sacrifices described in this morning's passage: every morning and evening a lamb is offered up with grain and oil, on Saturdays two additional

5. Ibid., 73.

lambs are offered with grain and oil, and the offering on the first day of the month consists of a whole inventory of livestock. A people who offer up this many sacrifices are going to exude a particular odor.

The aroma which the apostle Paul gives off could plausibly be understood as both the fragrance of wisdom and the pleasing aroma of a sacrificial offering, because the aroma that Paul exudes is the aroma of the crucified Christ who is both the wisdom of God and the true sacrificial offering. Paul understands his sufferings and afflictions in service of the Gospel to be his participation in the suffering and death of Christ and hence also his share in the power of Christ's resurrection. A chapter later, Paul adds, "We [apostles] always carry around in our body the death of Jesus, so that the life of Jesus may also be revealed in our body" (2 Cor 4:10). It is this participation in the death and, therefore, in the resurrected life of Jesus that gives Paul's life its aromatic quality. In the presence of the "apostle of the crucified Lord" some are overcome by the stench of death, while others savour the sweet fragrance of life, but everyone smells something.[6]

A couple of years ago, a friend of mine became somewhat of an international celebrity when he gave up eating solid foods for the season of Lent and sustained himself through drinking a fortified beer that he had specially brewed for the season.[7] As unusual as it sounds, my friend wasn't actually doing anything original. He was actually retrieving a Lenten discipline that was practiced by monks in medieval monasteries. Now, I'm not here to argue the merits of beer fasts or to defend my friend's decision to practice this unusual spiritual discipline. Rather, I want to draw attention to a discovery he made over the course of his fasting. He discovered that the longer he went without eating solid foods, the more his sense of smell seemed to be heightened. He came to notice that people smell like the food they eat. This wasn't some type of superficial or stereotypical observation which connected particular ethnic groups with the scents of particular spices. Rather, he came to recognize that *every* person gives off a subtle odor that reflects the foods that they have been eating. It even got to a point where he could make an educated guess as to what his wife and children had eaten on a particular day simply from how they smelled. Now, how much more should those who are gathered by the Lord to dine at his table give off a particular odor? Should not those in our world who are hungering for the bread of life smell something seeping from the pores of those who feast on Christ in faith?

6. The phrase "apostle of the crucified Lord" is taken from Michael Gorman's book, *Apostle of the Crucified Lord*.

7. For an account that appeared in a national Canadian newspaper, see Hopper, "Man will drink just beer."

The apostle Paul seems to think so. He writes, "For we are to God the pleasing aroma of Christ among those who are being saved and those who are perishing. To the one we are an aroma that brings death; to the other, an aroma that brings life" (2 Cor 2:15–16). But how do we account for these vastly different olfactory responses? After all, it is one and the same Paul who travels from town to town throughout the Mediterranean proclaiming one and the same Gospel message. It would seem that these differences in scent perception are rooted not in the "smellee," but rather in the "smellers." To play on a popular proverb, we could say that aroma is in the nostril of the sniffer. (Although, it doesn't quite seem to have the same ring to it, does it?) I learned this firsthand sixteen years ago when I was part of a ministry team that spent a couple of weeks serving in Taipei, Taiwan. While walking the streets and exploring the night markets, every so often I was overwhelmed by the scent of a terrible odor which quickly drowned out all other scents and smells. At first I thought maybe there was an open sewer or garbage dump somewhere in the area, or maybe a dog had died and was rotting in the alley, or maybe even a dog had fallen dead on top of a garbage dump within an open sewer! Eventually it dawned on me that this repulsive smell was coming from the stands of food vendors who were selling a Taiwanese delicacy known as "smelly" or "stinky tofu." Smelly tofu is a form of fermented tofu that is stewed, braised, or deep-fried and is often served with pickled cabbage, bamboo shoots, "thousand-year-old" eggs, or congealed duck blood. In 2011, smelly tofu made CNN's list of the world's most delicious foods.[8] Now I like to think that I am a fairly adventurous eater who likes to sample new and exotic cuisine, but the scent of the smelly tofu was enough to turn my stomach and dissuade me from getting anywhere nearly close enough to the vendor's stand to try it. However, for those who have acquired a taste for smelly tofu, the scent is not repulsive, but rather, in a way that remains incomprehensible to me, it is appetizing.

As an aromatic, apostolic people, the church does not set out to cultivate a particular odor, rather if we are faithful we will simply smell like people who have been with Jesus. For those who remain in darkness, a people whose life is patterned upon a first century crucified peasant will reek of failure, folly, and death. But for those whose hearts and minds have been illumined with the light of the resurrection, the vulnerable, humble existence of those walking in the way of the servant king will provide a whiff of glory. The church cannot force anyone to perceive the presence of the Lord of Glory in the form of the crucified one who dwells in its midst. This is solely the work of the Holy Spirit. Recognizing this remarkable convergence

8. CNNGo staff, "World's 50 best foods."

between the calling of an apostle and the ministry of the Holy Spirit, Paul exclaims, "Who is sufficient for these things?" or as the NIV puts it, "Who is equal to such a task?" (2 Cor 2:16).

The question of sufficiency or competency comes up again at the end of our passage, where Paul uses the "competency" word group three times in the span of two verses. The connection is somewhat masked in the NIV because it translates the word with the phrase "equal to the task" in 2:16 and later as "competent" in 3:5–6. Paul writes, "Not that we are competent in ourselves to claim anything for ourselves, but our competence comes from God. He has made us competent as ministers of a new covenant" (2 Cor 3:5–6). The competence of the aromatic, apostolic people of Christ is found in the God who has called and commissioned them. The word apostolic comes from the Greek verb *apostello*, which means "to send." The Latin translation of this word is *missio* from which we get our English word mission. So to say that the church is apostolic is simply another way of saying that the church is on mission. Sometimes we can be lulled into thinking that mission is solely the domain of missionaries; those strange and wonderful people who have a received a special calling from God to be his ambassadors in distant and exotic lands. This is an important calling and, to your credit, it is part of your enduring legacy here at Amberlea that you have been and continue to be a church that is committed to supporting and sending out missionaries so that the name of Jesus Christ may be known throughout the world. However, mission is not something that just happens overseas. Through his employment of the metaphor of the aroma of Christ, as well as the two other metaphors he mentions in the passage, namely the triumphal procession and the letter, Paul reminds us that the church is on mission wherever it finds itself. This is an important reality for you as a congregation to keep before yourselves at all times, and particularly during this time of profound cultural transition in Canada. Whether Canada was ever a "Christian" nation can be debated, but one would be hard pressed to argue that the Canada we live in today remains a Christian nation. On the one hand, we have those whom we could call "post-Christian," who have been exposed to just enough of the Christian faith to inoculate them against the real thing. On the other hand, people from all the nations of the world, who often have had no exposure to the Gospel at all, are now arriving at your doorstep. Pickering is now a mission field. However, if there is going to be a "genuine missionary encounter" between these two groups of people and the Gospel of Jesus Christ, there must be an apostolic people, a living and breathing, Gospel-shaped community capable of being encountered.[9]

9. The desire that there would be a "genuine missionary encounter" between the

Our passage this morning points us in this direction. All three of the metaphors Paul uses in this passage pertain to sensory phenomena and therefore are communicative realities. An aroma involves sensory information being transmitted through the nose and the olfactory system, which then contributes to the identification of the presence and character of an object. The other metaphors Paul employs—the triumphal procession and the letter—are visual and aural phenomena respectively. The church, the new covenant people, is a missional outpost planted by God in the midst of the world, so that the world may see and hear, taste and touch, and even smell the concrete reality of the Gospel. Mission is not simply something the church does, rather the church *is* mission. The church fulfills its missional calling through enacting its identity. The church gives off an aroma not because it is in the perfume industry, but simply because it is the body of Christ. It is his odor that the body exudes. Just as, in the words of the German pastor and martyr Dietrich Bonhoeffer, the Son of God came in the flesh, "incognito, as a beggar among beggars, as an outcast among outcasts, as despairing among the despairing, as dying among the dying,"[10] so also, will the church smell like the company it keeps, as it goes where Jesus goes and, in love, pours itself out as he poured himself out. But this body odor is a pleasing aroma unto God, and to the world it provides a whiff of the wisdom of the cross. So Amberlea Presbyterian Church, at the risk of sounding like a deodorant commercial let me leave you with these words of encouragement: Own your odor. Be who you are: the smelly people of God, the odorous body of Christ, the fragrance of life carried on the breeze of the Holy Spirit. To God be the glory in the church and in Christ Jesus throughout all generations, for ever and ever! Amen.

---

church and modern Western culture was one of the animating concerns of the writings of Lesslie Newbigin, particularly in *Foolishness to the Greeks*.

10. Bonhoeffer, *Christ the Center*, 107.

7

A Garden in the Wasteland

Chartwell Baptist Church

Clarkson Village, Ontario

Sunday, June 7, 2015

Galatians 5:13–26; Isaiah 35:1–7

F or four years, from 1992 to 1996, the city of Sarajevo lay under siege. Over the course of those four years the inhabitants of Sarajevo were subjected to continuous shelling and sniper attacks. An average of 329 shells per day rained down upon the beleaguered city and over the course of the siege over ten thousand people were killed and another fifty thousand were wounded.[1] The great city of Sarajevo was reduced to ruins. There was no public transit, no water, no gas, and no electricity. It was not unusual to find signs saying, "Beware of Snipers" posted on lampposts lining major streets. During those days Death was a constant companion to the inhabitants of Sarajevo. They could feel Death's icy cold breath on their necks each time they walked the streets and were forced to sidestep around the craters left behind from the falling mortars. They caught glimpses of Death's hooded figure lurking in the shadows each time they ventured out of their homes into the rubble of their desolated city. Death had visited the homes of their families, their friends, and their co-workers. Yet amid the swirling chaos and destruction which seemed to call life and everything associated with it into question, something amazing started to happen. People began to convert public park areas into gardens. These gardens not only helped to address the physical needs of the besieged city-dwellers by providing much needed fruit and vegetables, they also quickly became sites where people would gather

1. Horvitz and Catherwood, *Encyclopedia of War Crimes*, 382.

and linger together, sharing in conversation, in song, and in community. With the gardens came some hope for survival, a little security, and a sense that it was possible to do something. At the same time as these community gardens were sprouting up, in an act of resistance against the encroachment of chaos and death, people began to keep flowers, palms, lemon trees, and other exotic looking plants in the gardens in front of their homes and on their balconies. Despite the fact that, from a pragmatic perspective, these plants represented a completely useless investment of care and water, the message they communicated was invaluable. In the words of one who lived through the siege, it was as if those growing the exotic flowers and plants were saying, "We refuse to reduce ourselves to bare physical survival—our souls also need to survive!"[2]

I share this story from Sarajevo, because on some level it seems to resonate with the work and ways of God in our world. Our God is a gardener. In the beginning, when the Earth was but a dry and barren wasteland, God planted a garden and made all kinds of trees grow out of the ground (Gen 2:8–9). Similarly, the passage we heard from the book of Isaiah depicts the LORD bringing salvation to his beleaguered people and bringing healing to the entire creation through transforming the desert into a garden oasis. "The desert and the parched land will be glad; the wilderness will rejoice and blossom. Like the crocus, it will burst into bloom; it will rejoice greatly and shout for joy. . . . The burning sand will become a pool, the thirsty ground bubbling springs. In the haunts where jackals once lay, grass and reeds and papyrus will grow" (Isa 35:1–2, 7). It seems like somewhat of a bizarre strategy, to save the world through planting gardens in the wasteland and growing fruit on the frontlines, but that is exactly the type of work that our God is up to in our world.

This brings us to our passage from Paul's letter to the Galatians. This letter is Paul's attempt to ward off the teaching of Jewish Christian teachers who had infiltrated the congregations he had previously planted in Galatia.[3] Like a momma grizzly bear reacting to someone stepping between her and her cubs, in Galatians, Paul unleashes the full fury of his parental protective instincts in the attempt to spare his children from spiritual disaster. It appears that the teachers may have been saying something along these lines: "Now listen here Galatians, Paul is to be commended for bringing the Gospel to you, but unfortunately he didn't finish the work he started. He has left you without the resources you need to order your life together. It is only

2. The description of gardening in siege-stricken Sarajevo is largely dependent upon Maček, *Sarajevo Under Siege*, 76.

3. Here, and throughout this sermon, I am greatly indebted to J. Louis Martyn's magisterial commentary, *Galatians*.

through observance of the Law that you can hope to be victorious over the Flesh, which threatens to lead you into sin and corruption."

Now Paul agrees with the teachers that the Flesh is a force to be reckoned with, but Paul would never confuse the Flesh with some impulsive desire within human beings that can be mastered with the application of the proper technique and a little bit of elbow grease. Rather, for Paul, the Flesh is a power that holds human beings in bondage. We must not for a minute think that when Paul speaks about Flesh and Spirit that he is talking about some psychological drama that takes place within individuals as lower physical desires are encountered by the higher mental faculties. In fact, when Paul speaks about the Spirit and the Flesh, he is not talking about the human spirit and human flesh at all. What Paul has in mind is competing cosmic powers which act upon and within human beings. The Flesh is a power which creates chaos and leads to the breakdown of relationships and the shattering of community, isolating human beings from one another and from God. Under the influence of the Flesh, human beings are turned in upon themselves and imprisoned in selfishness, which results in enmity and alienation. For the enslaved human race, help must come from the outside. It must come from above. Observance of the Law is not the answer. Providing a set of moral guidelines to human beings enslaved under the power of the Flesh is as helpful as giving a roadmap to a blind man stranded on a desert island. What human beings need is not more religion or morality, but rather, a divine intervention. That is exactly what God has done in sending his Son and the Spirit of his Son into the world.

Paul understood that in the congregations of Galatia, the Holy Spirit had established a beachhead for the invasion of God's new creation into the midst of a broken and enslaved world. But the Flesh longed to take back this liberated territory. The first verse in our passage reads, "You, my brothers and sisters, were called to be free. But do not use your freedom to indulge the flesh; rather, serve one another humbly in love" (Gal 5:13). In this verse, Paul draws upon a word that is used in the Greek language to refer to a military base of operations.[4] In other words, Paul is saying, "Do not allow your freedom to become the occasion for the Flesh to set up a base of operations in your midst, instead be slaves of one another through love." Notice that Paul explicitly connects freedom with slavery to one another. How different this is from present day conceptions of freedom! According to the logic of the Gospel, freedom *from* is always connected with freedom *for*. Freedom is not some abstract indeterminacy where a person can determine themselves in whatever way is most appealing to them; that is in fact an illusion which

---

4. Martyn, *Galatians*, 485.

is simply another form of slavery. The American singer-songwriter and armchair theologian Bob Dylan had it right when he sang, "You're gonna have to serve somebody, / Well, it may be the devil or it may be the Lord / But you're gonna have to serve somebody."[5] Freedom from the power of the Flesh is accompanied by the freedom of adoption into the family of God. True freedom is the freedom to love and serve God and neighbor.

Jean Vanier, the son of former Governor-General of Canada Georges Vanier, began to experience the reality of this freedom when he welcomed two men with developmental disabilities into his home to live with him in 1964. This was the beginning of what would become the L'Arche movement, which now includes communities in thirty countries throughout the world. Vanier's experience of living in community with the developmentally disabled changed and continues to change his life. Reflecting on the subject of freedom, Vanier reflects, "Freedom lies in discovering that the truth is not a set of fixed certitudes but a mystery we enter into, one step at a time. It is a process of going deeper and deeper into an unfathomable reality."[6]

If we were to recast Vanier's thought in the language and terminology of the apostle Paul, we would say that freedom is walking in the Spirit. It is the Holy Spirit, the Lord and giver of life, who has brought freedom to Christians in Galatia and it is only by living by that same Spirit that freedom can be maintained. Attempting to live by the Jewish Law is not helping the Gentile Galatian churches, it is only leading to further conflict and disunity. To attempt to live by the Law is to return to living by human means. For the Galatians to take up living according to the requirements of Torah is essentially a denial of the Gospel on their part. In effect, they are saying that what was begun by a work of the Spirit, does not continue by the work of the Spirit, but is to be replaced by human religion or quite simply human effort. Their mindset—a mindset which seems to be very easy for the church in all times and places to slip into—seems to be that although this Christian thing began with God, it's now up to us to see it through. Such an outlook cannot help but lead to self-preoccupation and hence a return to the slavery of the flesh.[7]

5. Bob Dylan, "Gotta Serve Somebody," *Slow Train Coming* (Columbia Records, 1979).

6. Vanier, *Becoming Human*, 117.

7. Paul's polemics against Gentile Torah observance in Galatians should not be read as providing fodder for antinomian construals of the Christian faith. Even within the letter to the Galatians itself, Paul is prepared to speak of believers fulfilling "the law of Christ" (6:2). For further reflections on the place of the Law in the Christian life, see the earlier sermon on Psalm 119, "A Long and Winding Word."

So although the decisive battle has been won at the cross and ultimate victory is assured, the battle between the Flesh and the Spirit rages on and the church, wherever it finds itself—whether that be in Japan, Romania, or right here in Canada—always finds itself at the front lines of this cosmic conflict.[8] In light of this reality, Paul decides that the most helpful thing he can offer to the Galatians in their life together is a description of reality that can help them to recognize how the battle is going. As part of this description he provides two lists. One describes the works of the Flesh and the other describes the fruit of the Spirit.

The first thing to take note of is that these are descriptions, not prescriptions.[9] Paul is not prescribing a certain set of actions for the Galatians. He is simply describing what things will look like when the Flesh or the Spirit is at work within a community. In a sense, Paul is providing a diagnostic tool for the Galatian congregations to help them determine whether they are continuing to walk in the Spirit or to alert them if the Flesh is making inroads into their life together. If we look more carefully at the works of the Flesh—"sexual immorality, impurity and debauchery; idolatry and witchcraft; hatred, discord, jealousy, fits of rage, selfish ambition, dissensions, factions and envy; drunkenness, orgies and the like" (Gal 5:19–21)—we see a chaotic multiplicity of works. There is no logic to the listing or grouping of the works of the Flesh. They just intrusively appear, popping up one after another in random ways like thorns and thistles. The chaotic multiplicity inherent in the listing of the works of the Flesh is perhaps symbolic of the divisive effect that these works have upon the life of the community. The works of the Flesh are things that destroy unity within a community and break down relationships. The works of the Flesh stand opposed to the healthy life of a congregation or community. Wherever and whenever we see these community-threatening works of the Flesh rearing their heads within the life of the church, it should cause us to step back and ask whether we are indeed being led by the Spirit in that area of our life together or whether the Flesh has been allowed to set up a base of operations in our midst.

In contrast to the multiplicity and divisiveness of the works of the Flesh stands the singularity and unity of the fruit of the Spirit.[10] While there are many works of the Flesh, there is only one fruit of the Spirit. There is only one fruit of the Spirit, because there is only one Lord Jesus Christ. Through his listing of the fruit of the Spirit, the apostle Paul has placed

8. On the previous Sunday, the congregation had welcomed home missionaries who had been serving in Japan and heard from a missionary involved in providing direction for Romanian orphanages.

9. Martyn, *Galatians*, 496.

10. Betz, *Galatians*, 283.

before our eyes a portrait of the Lord Jesus Christ, in whose likeness we are being conformed through the work of the Holy Spirit. The church is God's garden. The community of disciples is the plot where the Holy Spirit is nurturing and bringing forth fruit so that the world may see in us the image of Jesus Christ. For this reason, the fruit of the Spirit must not be mistaken for private feelings or emotions, rather, they are rightly looked upon as concrete, practical ways of being in the world and relating to one another that are brought forth by the Holy Spirit. The fruit of the Spirit are characteristics that build and support community. They are ways of relating to one another that reflect God's way of relating to us in Jesus Christ. When Paul talks about the fruit of the Spirit, he is telling us that God is actively at work doing something in the midst of our broken world. Amid the chaos and violence of the surrounding world, the Holy Spirit is bringing forth God's new creation people, a people who truly care for one another and receive each other as a gift from God. They are the first-fruits of the victory of Christ and a foretaste of the future redemption that awaits the entire world.

This past week marked the passing of the great New Testament scholar J. Louis Martyn. Martyn devoted a significant portion of his life to studying and writing about Paul's letter to the Galatians. In one of his books, Martyn tells a wonderful story stemming from the civil rights movement in America that captures the essence of the picture that Paul is painting for the churches in Galatia.[11] Imagine that you are sitting in the pews of Sixteenth Street Baptist Church in Birmingham, Alabama. It is May of 1963. The campaign organized by the Southern Christian Leadership Conference to desegregate one of the South's most racially segregated cities was well under way. Each evening the black community gathered in the church to pray and sing and hear a word of encouragement. On one particular night, after the congregation had assembled and sung a few songs, a guest speaker who was a professional athlete from the northern part of the United States took to the pulpit. He began by saying, "You people are doing a great thing here in Birmingham." There was an awkward shuffling of a few feet, but he continued and again stated, "It is a great thing you people are doing here." There was some more shuffling of feet, some coughing, and a few murmurs. The athlete spoke for a few more minutes and then once again said, "The whole world has its eyes fixed on you, because you are doing a great thing here in Birmingham." At this point one of the elders, who was standing in the side aisle, having given up his seat in the pew because of the large crowd that had assembled, called out in a polite, but firm voice, "*We* are not doing this. *God* is doing this!"

11. Martyn, *Theological Issues*, 284–85.

In 1856 Captain Edward Sutherland, a widower with seven children, moved his family to Clarkson Village. He quickly recognized the horticultural potential of this region and is believed to have introduced strawberry and raspberry cultivation to the area. Clarkson eventually became known as the Strawberry Capital of Ontario. In 1915 a sign was erected in the Clarkson train station declaring, "Through this station passes more strawberries than any other station in Ontario."[12] One hundred years later, a labyrinth of winding asphalt lined by structures of brick and steel covers the ground where strawberries once grew. Yet amid this concrete wasteland, God is cultivating a garden plot by the lake. Strawberries may have been in abundance at one time, but the harvest God now intends is love, joy, peace, patience, kindness, goodness, faithfulness, gentleness, and self-control. Our God is a gardener and his Spirit is cultivating something beautiful amid the rubble of a world that has lost its way. He is forming the image of his Son Jesus Christ in the church—the hope of the world amid the ruins. Let's not miss it. Let's not turn our backs on it or take it for granted. Since we live by the Spirit, let us walk by the Spirit, for if Christ has set us free, we are free indeed!

12. Clarkson BIA, "History of Clarkson."

8

"The Clothes Make the Man"

Caledonia Congregational Church

Caledonia, Ontario

Sunday, August 2, 2015

Colossians 3:12–17

I f you've watched any television at all over the past year, you've probably seen the Trivago guy. He's the middle-aged, messy-haired, rumpled-shirt-wearing, five-o'clock-shadow-sporting, too-long-pants-wearing, belt-less pitchman for the hotel internet search engine Trivago. Or at least that's what he used to look like, until Trivago responded to the public outcry by giving him a makeover and making him the star of what seems to be an exponentially increasing series of commercials. It was about a year ago that the dishevelled Trivago guy began his rise to prominence as an internet and media sensation. Articles about him appeared in the *Globe and Mail* and the *Toronto Star*, CNN ran a series of stories about him, and "Trivago guy" was a popular Halloween costume this past year.[1] There were a variety of diverse opinions expressed online about the pre-makeover Trivago guy, but at the most basic level the problem seems to have been rooted in the wide-spread perception that the Trivago guy was not properly dressed for his context. People looking for a clean and comfortable hotel room are not interested in taking advice from someone who looks like they don't know how to shave, shower, or use an iron. When it comes to advertising, clothes really do make the man and the Trivago guy's wardrobe was found wanting.

1. Krashinsky, "Trivago spokesman"; Demara, "Trivago Guy"; Hunter, "Does 'Trivago Guy' need a makeover?"; Leopold, "'Trivago Guy' gets a new look."

In our passage, the apostle Paul is at pains to communicate to the Colossians how important it is that their clothes fit their context. Leading up to this section of the letter, Paul has told the Colossians that they have been placed within an entirely new reality through their burial with Christ in the waters of baptism and their being raised to new life in Christ through faith. This change of dominion had to be matched by a change of clothes. It simply would not be fitting for those adopted into the family of the King to appear in the filthy, ill-fitting clothes of their previous existence. Instead they should be found appareled in the robes of the royal family. The first word that we must hear this morning as we delve into this passage outlining the glorious apparel of the saints are the first words of the passage: "as God's chosen people, holy and dearly loved" (Col 3:12). This declaration is shorthand for the good news of the Gospel. God has taken the initiative. He has chosen to make us, people who were once his enemies, into his friends. We are children of the King. We are holy and dearly loved. These words—"as God's chosen people, holy and dearly loved"—are the foundation for all that follows. As if to underscore this point, Paul weaves throughout this passage a whole constellation of words derived from the Greek word for grace: *charis*. Unfortunately this doesn't come across in our English translations. The words Paul uses for the instruction to forgive in verse thirteen, to be thankful in verse fifteen, to sing with gratitude in verse sixteen, and giving thanks in verse seventeen, all have the Greek word for grace (*charis*) as their stem. All that follows is bathed in this ethos of grace; the grace that has adopted us into God's royal family.

For the apostle Paul, how we are to live flows out of who we are. To put it another way, ethics is inseparable from identity. That's why the first question of Christian ethics is not "what should I do?" but rather "Who am I?" and following from that, "What type of person am I called to be?"[2] This is on display in our passage this morning. When Paul reaches into the wardrobe for the characteristic garments of new life in Christ, the first thing he pulls out is not a set of rules or a collection of principles, but rather something that more closely resembles what we might call virtues or character traits. Now the ancient Greco-Roman world had no problem talking about virtue, but the virtues that Paul describes are not the fancy garments which lined the racks of the Greek philosophical schools. The philosophers spoke of the cardinal virtues—justice, prudence, courage, and temperance—but

---

2. This way of formulating the Christian ethical question and the insights of the remainder of the paragraph are indebted to Stanley Hauerwas's pioneering work in the field of Christian ethics. His early insights regarding the importance of character, narrative, and community for Christian ethics come to maturity in *The Peaceable Kingdom*.

these are not the character-traits spoken of by Paul.[3] Instead, Paul tells the Colossians that they are to be clothed with "compassion, kindness, humility, gentleness, and patience" (3:12). It's not that Paul was necessarily opposed to the virtues of the Greek philosophers, rather, he was working out of an entirely different trunk of clothes. Followers of Christ must be clothed in the virtues that emerge from the story of the God of Israel and his Messiah Jesus. In this story we encounter the God who, in bringing his people up out of slavery in Egypt, identifies himself as "The LORD, the LORD, the compassionate and gracious God, slow to anger, abounding in love and faithfulness, maintaining love to thousands, and forgiving wickedness, rebellion and sin" (Exod 34:6). This identity statement is then concretely displayed in the life of the Messiah Jesus, God's holy and beloved Son. The one who came to Jerusalem, gentle and humble, riding on a donkey. The one who "being in very nature God, did not consider equality with God something to be used to his own advantage; rather, he made himself nothing by taking the very nature of a servant, being made in human likeness. And being found in appearance as a man, he humbled himself by becoming obedient to death—even death on a cross!" (Phil 2:6–8). So when the apostle Paul tells the Colossians to clothe themselves with "compassion, kindness, humility, gentleness, and patience," he is telling them that they should be clothed in nothing less than the character of God.[4]

This insight is further reinforced when Paul goes on to tell the Colossians that the belt which completes the whole ensemble is love. Love must be put on overtop of all the other virtues, for love is from God. In fact, as the Scriptures tell us, "God *is* love" (1 John 4:8). Without the love of God to tie everything together, the Christian moral outfit lacks cohesion and remains woefully incomplete. Just ask the Trivago guy, he'll tell you about the importance of a good belt! The great theologian of the Middle Ages, Thomas Aquinas, offers us some help at this point. Aquinas insisted that love is the form of the virtues.[5] What he meant by this was that without love the other virtues are nothing. For evidence of this we need to look no further than the text of Colossians itself. While Paul instructs the Colossians in our passage to clothe themselves with humility, earlier in the letter he had warned them of the danger of false humility (2:18). Only as humility and all of the other virtues are taken up *by* and directed *to* the love of God in Christ can we speak of them as being *Christian* virtues. The Christian life is not about making something of oneself—even making oneself into a virtuous person—rather it is about losing

3. Barth and Blanke, *Colossians*, 418.
4. Barth and Blanke, *Colossians*, 418–22; Seitz, *Colossians*, 161–62.
5. Aquinas, *Summa Theologica*, 2.2.23.8.

oneself in the love that has been shared for all eternity between the Father, the Son and the Holy Spirit and thereby finding one's true self in Christ. The new self that we discover in Christ is constituted by the love of God and therefore is a profoundly relational self. The old selfish man of sin has been buried in the waters of baptism and we have been raised to new life as members of the body of the new human being, Jesus Christ. The whole point of the cross and resurrection of Christ and the pouring out of the Spirit, Paul is at pains to tell us in Colossians, is so that there may be a people who live out of the reconciliation accomplished by Christ on the cross and therefore live at peace with God, with one another, and with the entire creation. This new creation community, whose composition transcends all divisions and whose life together is permeated by the self-giving love of God, images the God revealed in the face of Christ and therefore fulfills the vocation for which human beings were created in the beginning.

At this point, we might be tempted to ask how the character of God is formed within such a community. I would suggest that it is this very question that informs the transition from the discussion of the virtues of the company of disciples in verses twelve through fourteen to the discussion of the practices of the worshipping community in verses fifteen through seventeen. In describing the practices that are to characterize the corporate life of the congregation, Paul writes, "Let the peace of Christ rule in your hearts, since as members of one body you were called to peace. And be thankful. Let the message of Christ dwell among you richly as you teach and admonish one another with all wisdom through psalms, hymns, and songs from the Spirit, singing to God with gratitude in your hearts. And whatever you do, whether in word or deed, do it all in the name of the Lord Jesus, giving thanks to God the Father through him" (Col 3:15–17). It seems to me that Paul is suggesting that it is through participation in these Christ-shaped practices that the Holy Spirit forms a people who are clothed with compassion, kindness, humility, gentleness and patience.[6] It is through learning the skills necessary to become true worshippers of God that the people of God are shaped in the image of the God they worship. This is a key insight of the Old Testament prophets and poets. These men of God insisted that human beings come to resemble what they worship. In Psalm 115 we read, "But their idols are silver and gold, made by human hands. They have mouths, but cannot speak, eyes, but cannot see. They have ears, but cannot hear, noses but cannot smell. They have hands, but cannot feel, feet, but cannot walk, nor can they utter a sound with their throats. Those who make them will be like them, and so will all who trust in them" (vv.

---

6. Seitz shares a similar judgment in *Colossians*, 163–66.

4–8). The psalmist is clearly telling us that in worshipping deaf and dumb idols, human beings themselves become deaf and dumb. The warning for us today in our consumeristic society is that if we ever find ourselves asking the question "What am I getting out of worship?" there is a good chance that we are worshipping an idol and that idol might very well be ourselves. Now it is true that we will get a lot out of worship, but this only occurs as we abandon our conceptions of getting something out of worship and join our voices to those of the apostles saying, "Lord, teach us to pray" (Luke 11:1). We must learn to be worshippers and to be a disciple involves giving oneself over to the discipline of a people who have learned to worship in the Spirit and in truth. As we enter fully into the worshipping life of God's people, we discover that through our participation in these Christ-shaped practices the Spirit clothes us in the character of Christ. In assembling week after week to give thanks, we are made into a thankful people. In committing ourselves to teaching and admonishing one another in all wisdom, we become a people who are truly wise. In joining our voices with one another to sing psalms, hymns, and spiritual songs with gratitude in our hearts to God, we find that we are made to be grateful people whose hearts beat to the melody of God's love.

The fact that Paul expands upon the virtuous apparel of the Colossians with instructions concerning bearing with and forgiving one another demonstrates that Paul is no starry-eyed idealist. Although there is something inherently attractive about the life shared by the disciples of Jesus Christ, no disciple can ever make the claim to have arrived. We all continue to be works in progress, with the result that life in community can be difficult. In fact, it can be incredibly difficult for addicts like ourselves, who are recovering from our habituation to the radical egocentricity of sin. The German pastor and martyr Dietrich Bonhoeffer recognized that one of greatest threats to Christian community is the refusal to recognize how difficult it is to truly live in community. In his spiritual classic, *Life Together*, Bonhoeffer observes:

> On innumerable occasions a whole Christian community has been shattered because it has lived on the basis of a wishful image . . . Every human idealized image that is brought into the Christian community is a hindrance to genuine community that must be broken up so that genuine community can survive. Those who love their dream of a Christian community more than the Christian community itself become destroyers of that

Christian community even though their personal intentions
may be ever so honest, earnest, and sacrificial.[7]

If Bonhoeffer is right, and I think he is, then we must not allow our
idealized images of church life to undermine our real life in community
with our brothers and sisters in Christ. Real life in community, however,
is messy and difficult. Therefore, Christians must be willing to bear with
each other and forgive whatever grievances they have against one another. It
seems to me that many of the problems that arise in church life today can be
traced back to the confusion of forbearance and forgiveness. There appears
to be many congregations that are intent on forbearing what really needs
to be forgiven, and, not as commonly, there are some that want to forgive
what should simply be borne. Forbearance is necessary because, as Paul says
in the verse immediately preceding our passage, in Christ's church there is
neither "Gentile or Jew, circumcised or uncircumcised, barbarian, Scythian,
slave or free" (Col 3:11). We are all wonderfully weird and wacky in our own
unique way, but Christ has called us to live together in peace. In the close
space of community, we will inevitably grate up against one another with all
our glorious idiosyncrasies. Forbearance requires the maturity to recognize
that my personal tastes and preferences are not the same thing as the law of
God. As a result, just because something annoys me or someone does things
differently than I would, it doesn't mean that what they are doing is wrong
or that it should be the cause for the breaking off of my relationship with
that person. In this way, forbearance is a form of dying to self.

Forbearance may involve turning a blind eye, but forgiveness involves
bringing out into the open. The Christian community cannot overlook sin,
for sin in its very essence is the destruction of community. We bear one
another's brokenness, but we must forgive each other's sins. Forgiveness is
necessary because we are recovering sinners, who all too often resort to our
old selfish ways, with the result that we hurt and harm one another. Without
forgiveness there is no way that the community can go on when relationships have been damaged in this way. Now it's true that the community may
continue to exist at the surface level, but these unreconciled relationships
are like festering wounds that serve as incubators for infections that can
spread throughout the entire body. The wounds inflicted by sin must be
exposed to the air, so that the healing balm of forgiveness may be applied.
Forgiveness involves the struggle to rightly name the offense, so that it may
then be released, and all parties may be restored to relationship with one
another. Forgiveness involves all parties undergoing a type of death. The one
who is forgiven suffers the death of having their offense named and brought

7. Bonhoeffer, *Life Together*, 35–36.

to light. The one who forgives must die to their desire to enact vengeance and seek retribution. We see these dynamics of forgiveness on clear display in the cross of Christ where the ugliness of humanity's sin was made painfully visible for all to see when we crucified the Lord of glory. Yet in spite of our murderous intentions, Jesus interceded for us praying, "Father, forgive them" (Luke 23:34). Because we have been forgiven, we can't imagine being anything other than a forgiving people.

While the Trivago guy became a media sensation on account of his disheveled appearance, more recently an impromptu photograph of two well-dressed people went viral last month. In the photograph we see an older African-American man sharply dressed in a suit and white gloves holding open a heavy wooden door for a little girl clothed in her Sunday-best dress.[8] It could have easily been a Norman Rockwell painting, depicting a scene from a cherished past—a time when people were truly civilized and when they still got dressed up for church. But this picture was not a scene from some bygone era, it was taken just a few weeks ago on June 21. The little girl in the photo is the daughter of a New York church-planter who travels across the country helping congregations in crisis.[9] The large wooden doors were the doors of Mother Emanuel African Methodist Episcopal Church in Charleston, South Carolina, as they were opened for worship for the first time following the horrific shooting which claimed the lives of nine of the church's members. It is true that on that Sunday many of those in attendance, like the usher and the little girl appearing in the photo were elegantly dressed in their finest clothes. However, more significantly, in the days and weeks which have followed the shooting the members of Mother Emanuel have showed themselves to be a people who are truly well-dressed—a people clothed with compassion, kindness, humility, gentleness, and patience.

On the day of the bail hearing for Dylann Roof, family members of the murdered parishioners arrived at the court-room and were given the opportunity to address the twenty-one-year-old shooter. One after another, these family members extended words of forgiveness to the young man who had so grievously harmed them and taken the lives of their loved ones. This surprisingly gracious response in the wake of the perpetration of such horrific evil has captured the attention of the watching world, leaving commentators simultaneously amazed, mystified, and even angered. Some have claimed that this forgiveness was offered too hastily and too freely. However,

8. Fleming Rutledge drew attention to this photograph in "A Norman Rockwell scene."

9. Swanson, "What the aftermath of the Charleston shooting looked like."

if you listen carefully to the words of those who spoke, you'll discover that there is nothing cheap about this forgiveness. They speak freely and openly of their pain, they name the horrific act for the evil that it was, and one of the speakers even calls the young man to repentance. This is not cheap forgiveness, this is forgiveness that has been won at the cost of the broken body of the Son of God who hung upon the cross. But why should we expect anything less? For the shootings were not merely an act of terror inspired by racial hatred, they were also an assault upon the body of Christ. As members of the body of Christ, the people of Mother Emanuel know that evil and hatred can only be overcome by goodness and love.

Listen to the words of the family members who appeared before the court.[10] Nadine Collier addressed the young man saying, "I forgive you. You took something very precious away from me. I will never get to talk to her ever again. I will never be able to hold her again, but I forgive you, and have mercy on your soul. . . . You hurt me. You hurt a lot of people. If God forgives you, I forgive you." She was followed by a relative of Myra Thompson who added, "I would just like him to know that, to say the same thing that was just said: I forgive him and my family forgives him. But we would like him to take this opportunity to repent. Repent. Confess. Give your life to the one who matters most: Christ. So that He can change him and change your ways, so no matter what happens to you, you'll be okay." A little later, the sister of DePayne Middleton Doctor addressed the court with these words, "For me, I'm a work in progress. And I acknowledge that I am very angry. But one thing that DePayne always enjoined in our family . . . is she taught me that we are the family that love built. We have no room for hating, so we have to forgive. I pray God on your soul."

The gracious response of the family members of those who were murdered is truly staggering, but we completely misunderstand that response if we isolate it from its broader context within the life of Mother Emanuel Church. The decision to forgive was not really a spur of the moment choice for those family members. In many ways, the decision to forgive had been made long before that fateful day when Dylann Roof decided to attend Wednesday night Bible study. Perhaps we could more accurately say that the decision faced by the people of Mother Emanuel was not whether to forgive, but rather whether they would be true to themselves. In the early days of their congregation their church building had been burned to the ground by white slave-holders and a few years later it had been razed by an earthquake.[11] In

10. The following quotations were reported in Izadi, "The powerful words of forgiveness."

11. Emanuel African Methodist Episcopal Church, "'Mother Emanuel' A.M.E. Church History."

the crucible of the American south, the congregation of Mother Emanuel have again and again found themselves, much like Shadrach, Meshach, and Abednego, thrust into the midst of the fiery furnace (Dan 3). Yet through all their tribulations they have continued together in prayer, in worship and in Bible study, clothing themselves in the garments of compassion, kindness, humility, gentleness, and patience. Much like Shadrach, Meshach, and Abednego, they have again and again discovered that there is another who walks with them through the flames. As a result, the question posed to them by the cruel events of June 17 was not whether they would forgive, but whether they would show themselves to be the people that the Spirit had made them to be over the course of their community's ongoing commitment to letting the peace of Christ rule in their hearts and the message of Christ dwell richly among them as they taught and admonished one another with all wisdom through psalms, hymns and songs from the Spirit, singing to God with gratitude in their hearts.

The well-dressed people of Mother Emanuel have captured the eyes and imaginations of the watching world. When Mother Emanuel re-opened its doors for worship on June 21, people came from across the United States to offer their support and to be a part of the historic moment. One visitor, a white man of no particular faith commitment was heard saying, "I came down here because I was so moved by their grace, humility and courage. I'm more angry than they are, but I want a dab of their grace."[12] There is an alternative to the hatred, division and violence of our broken world and God is making this alternative known through clothing a people in the character of the one who is himself the presence of God's peaceable kingdom—the Lord Jesus Christ. God has set his people on the runway to model before the watching world a whole new wardrobe. The world would not be able to imagine this Spirit-led, Christ-shaped way of life apart from the presence of God's well-dressed people. So Caledonia Congregational Church, "as God's chosen people, holy and dearly loved, clothe yourselves with compassion, kindness, humility, gentleness and patience." And, of course, don't forget to wear your belt!

12. Ravitz, "After Confederate flag comes down." I have reversed the order of the two clauses which make up the final sentence.

Part II

Preaching through the Christian Year

9

"Let Heav'n and Nature Sing!"

Bridlewood Presbyterian Church

Scarborough, Ontario

Sunday, December 14, 2014

Luke 1:26–38, 46–55

Advent

Over the last couple of months, I've been slowly watching my way through *The Bible*, the self-proclaimed "Epic Miniseries" produced by Roma Downey and Mark Burnett. Just a couple of days ago, I watched the segment depicting the annunciation to Mary and the birth of Jesus. As to be expected, some aspects of the story were left out and others were creatively modified to fit the constraints of the series. The end result was certainly dramatic and it made for compelling television. However, there was something about it that seemed just a little off. It's hard to blame the producers though. After all, they had the difficult task of adapting for the television screen material that is actually much better suited for the bright lights of Broadway. The first two chapters of the Gospel of Luke much more closely resemble a musical than they do a television drama. The characters in these opening chapters are constantly bursting into song. It all begins with Mary, whose magnificent song has been a source of inspiration for composers and song-writers for centuries (Luke 1:46–55). Not long after Mary's song has drawn to a close, the spotlight shifts to old Zechariah, who had been living in silence for nine months. As soon as Zechariah's lips are opened following the birth of his son, John the Baptist, he bursts into exuberant song (Luke 1:68–79). Next a choir of angels takes the stage to mark the birth of the Messiah (Luke 2:13–14). Following that, another singing senior gets into the swing of things as Simeon serenades the promised child in the Temple (Luke 2:29–32). Forget *The Bible: The Epic Miniseries*, we need "The Nativity: The Broadway Musical!"

The musicality of the opening chapters of the Gospel of Luke seems appropriate, for the singing accompanies the coming in the flesh of the Word that has been sung from all eternity by the Father on the breath of the Holy Spirit. The harmonious melody, which has resounded within the life of the triune God from before the beginning of time, was now about to perfectly sound forth in the life of the child conceived in Mary's womb.[1] Although no one could have anticipated this development which saw the great composer taking up a chair within the symphony of creation, those who have beheld his glory can read backwards and hear traces and echoes of the divine melody throughout the sacred story. Long before all worlds were made, the harmonious melody of the Father's song of delight in his Son and the Son's song of undying love for his Father were carried on the eternal breath of the Holy Spirit. Even though this love song was complete and perfect in itself within the life of the triune God, God did not aspire to keep this melody to himself. It was God's desire to share its melodious strains with others outside of God's own life. So the melody that had eternally resounded within the life of God now sounded forth for the first time outside of God bringing all of creation into being. As John the Evangelist memorably put it, "In the beginning was the Word, and the Word was with God, and the Word was God. He was with God in the beginning. Through him all things were made; without him nothing was made that has been made. In him was life, and that life was the light of mankind" (1:1–4). To transpose John's assertion into a slightly different key, we could say that the Word is the melody that resounds through all of creation. The music of the spheres, the dance of life, the symphony of creation—they are all set to the song of the Son.

But something has gone wrong. The divine melody has become occluded by an array of shrill notes and dissonant voices. It has become difficult to discern whether the symphony of creation is playing any score at all. The human desire to make one's own kind of music has resulted not in virtuoso performances, but in a cacophony of competing voices. Having lost the melody, we are easy prey to the counterfeit choruses that clamour and

1. Ken Michell, the Director of Worship at Bridlewood Presbyterian Church, rightly pointed out to me afterwards that, strictly speaking, a "harmonious melody" is a contradiction in terms. While musically suspect, the phrase "harmonious melody" may nonetheless helpfully point us to the mystery of difference-in-unity which characterizes the life of the triune God. If the term harmony were used by itself we would run the risk of losing sight of the fact that the Son is the exact imprint or repetition of the Father (*homoousios*, in the terminology of the Nicene Creed). If we simply employed the term melody, we would risk conflating the Father and the Son.

compete for our attention: money, sex, power. The songs of sirens like these result in idolatry and injustice and ultimately lead to death. Our inability to hear and heed the divine melody presents not only a moral problem, but also a cosmic threat. Our tone-deafness has thrown the entire creation into disarray. Sharp staccato notes ring out at seemingly random times: tsunamis, earthquakes, Ebola, cancer. The entire creation seems to teeter on the edge of sonic anarchy.

But God did not give up on his broken world. He continued to sing over his creation. He called out Israel as his treasured possession to prepare for the day when he would sing his song of love divine not only over creation, but also in and through creation. Fittingly, this peculiar people were a singing people. When the LORD brought the Israelites up out of slavery in Egypt by parting the waters of the Sea and leading his people across on dry ground, Miriam, the sister of Moses, took up the tambourine and sang, "Sing to the LORD, for he is highly exalted. Both horse and driver he has hurled into the sea" (Exod 15:21). The celebrated king who united the twelve tribes under the banner of a single kingdom and established the capital city of Jerusalem was equally renowned for his musicianship and may go down as history's most famous song-writer. His catalogue of hits, including the chart-topping, "The LORD is My Shepherd" (Ps 23), are still sung and celebrated to this day. As the beleaguered kingdom of Israel divided and eventually fell to foreign invaders, God raised up prophets within the ranks of his people. Their hopeful promises of restoration and new creation often took on lyrical form. Following his announcement of the coming dreadful day of judgment, the prophet Zephaniah shared the following words of comfort: "The LORD your God is with you, the Mighty Warrior who saves. He will take great delight in you; in his love he will no longer rebuke you, but will rejoice over you with singing" (3:17). There were dramatic crescendos in the history of Israel—Sinai, the dedication of the Temple, King Josiah's reforms—moments when the divine melody majestically sounded forth for all to hear. However, there were also times, due to apostasy within and persecution without, when the divine melody was barely audible. Through it all, the LORD remained faithful to his people and preserved the memory of the melody in the ears of a faithful remnant.

We don't know much about the teenage girl chosen to carry the Son of the Most High in her womb, but we do know that Mary is a daughter of Israel—the people of the promise. This helps to explain the militant character of Mary's song. In Mary's day the people of Israel were prisoners in their own land, suffering under a cruel Roman occupation force. Only a daughter of Israel, only a member of the people who had suffered so much for the sake of God's promise, could sing a song like the Magnificat. Mary's song reminds us that joy is not to be confused with happiness. Happiness is dependent on external circumstances and the whims of fortune. Joy comes from a deeper place. It is a gift of God rooted in the promises of God. As Mary's song demonstrates, joy can be angry. Joy never makes peace with injustice. Joy rails against illness and death. Joy recognizes that the way things are is not the way they have to be. Joy knows that one day, by God's grace, all things will be made right. In her song celebrating the impending arrival of the promised and long-hoped-for Messiah, Mary skillfully weaves together the language of the Torah, the song of Hannah, and the Psalms of David into a new song of joyful praise.[2] As Mary's song attests, the promises of God were finally coming true, but in a way that no one could have ever expected.

The first hint we get of the subversive nature of this coming king and his kingdom is that the angel Gabriel is sent not to a princess in a palace in Jerusalem or even Rome, but rather to a young, unmarried peasant-girl in the backwaters of Galilee. Mary's jubilant song further emphasizes the upside-down nature of the Messiah's reign: the proud are scattered, rulers are brought down from their thrones, the humble are lifted up, the hungry are filled with good things and the rich are sent away empty. To be clear, this kingdom is not really upside-down. It only appears that way because we are standing on the ceiling. In a world of war, the arrival of the Prince of Peace cannot help but be disruptive. In a world of cold cruelty and indifference, the flame of love will be experienced as scorching hot. In a world enshrouded in the darkness of falsehood, the light of life will necessarily be perceived as blinding. There is a disruptive, even shocking, character to the entrance of the divine melody into a world filled with dissonant human voices.

The theme of finding grace inside a sound has become an increasingly prominent theme in the music of the Irish rock band U2. Their previous album even included a soaring anthem which, in a nod to Mary, was entitled, "Magnificent."[3] Their recently released album, *Songs of Innocence*, which generated a great deal of controversy on account of its free distribution to all iTunes users, continues to develop the theme as it explores some of the band's formative experiences from their teenage-years. The lead single and first song on the album, entitled "The Miracle (of Joey Ramone)," describes the liberating experience of hearing the punk-rock music of the Ramones for the first time. However, it was during their teenage years that three members of the band were also first gripped by the Gospel. As in most U2 songs, there appears to be more going on than first meets the eye, or better,

2. Jeffrey, *Luke*, 33.

3. The explicit reference to the inspiration of the Magnificat is found in the following interview with Bono: Brian Hiatt, "Hymns for the Future."

ear. The first verse ends with the confession of a young man, "I wanted to be the melody, above the noise, above the hurt."[4] After a short bridge, the song launches into its first chorus, which is surely a riff on the lead singer Bono's favourite hymn, "Amazing Grace."[5] "I woke up at the moment when the miracle occurred / Heard a song that made some sense out of the world / Everything I ever lost, now has been returned / In the most beautiful sound I'd ever heard."[6]

When the strains of the divine melody catch our ear, they awaken us from our slumber and the world begins to look and sound different. Like Mary, those who have heard the opening chords of the divine melody, cannot keep themselves from singing.[7] The baby conceived in Mary's womb does not merely create a people who sing with their voices. Upon his arrival, the song-in-the-flesh begins fashioning a people whose lives resonate with the divine melody. The one, holy, catholic and apostolic church has rightly recognized Mary as the mother of our Lord, but what has often been overlooked is that Mary was also the first disciple.[8] Luke makes this clear later in his Gospel by including a couple of brief sayings of Jesus about family. On one occasion, when he was teaching a large crowd, someone said to Jesus, "Your mother and brothers are standing outside, wanting to see you." Jesus replied, "My mother and brothers are those who hear God's word and put it into practice" (Luke 8:19–21). On another occasion, when Jesus was once again teaching a large crowd, a woman called out, "Blessed is the mother who gave you birth and nursed you." To this Jesus replied, "Blessed rather are those who hear the word of God and obey it" (Luke 11:27–28). Far from marginalizing Mary, these comments actually establish her as the preeminent disciple. When the angel Gabriel proclaimed God's word to her, Mary replied, "Behold the handmaid of the Lord; be it unto me according to thy word" (Luke 1:38, KJV). Mary is first and foremost a disciple and because she is a disciple she becomes the mother of her and our Lord. The ancient Church Fathers reflected this reality when they insisted that Jesus was conceived through Mary's ear as she heard and clung to the word of God in faith.[9]

---

4. U2, "The Miracle (of Joey Ramone)," *Songs of Innocence* (Island, 2014).

5. Scharen, *One Step Closer*, 140.

6. U2, "The Miracle."

7. There is an allusion here to the Robert Lowry's (1826–1899) hymn, "How Can I Keep from Singing?" which also sometimes appears in hymnals under the title, "My Life Flows on in Endless Song."

8. Brown, *A Coming Christ*, 60–66.

9. Benedict XVI, *Jesus of Nazareth*, 36–37.

The song of Mary, the first disciple, gives us some clues about the nature of discipleship. On the one hand, disciples are not simply whistling their own tunes; rather, they are drawn up into the great anthem of salvation. This is reflected in the deep indebtedness of Mary's song to the Scriptures of Israel. On the other hand, disciples are not simply cookie-cutter repetitions of a simple melody line as in some crass commercial jingle. Rather, as the image of Christ takes form in the members of his body, the result is endlessly new variations on the eternal theme. This is evident in the way Mary takes up the Scriptures of Israel, but employs them in an entirely new way. I think there is something here for you as you think about the calling of Bridlewood Presbyterian Church to make disciples of all nations in this particular corner of Scarborough.[10] On the one hand, you must avoid the dangers of unreflective obsession with new fads and innovations. This is often simply a form of catering to autonomous human beings who desire to sing their own song in defiance of the divine Maestro. On the other hand, nothing can squelch the Spirit faster than the conservative impulse preeminently displayed in the refrain, "But that's how we've always done it." Disciples are called to the art of improvisation.[11] A skilled improviser does not just randomly play notes off the top their head, rather their ability to improvise emerges from their schooling in the rudiments of their craft. Like a skilled jazz musician who has studied her scales, developed her understanding of chord-progressions, and is conversant in the history of music, disciples must be rooted in the story of God as it has been presented in the Scriptures and as it has been lived out in their particular community. However, the community of disciples must always be open to new variations on the theme as the Holy Spirit plays the melody of Christ's redeeming and reconciling love through his people.

John Perkins put it this way: the Christian life is nothing other than "the outliving of the in-living Christ!"[12] Perkins is, in a way, also part of your story here at Bridlewood. In 1994, you sent a group of young people on a short-term mission trip to Mendenhall, Mississippi, where Perkins had established a ministry to help the poor in rural Mississippi begin to meet their own needs. Like Mary, Perkins was an unlikely choice to be a disciple assigned important kingdom responsibilities.[13] He was born into

10. The congregation at Bridlewood was in the midst of a pastoral transition and was about to embark upon a pastoral search following the departure of a long-standing and beloved lead pastor.

11. Samuel Wells skillfully develops this theme in his book *Improvisation*.

12. Perkins, *With Justice for All*, 18.

13. Perkins recounts his own journey of discipleship in his autobiography, *Let Justice Roll Down*. Many of the key events in his life are also recounted within *With Justice*

an African-American family of share-croppers and bootleggers. After his mother died when he was seven months old, his father left him with his grandmother and skipped town. He dropped out of school after grade three. As a teenager, he held his bleeding brother in his arms as they rode to the hospital after his brother, a veteran of the Second World War, was shot by white police officers less than a year after returning from Germany. His brother eventually succumbed to his wounds and Perkins fled to California, never to return to Mississippi again—or so he thought. But something happened in California. While growing up Perkins had possessed nothing but disdain for religious folk. In California he found himself caught up in the song of salvation. It began with a group of women who started taking Perkins's son to Sunday school. Soon Perkins himself began to notice the chords of a different melody sounding forth in the life of his son. It wasn't long before this divine melody took root within his own soul.[14] He began visiting local prisons to share the good news of the Gospel with the incarcerated men. The prisoners were predominantly young, black men, many of whom, like him, had moved to California from the South, but, unlike him, had been unable to overcome the odds of a system stacked against them. As he talked with these young men, Perkins began to sense that God was calling him back to Mississippi. In 1960, Perkins and his family returned to Mississippi, eventually settling in the ghetto in Mendenhall. This move became the basis for the first of what Perkins later came to understand as the three "R's" of community development: relocation.[15] Years later, a large white mega-church asked Perkins to come and share with them how they could reach their black neighbours with the Gospel. Perkins's answer was simple. He told them when a black family buys the house beside you and moves in next-door, you don't move out six months later.[16] As Perkins continued his work in community development in Mendenhall, he observed that the town was losing its best and brightest young people to the big cities where there were jobs and opportunities. This led Perkins to commit himself to the second "R" of community development: redistribution. When Perkins speaks of redistribution what he has in mind is not the forceful taking of wealth from the rich and giving it to the poor in the spirit of Robin Hood, but a community that lives together and shares their material resources, their professional skills, and their life experiences in the Spirit of the Gospel. It

---

for All.

14. Charles Marsh helped me to see the "musicality" of Perkins's life through his essay, "The Power of True Conversion" in Marsh and Perkins, *Welcoming Justice*, 53–71.

15. Perkins explicates his understanding of the three "R's" in *With Justice for All*.

16. Perkins, "Quiet Revolution."

was in 1970 that Perkins was struck by the final "R" of community development: reconciliation. On a February night, a van full of students who had been participating in a civil rights march was stopped by the police and the students were arrested and taken to the station. Perkins was called to post bail. When he arrived at the jailhouse, he was met by a dozen highway patrolmen. It was a trap! Perkins recalls slipping in and out of consciousness over the course of the night as the white police officers beat him to within an inch of his life. As he lay on his hospital bed recovering from the attack, tempted to despair, the song of the reconciling and redeeming love of Christ welled up within him and a vision of Christ on the cross formed in his mind. Reflecting on this vision, Perkins observed, "He too was arrested and falsely accused. He too had an unjust trial. He too was beaten. Then he was nailed to the cross and killed like a common criminal. But when he looked at the mob that had crucified him, He didn't hate them; He loved them! And he prayed, "Father, forgive them; for they do not know what they were doing."[17] At that moment Perkins realized that he was called to a ministry of community development that was inescapably committed not only to relocation and redistribution, but also to reconciliation, particularly between people of different races. Perkins came to recognize that the song of the crucified one is not a solo to be sung by a lone disciple. Rather, it is a melody carried by a choir of disciples who have learned that their lives are meant to harmonize with others, even those who are least like them, until the music swells into a joyful and irresistible chorus. Perkins recognized that the risen Christ continues to sing today through his body. The song which sounds forth from the life of the church invites men and women to find their lives through losing themselves in the melody that brought the worlds into being. The song of love to the loveless shown. The chorus that is the destiny of all creation.

The world ends not with a bang or a whimper, but with a song. The creation groans with longing, in eager expectation waiting for the curtain to go up on the final number. To quote U2's song "The Miracle" one last time: "I woke up at the moment when the miracle occurred / I get so many things I don't deserve / All the stolen voices will someday be returned / The most beautiful sound I'd ever heard."[18] On that day, all of the voices prematurely silenced by calamity and injustice will be returned and they will join with all of the saints and the creation itself in singing: "Hallelujah! For our Lord God Almighty reigns" (Rev. 19:6)! "To him who sits on the throne and to the Lamb be praise and honor and glory and power for ever and ever" (Rev 5:13)! So let heav'n and nature sing, let the fields and floods, rocks, hills and

17. Perkins, *With Justice for All*, 109–10.
18. U2, "The Miracle."

plains repeat the sounding joy and let every heart prepare him room—for the living Christ delights to sing his song of salvation to and in and through us until all of creation is taken up in a great tidal wave of praise.[19] Maranatha! Come, Lord Jesus.

19. The first part of this sentence consists of numerous references to Isaac Watts's great Advent hymn "Joy to the World!" (1719) which was sung during the service of worship.

10

When a Hallmark Christmas
Isn't Good Enough

Good Shepherd Community Church

Scarborough, Ontario

Monday, December 24, 2007

Luke 2:1–20

Christmas Eve

I f you've been following the entertainment news, you may be familiar with the uproar that has accompanied the release of the film adaptation of Philip Pullman's novel *The Golden Compass. The Golden Compass* is the first installment of a fantasy trilogy that has been described as "an atheist's answer to *The Chronicles of Narnia.*"[1] Its release has caused a furor among some Christian groups who are urging their supporters to boycott the film. In the wake of this controversy a quick-witted United Reformed pastor in Wales has written a delightfully provocative column in which he argues that what we as Christians really ought to be boycotting is not *The Golden Compass*, but rather children's nativity plays.[2] I'm sure you've probably all either seen one in person or on video, or at the very least heard about these cute productions in which kids dress up in bathrobes and drape towels over their heads so that they can fill the role of the shepherds in the Christmas story. Maybe you've even been the parent of one of the three lucky chil-

---

1. Unfortunately I am no longer able to locate the source of this quote. I am sure it came from one of the movie reviews that was circulating at the time. For a review from that time that makes a similar connection between Pullman's *His Dark Materials* trilogy and Lewis's *The Chronicles of Narnia*, see Chattaway, "Chronicles of Atheism."

2. Fabricius, "Boycott Nativity Plays!"

dren who in addition to experiencing the thrill of wearing their bathrobe to church also got to add a bit of jewelry to their costume and carry an empty shoebox, which of course immediately makes them one of the wise men! I've even seen pictures of myself as a child preparing to participate in one of these nativity plays draped in a white robe with large heart-shaped cardboard cut-out wings lined with tinsel attached to my back.

These are the type of nativity plays that the pastor in Wales is urging Christians to boycott, going so far as to suggest, in tongue-in-cheek fashion, that he may even picket in front of any local churches who are planning on staging such a production. His concern is not for the children involved in the nativity plays. He admits that dressing up and playing the role of a character in a nativity play probably helps the children to learn and enter into the story. His concern is that these plays are corrupting the children's parents and the other adults who look on adoringly, gushing, "Isn't it sweet," while the flashbulbs of digital cameras erupt throughout the audience. You know what? He has a point. Absorbing ourselves as adults in children's nativity plays could trick us into thinking that the Christmas story is all "sweetness and light." Now, it certainly is light, but it is light in the darkness and it's definitely not sweet.

You'd never get that impression though from looking at the covers of our Hallmark greeting cards with their chubby cherubim, wonder-filled wise men, and doting donkeys. The romantic images on these greeting cards make it appear that a cold cave or stable surrounded by animals is the most obvious place to deliver a baby. But we can't just blame the greeting card companies or the entertainment industry for this romanticization or sentimentalization of Christmas. We Christians are not without our share of the blame. After all, we are the ones going gaga over children's nativity plays and singing Christmas carols which include such lines as, "The cattle are lowing, the Baby awakes, but little Lord Jesus no crying he makes."[3] Think about that for a second. You've got a newborn baby sleeping in a feeding trough in a cold, dark, damp cave, when suddenly he is jolted awake by the noises coming from a group of large, smelly animals and you're telling me that baby is not going to cry? Now, "Away in a Manger" will always have a special place in my heart, as I've sung it since I was a small child appearing in nativity plays, but that line is evidence of simply preposterous hymn writing.

However, we don't stop with merely sentimentalizing the Christmas story through our songs and plays, we've moved beyond that to sentimentalize our entire celebration of the season to which the story has given birth. Family and acquaintances that don't have the time of day for each other

---

3. John T. McFarland, "Away in a Manger," (1892).

the rest of the year are all of a sudden expected to come together in peace and harmony. We wrap gifts and gather around the Christmas tree with our loved ones in the hopes of creating our own Hallmark Christmas moment; something that gives us a warm and fuzzy feeling inside that goes beyond being accounted for by the rum in our eggnog. This is even a strong temptation for us here in worship on Christmas Eve. On no other day is there such pressure on the pastor and others involved in planning and leading worship to create an experience for the congregation—to choose the right songs that bring back cherished memories from Christmases past and to establish a warm and soothing environment basked in candlelight.

Yet, after our time together tonight has passed, after we've unwrapped the presents tomorrow, and after we've carved the turkey and shared meals with family and friends over the next few days—it's back to real life. It's back to menial tasks and irksome jobs; back to petty squabbles with co-workers and getting children off to school. It's back to the daily grind of lives and circumstances that don't look at all like the cover of our Hallmark greeting cards or even a Christmas Eve congregation bathed in the warmth of candlelight. It's no wonder then that some people only come to church on Christmas Eve and avoid coming the rest of the year. For if this Christian thing is only about feeling warm inside as we sing familiar carols and bask in the glow of candlelight, then it really doesn't have anything to do with the rest of the year or the rest of our lives.

If you've come here tonight looking for your annual fleeting Hallmark-moment fix, then there's a good chance that you're going to leave tonight disappointed with this message.[4] But I don't have any apologies for you. As a congregation we've suffered too much loss, we've experienced too much hurt over the past year, and especially over the past few weeks, to settle for a Hallmark Christmas. We need something more than a sentimental moment that warms our hearts for an evening, or a day, or even a week. We need something more profound than a tender birth scene or a celebration of babyhood or of families. We need something more than mere sentimentality this Christmas.

Moving beyond our own existential needs, there's actually nothing particularly sentimental in the Christmas story itself. What's sentimental about a beaten down group of people being terrorized by the political superpower that occupies their land? What's touching about an eighty-five mile uphill-trek through rugged wilderness in order to register for a census that is conducted simply for the sake of extorting more taxation money from

4. This did, in fact, happen for at least one woman. The following year, she approached me after worship on a Sunday morning in Advent and proceeded to tell me how my sermon had ruined Christmas for her and her family.

an occupied people?[5] Is there anything particularly endearing about an unplanned, teenage pregnancy? What's romantic about experiencing labor pains in a cold, damp cave surrounded by livestock?[6] What about welcoming a group of shepherds—outsiders who spent their lives alone outdoors with sheep as their only company—as your baby's first visitors? That's certainly not romantic, it's just plain weird!

Now, I know some of you are probably thinking, "What about angels? Surely the presence of the angels resonates with our romantic conceptions of this festive season? Surely there's something special about the presence of the angels?" And you're right, there is something special about the presence of the angels, but these are not like the chubby cherubim that you might find atop Grandma's Christmas tree. These angels are "a great company of the heavenly host" (Luke 2:13). In other words, this is an army of angels—a celestial invasion force—amassing along the border of heaven and earth! No wonder the shepherds were terrified. What we originally thought was an endearing passage at the beginning of Luke's Gospel actually turns out to be the beginning of a war story. It is the beginning of the account of God's invasion of the cosmos.

This invasion does not resemble any of the military campaigns that we're familiar with from our history books. God's invasion of the world turns everything upside down. This is apparent in the appearance of the angels who arrived on the scene proclaiming the good news of the Savior's birth, which has inaugurated an era of peace. These phrases: "good news," "Savior," "peace on earth," are taken directly from the Roman imperial propaganda of the time where they were used to describe the "good news" of the birth of Caesar Augustus, the "Savior" who had established the *pax Romana* (the Roman peace) throughout the known world.[7] The terms make quite a bit of sense when they are connected with Caesar Augustus, the most powerful man on the planet at that time, but when they are applied to a vulnerable little baby born to a peasant couple "wrapped in cloths and lying in a manger" (Luke 2:12), the entire world is turned upside down.

The angels appeared to the shepherds saying, "the God of peace is invading our world and if you want to find him, go look in the animal shelter among the hay and the manure." The nativity story actually turns out to be one of the best arguments for the church today. For it tells us that if we want

5. Fitzmyer, *Luke I-IX*, 405–6.

6. In the second century, Justin Martyr suggested that Joseph and Mary took up quarters in a cave after they were unable to find a room in Bethlehem. Justin Martyr, *Dialogus cum Tryphone Judaeo*, 79, quoted in B. Witherington III, "Birth of Jesus," in Green et al., *Dictionary of Jesus and the Gospels*, 70.

7. Brown, *Adult Christ at Christmas*, 18; Green, *Luke*, 121–24.

to find God, the place to look for him is not in the halls of power, nor in the depths of personal spirituality or religious experience, rather God is found among the strange people that he has called together, right there amid the straw and stench.

We must not fool ourselves into thinking that the manger was just a phase in Jesus' life that he would eventually outgrow. Rather, from the moment he was born right until he died, Jesus' life was lived out amid the hay and the manure. He was born in a stable. Along with his parents, he lived the first few years of his life as a fugitive in a foreign country (Mat 2:13–23). At some point when he was a teenager or young man he suffered the death of his father, Joseph. Once he began his ministry, he lived as a homeless person, who had "no place to lay his head" (Luke 9:58). He traveled around Galilee and Judea eating and drinking with the untouchables, those deemed to be the lowest dregs of society: the tax-collectors, prostitutes, and lepers. The wonderful line from "Hark! The Herald Angels Sing," which exclaims, "veiled in flesh the Godhead see," applies just as much to the rest of Jesus' life as it does to the babe in the manger.[8]

For the entire length of time that Jesus roamed throughout Galilee and Judea, he was engaged in combat with the forces of darkness, enacting the reign of God in the midst of a broken world. He drove out the demons that sought to hold people back from experiencing the fullness of life. He breathed life into the broken bodies of the sick and infirm. He overturned the tables of the money-changers who sought to make a profit on the backs of the poor and the marginalized. He called the religious establishment into question and caused the political authorities to look over their shoulders. These were the invasive actions of God-in-the-flesh. Yet it was all a little too much for the powers that be, so when God-in-the-flesh appeared on the scene, "church and state" aligned together to kill him. This turn of events is already foreshadowed in Luke's telling of the Christmas story when he makes use of the threefold sentence, "wrapped him in cloths and placed him in a manger, because there was no guest room available for them" (2:7). This is later echoed near the end of Luke's Gospel when Joseph of Arimathea took down Jesus' body from the cross, "wrapped it in linen cloth and placed it in a tomb cut in the rock, one in which no one had yet been laid" (23:53).[9]

Jesus endured all that the world could throw at him, even the cruel and humiliating death reserved for the most reviled of criminals. In evoking such opposition to his ministry, the Prince of Peace revealed the violence that under-girds the societies of our world. When he who is the way, the

---

8. Charles Wesley, "Hark! The Herald Angels Sing" (1739).

9. Green, *Luke*, 124.

truth, and the life was hung upon the cross, the claims for allegiance made by the powers of this world were revealed as the falsehoods they really are. And when Jesus was raised up from the dead on the third day, we were given assurance that Jesus' patient endurance and faithful obedience to his Father in the face of his unjust suffering was actually his triumph over the forces of darkness which sought to destroy him. The empty tomb joins with the empty manger in calling out to us: Behold this man, Jesus. He is Emmanuel—God-with-us. In him the Most High has drawn near, invading our world and setting things right. He has overcome evil with good. He has overwhelmed the darkness with pure light and has conquered hatred with love incarnate.

This is the way of God in the world. This is the victory of Christ and we too have been invited to join in the victory procession and follow in the way of Jesus. He has left special gifts for us underneath the tree so that we may withstand the forces of darkness that linger on in this world, somehow not realizing that their time is up. There's a whole new wardrobe for us waiting to be unwrapped and tried on: a belt of truth, a breastplate of righteousness, shoes of peace, a shield of faith, a helmet of salvation, and the sword of the Spirit (Eph 6:14–17). It's all we need to stand firm against the forces of darkness, for they have already been defeated and although they may rage and conspire against us, they cannot ultimately triumph over us, for the victory belongs to the Lord.

So join with me tonight in lighting a candle in defiance of the darkness in our world that, whether it acknowledges it or not, already stands defeated in Christ. Lift the candle high and hold it out from yourself. Let it shine out in protest against the darkness. Let it shine in protest against the multinational corporations who rule over the global economy, making incredible wealth on the backs of the poor. Let it shine in protest against a society that prides itself on its openness in welcoming doctors, lawyers, and professionals from countries throughout the world, but then is unwilling to employ them in their professions and forces them to flip burgers instead. Let it shine in protest against the stock-piling of weapons and war-mongering which seems to have captured the imaginations of the worlds' leaders. Let it shine in protest against AIDS, Alzheimer's, cancer, frontal lobe dementia, Crohn's disease and all of the other illnesses at whose hands our loved ones have suffered. Let it shine in protest against the tsunamis, earthquakes, famines, and floods that inflict such damage upon our world, and in protest against the patterns of life and consumption that may be causing them. Let it shine in protest against the exploitation of the powerless and those whose voices are not heard: the unborn, the elderly, the mentally ill, all those who are out of sight and so often out of mind. And finally, let it shine in protest against the darkness that still remains within our own hearts.

Let us light candles and sing together in protest against the darkness in the name of Jesus Christ, the light of the world, who is making all things new. For "the night is nearly over; the day is almost here" (Rom 13:12). So let us together lift our candles and let our light shine in the darkness as we await the coming of the dawn. Let us join with the great army of angels in hailing the arrival of the heaven-born Prince of Peace, as we celebrate the victory of the risen Sun of Righteousness.[10]

---

10. This last sentence contains multiple references and allusions to the third verse of "Hark! The Herald Angels Sing," which was sung immediately following the message as the flame of the Christ candle was used to light candles held by members of the congregation who, in turn, lit the candles of their neighbours.

11

Being on Pilgrimage Sure Is No Vacation!

Good Shepherd Community Church

Scarborough, Ontario

Wednesday, February 22, 2012

Isaiah 58:1–12; Mark 1:14–15, 2:13–17

Ash Wednesday

It's hard to believe that Ash Wednesday and the Season of Lent are already upon us. Ash Wednesday has traditionally been the least attended worship service of the year here at Good Shepherd. I suppose there are plenty of reasons for the relatively small Ash Wednesday gatherings. The service does take place on a weeknight, which places it in direct competition with regular family, work, and other weekly commitments. Not only does it take place on a weeknight, it takes place on a weeknight in February or early March, when the evenings are normally cold, dark and dreary. One has to be particularly motivated to leave the house on such an evening. Some people are probably put off by the very thought of putting ashes upon one's forehead. After all, it is not, by any stretch of the imagination, something that is culturally accessible or wildly popular. I have yet to hear of any major retail outlets introducing a line of sackcloth tracksuits just in time for Ash Wednesday. In a society in which people probably spend more time and money on keeping their faces clean than at any point in history, the thought of smearing ashes on one's forehead is counterintuitive, to say the least. However, there is clear biblical precedent for the practice of placing ashes upon one's head as a sign of humility and repentance. Job repents in dust and ashes after being questioned by the LORD (Job 42:6). After suffering a terrible defeat at the hands of the men of Ai, Joshua and the elders of Israel tore their clothes and sprinkled dust on their heads, as they fell facedown before the LORD (Josh 7:6). In the face of the impending judgment of the LORD at the hands of the Babylonian invaders, the prophet Jeremiah urged the people of Jerusalem to put on sackcloth and roll in ashes (Jer 6:26). In the book of Esther, when Mordecai discovered Haman's plot to wipe out the Jewish people, Mordecai and many of his Jewish kinsmen, in their great distress, donned sackcloth and ashes (4:1–3).

Beyond the strangeness of putting on ashes and the difficulty of getting out on a weeknight in February, I think there may also be a more profound spiritual reality at play. Perhaps the reason Ash Wednesday is the least popular worship service of the year is that we'd rather not face the harsh reality that we are dust and to dust we will return (Gen 3:19).[1] We'd rather not be reminded of the fact that we are frail creatures, utterly dependent upon God's mercy and grace at all times and in all circumstances. Nor are we particularly interested in acknowledging our need for repentance. Not only do we like to look upon ourselves as being self-sufficient, we also like to think that we have arrived. We'd rather not be reminded that we are each a work-in-progress. Repentance? No, that's for drunkards and crack-heads, pedophiles and home-wreckers, and families named Kardashian. It's certainly not for nice Christians like us. Repentance? I don't think so—been there, done that—it's time to move on to bigger and better things.

"Not so fast!" the Protestant Reformer Martin Luther would growl if he were with us tonight. If Luther were our pastor, tonight might find him traveling from house to house, hammering a copy of his ninety-five theses onto each and every door, so that all could read his first thesis: "When our Lord and Master Jesus Christ said, 'Repent' [Matt. 4:17], he willed the entire life of believers to be one of repentance."[2]

Of course, at this point I have to realize that I'm preaching to the choir. You are all here. We are the ones who get it. We understand the importance of this night and the ashes. But then—all of a sudden—the LORD's indictment of the people of Israel through the mouth of the prophet Isaiah rings out against us. "Is *this* the kind of fast I have chosen, *only a day* for people to humble themselves? Is it *only* for bowing one's head like a reed and for lying on sackcloth and ashes? Is *that* what you call a fast, a day acceptable to the LORD?" (58:5; italics mine). The word of the LORD sounding forth through the prophet Isaiah leaves us to ponder whether, at our core, we are simply good religious people: people like those who in Isaiah's day were using

1. The application of the ashes to the forehead of each person is accompanied by the words: "Remember you are dust, and to dust you shall return."

2. Luther, "Ninety-Five Theses or Disputation on the Power and Efficacy of Indulgences," in *Luther's Basic Theological Writings*, 21.

religious rites and observances as a way to hide from the rightful claim of God upon their lives. Is setting aside a night to repent and place a few ashes upon our foreheads simply a clever religious way of evading the hard work of daily repentance to which we are called? Is the great fast of Lent that we enter into tonight simply a spiritualizing tactic for avoiding the kind of fasting that God has chosen: "to loose the chains of injustice and untie the cords of the yoke, to set the oppressed free and break every yoke? Is it not to share your food with the hungry and to provide the poor wanderer with shelter—when you see the naked, to clothe him, and not to turn away from your own flesh and blood?" (Isa 58:6–7). It would seem that what the LORD is interested in cultivating in his people is not simply a more fervent level of religiosity or even what we might call a deeper spirituality. Rather, it seems that what the LORD is interested in is comprehensive, personal transformation. Victor Shepherd, who was my theology professor back when I was a seminary student, never tired of reminding the class that the root command of Scripture is: "Be holy because I, the LORD your God, am holy" (Lev 19:2).[3]

I've recently been introduced to the work of Ronald Heifetz, a professor at Harvard's Kennedy School of Government, who teaches and writes on leadership.[4] Now, to be honest, I'm not normally impressed by leadership literature, especially Christian leadership literature. It often seems to be neither insightful, nor particularly Christian. Heifetz, however, does not appear to write from any particular faith perspective, but he does introduce some terminology around change that I think can be used to illuminate some central aspects of the Christian life. Heifetz identifies two types of challenges that leaders and organizations face, each requiring different types of responses. He calls them technical problems and adaptive challenges.[5] Technical change is necessary when the problem has been clearly identified and the solution and how the solution should be implemented are clear. Technical problems can be solved by simply calling upon the right expert or implementing the right program or procedure. For example, if the muffler falls off my car, what I have is a technical problem. I simply have to take my car in to the mechanic who has the appropriate set of skills and know-how to install a new muffler. Adaptive change, on the other hand, is necessary when the nature of the problem, the solution, and its implementation are more complex and less than clear. Adaptive change requires drawing upon the wisdom of the entire community, discerning the times, and being will-

---

3. Shepherd, *Our Evangelical Faith*, 18.

4. Thanks to Arthur Boers for introducing me to Heifetz's work.

5. This distinction is introduced in and employed throughout his seminal work: Heifetz, *Leadership without Easy Answers*.

ing to undergo deep personal transformation, as the community may be called upon to revisit its priorities, beliefs, habits, and loyalties. Human beings naturally prefer technical solutions to problems because they don't cost us anything. We simply "plug in" the solution and continue on with things as they were. For this reason, the promises made by politicians running for election are usually technical solutions. Basically, the politician says, "I will apply my specialized knowledge to develop a plan that will maintain the current level of government services without raising taxes." The politician who proposes an adaptive solution to a problem like raising taxes or cutting key services or some other thing that necessitates a change in behaviour on the part of the electorate will suffer at the polls. Just ask Jimmy Carter. In the face of the energy crisis of 1979, when he was President of the United States, Carter had the nerve to go on television and urge the American people to cut down on their consumption. In the words of that famous speech, Carter observed, "In a nation that was proud of hard work, strong families, close-knit communities, and our faith in God, too many of us now tend to worship self-indulgence and consumption. Human identity is no longer defined by what one does, but by what one owns. But we've discovered that owning things and consuming things does not satisfy our longing for meaning. We've learned that piling up material goods cannot fill the emptiness of lives which have no confidence or purpose."[6] Therefore, Carter continues, "I'm asking you for your good and for your Nation's security to take no unnecessary trips, to use carpools or public transportation whenever you can, to park your car one extra day per week, to obey the speed limit, and to set your thermostats to save fuel. Every act of energy conservation like this is more than just common sense—I tell you it is an act of patriotism."[7] That's the not type of thing you say if you're hoping to be re-elected. Sure enough, a year later Jimmy Carter was steamrolled by Ronald Reagan in the presidential election, becoming the first sitting American president since 1932 not to be re-elected.

Don't be fooled! God is not running for election. He is not pandering for votes by proposing quick-fix technical solutions to make our lives more comfortable. He has no need of a Super Pac or a string of high-profile celebrity endorsements. God is not concerned about his approval ratings. Jesus is Lord whether any of us choose to acknowledge him or not. God created us without our consent and he raised Jesus Christ from the dead and enthroned him as ruler and Lord despite our opposition. However, as

6. Jimmy Carter, "Energy and National Goals: Address to the Nation (July 15, 1979)," in *Public Papers*, 1237.

7. Ibid., 1240.

the fourth century Church Father St. Augustine once observed, the God who made us without us, will not save us without us.[8] He loves us too much to leave us the way we are. The same command of the Lord comes to us in various forms throughout the Scriptures. In Romans we hear, "Do not conform to the pattern of this world, but be transformed by the renewing of your mind" (12:2). In Leviticus, God tells his people, "I am the LORD, who brought you up out of Egypt to be your God; therefore be holy, because I am holy" (11:45). And in the Gospels, Jesus begins his ministry by proclaiming, "The time has come. The kingdom of God has come near. Repent and believe the good news!" (Mark 1:15). Whatever the Lord commands of us, he also enables and empowers us to do. This doesn't mean that it will come easily or naturally to us. Our default setting as fallen human beings is to prefer technical solutions to the type of adaptive change that the Lord desires to work in our lives. We would much rather make an external change than face up to the reality that the first thing God desires to save us from is ourselves. We are always tempted to believe that there is some type of shortcut to personal holiness and congregational health that gets around the need for us to become new people. A subtle example of this is on display in the Christmas carol, "Away in a Manger," which provides an overly sentimental, romanticized picture of the events of Christmas. "The cattle are lowing, the baby awakes, the little Lord Jesus, no crying he makes."[9] Really? No crying? Come on! But enough of that. Tonight I am going to speak in defense of the carol in the face of some contemporary revisionists who have attempted to change the words. In recent years, in several different contexts I've noticed that the final line of the song has been changed from "and fit us for heaven, to live with Thee there" to "and take us to heaven, to live with Thee there." Only one word has been changed, but the theological stakes are extremely high. The original version of the song—"fit us for heaven, to live with Thee there"—implies what Christians have traditionally referred to as sanctification, the process by which believers are made holy as their wills and desires are aligned with the will of God as they are conformed to the image of Christ through the work of the Holy Spirit. The revised version of the song—"take us to heaven"—is pure religious escapism and does not reflect biblical faith at all. The original version implies adaptive change; we must be transformed, if we are to be the type of people who will be able to endure dwelling in the Lord's presence. The revised version reflects a simple technical change mentality. The problem is external to us; namely, we are not yet in heaven. The solution is that God will take us there. There is no thought that

8. Augustine, *Sermo* 169.11.13, quoted in *Catechism of the Catholic Church* 8.1847.
9. John T. McFarland, "Away in a Manger," (1892).

the problem may not only be external to us, but that it also resides within us. There seems to be no recognition that not only do external circumstances need to change, but we need to be worked over by the Holy Spirit and hammered into shape upon the anvil of the living Word of God.

The question that we as God's people need to ask ourselves is whether we are a family going on vacation or a people setting out on pilgrimage? The differences between a vacation and a pilgrimage are revealing. A vacation is self-chosen. A pilgrimage only occurs in response to a call. One heads to a vacation destination in order to escape from reality. The destination of a pilgrimage is the ultimate reality itself. Travel is incidental to a vacation; the faster you can get to your destination the better. Conversely, the journey is an inseparable and essential part of a pilgrimage. With respect to a vacation, it matters little whether you travel by plane, train or automobile. On the other hand, when it comes to a pilgrimage, the way that the way is traveled must be in keeping with the character of the final destination. A vacation, at its core, is about the self consuming things, whether that is soaking in the sun, taking in the sights, or wolfing down the local cuisine. A pilgrimage, on the other hand, is fundamentally about the self being consumed by the all-consuming holiness of God.

We are a people set on pilgrimage by the living God. Our pilgrimage is not for a year or a season. Our pilgrimage extends for the duration of our lives or until Christ returns in glory, whichever comes first. The people of God are always in transition.[10] As the author of the letter to the Hebrews puts it, "For here we do not have an enduring city, but we are looking for the city that is to come" (13:14). In Jesus Christ we have been given a share in the great adventure called kingdom.[11] When left to our own devices, we could do nothing more than stumble around, lost in the darkness; God made his light to shine upon us and set us upon the Way. Over the course of the journey, the Lord intends to transform us, so that we may be the type of people who are fit for our destination when we arrive. The danger is that if we are not transformed, we run the risk of the hell of spending eternity in heaven with a God whom we have not learned to love or desire. It is through the work of daily lifelong repentance that the Lord makes us holy. We must be sure we are not confused about repentance: "Repentance is not preoccupation with an unsavoury past."[12] We will, however, discover that as we learn to name our sins in the presence of Jesus Christ and one another that

10. The congregation was, at that time, in a transitionary period between lead pastors.

11. Hauerwas, *Sanctify Them in the Truth*, 199.

12. Thomas J. Talley, quoted in Neil Alexander, "An Introduction to Lent," in Webber, *Services of the Christian Year*, 227.

their power over us is broken. As pilgrims, we do not back into the future like Lot's wife (Gen 19:26), preoccupied with where we've been. Rather, our gaze is focused upon him who goes before us—"the pioneer and perfecter of faith" (Heb 12:2). We long to follow so closely behind him that our faces are covered by the dust rising up from his sandals. Repentance, then, is the daily reorientation of our lives to the mercy of God in Jesus Christ that allows us to acknowledge our constant dependence upon God and daily receive anew our lives as gifts from him. In repentance, we cast our cares upon the Great Physician in the recognition that we are among the sick, the sinners, and the lost that Christ came to save. As our gaze is focused upon Christ, through the work of repentance, we are freed to acknowledge that "we are dust and to dust we will return." This is infinitely good news. First, because it frees us from the idolatrous desire to be our own gods, and second, perhaps more importantly, because our Lord is in the habit of making something beautiful out of dust and ashes. Just ask Hannah, who was given a son by the LORD after enduring years of being barren. She will tell you, "[The LORD] raises the poor from the dust and lifts the needy from the ash heap; he seats them with princes and has them inherit a throne of honor" (1 Sam 2:8). Or ask the blind man who had his sight restored when Jesus took dust from the ground, made mud out of it, and applied it to his eyes. He'll tell you what Jesus is able to do with a handful of dust and ashes (John 9:6–7). Or listen to the apostle Paul, who reminds us that "we have this treasure in jars of clay to show that this all-surpassing power is from God and not from us" (2 Cor 4:7). So hear afresh the words of our Lord, the good news of the Gospel, "The time has come. The kingdom of God has come near. Repent and believe the good news!" (Mark 1:15).

12

The Road to Calvary Passes
through Flossenbürg

Knox Presbyterian Church

Toronto, Ontario

Sunday, March 27, 2011

Mark 8:27—9:8

Lent

An expectant hush fell over the auditorium as the impossibly-young-looking, broad-shouldered, bespectacled professor stepped to the lectern at the University of Berlin. The year was 1933. Just a few months earlier, Adolph Hitler had been appointed as the Reich Chancellor of Germany and the nation had begun its terrifying descent into barbarism. A week later, students and Nazi storm troopers would assemble on the university campus to burn hundreds of volumes of books. Among the books burned were the works of Heinrich Heine, who had, a century earlier, written the chilling prediction, "Where they burn books, they will ultimately also burn people."[1] Astoundingly, in the midst of these tumultuous events, over two hundred bleary-eyed students assembled at 8:00 am on a Saturday morning to hear the opening lecture of Dietrich Bonhoeffer's course on Christology. The carefully-measured opening words of Bonhoeffer's lecture pierced the hush which had fallen over the lecture hall:

> Teaching about Christ begins in silence. 'Be still, for that is
> the absolute', writes Kierkegaard. That has nothing to do with

1. Heinrich Heine, *Almansor*, quoted in Rasmussen, editor's introduction to Bonhoeffer, *Berlin*, 4.

the silence of the mystics, who in their dumbness chatter away secretly in their soul by themselves. The silence of the Church is silence before the Word. In so far as the Church proclaims the Word, it falls down silently in truth before the inexpressible: 'In silence I worship the unutterable' says St. Cyril of Alexandria. The spoken Word is the inexpressible; this unutterable is the Word. 'It must become spoken, it is the great battle cry' proclaims Luther. Although it is cried out by the Church in the world, it remains the inexpressible. To speak of Christ means to keep silent; to keep silent about Christ means to speak. When the Church speaks rightly out of a proper silence, then Christ is proclaimed.[2]

At several points in our passage from the Gospel of Mark, the apostle Peter fails to speak rightly out of a proper silence. Peter first comes into the spotlight when, in response to Jesus' question, "Who do you say I am?" he announces on behalf of the Twelve, "You are the Messiah" (Mark 8:29). The careful reader of Mark's Gospel has been waiting for this very moment. Mark began his Gospel with the words, "The beginning of the good news about Jesus the Messiah, the Son of God" (1:1). However, within the eight chapters that follow, not a single character within the story recognizes that Jesus is the Christ. It is only here at the halfway point of the book that someone finally realizes that Jesus is the Messiah. However, no sooner have the words left Peter's lips, than Jesus shockingly rebukes Peter for it. The phrase as it appears in the NIV, "warned them not to tell anyone" is a rather weak translation of the Greek word which could simply be translated as "rebuked." It is the same word which is used earlier in the Gospel of Mark to describe Jesus' rebuking of the unclean spirits (1:25, 3:12) and it is the same word which the NIV does later translate as "rebuked" when it occurs later in our passage (8:32, 33).[3] This raises the question, Why would Jesus rebuke Peter for identifying him as the Messiah when Mark has already told us at the beginning of his Gospel that Jesus is, in fact, the Christ?

A clue is found in the strange story of the healing of the blind man at Bethsaida which occurs immediately before this morning's passage (Mark 8:22–26). In that passage a blind man is brought to Jesus. Jesus leads the blind man outside the village, spits on the man's eyes and lays hands on him. He then asks the man if he sees anything and the man replies, "I see people; they look like trees walking around" (v. 24). Jesus places his hands on the man a second time and this time the man's sight

---

2. Bonhoeffer, *Christ the Center*, 27. Quotation adapted slightly for oral performance.

3. Hooker, *Mark*, 203, 206.

is fully restored. The fact that this story occurs immediately before the events of our passage suggests that it is significant for how we are to understand Peter's confession. Peter's acclamation of Jesus as the Messiah is an indication that the eyes of the disciples are beginning to be opened to perceive the true identity of Jesus. However, like the blind man who at first only saw trees walking around, the eyes of the disciples have only been "half-opened."[4] They are correct in recognizing Jesus as the Messiah, but at this point they have no understanding of what true Messiahship entails. Peter and his companions had very definite conceptions about how the Messiah would come, how the Messiah would act to save the people of Israel, and how the Messiah would rule the nations, but these conceptions stand in stark contrast to the path that has been laid out for Jesus.

The fact that this conversation between Jesus and his disciples occurs on the way to Caesarea Philippi further sharpens the contrast.[5] The city of Caesarea Philippi was constructed by Herod the Great and later enlarged by his son Philip, who renamed it in honour of Caesar Augustus; hence the name Caesarea Philippi or Philip's Caesarea. A large white marble temple was constructed for the worship of Caesar, the self-proclaimed Savior of all men who sought to bring "peace" to the entirety of the known world through the flexing of his imperial muscle. In ancient times, Caesarea Philippi was the site of a shrine for the Greek god Pan, the famous player of the pan flute. Pan was known as the god of shepherds, flocks and mountain wilds, and was believed to be able to incite fear and terror with his music. Caesarea Philippi was also a site where the Canaanite storm-god Baal had been worshipped. Caesarea Philippi, with its matrix of cultural, political, and religious influences in some ways resembles our own city of Toronto: where the tycoons of the business world gather on Bay Street; where the movers and shakers of the political realm assemble at Queen's Park and City Hall; where the media moguls at Rogers, CBC, and City TV beam their programming out to the world; where the modern-day gladiators of the rink and the hardcourt meet to do battle at the Air Canada Center; and where the intelligentsia pontificate from the lecterns of the lecture halls at any of our city's three universities. In the face of the ancient equivalents to our modern-day power brokers, Jesus, the truly divine one, turns to his disciples and insists upon the humble title Son of Man or quite simply "the Human One."[6] He then goes on to describe a path that involves the renunciation of

4. Hooker, *Mark*, 200.

5. The description of Caesarea Philippi which follows is indebted to Witherington, *Mark*, 240; and J.R. McRay, "Caesarea Philippi" in Evans and Porter, *Dictionary of New Testament Background*, 178–79.

6. The *Common English Bible* has elected to render *huios tou anthrōpou* as "the

all power in terms of the world's understanding. He sketches the portrait of a path which will ultimately end in humiliation, suffering, and death.

Peter does not want to hear any more of this nonsense. Rejection, suffering, and death? That is no way for a Messiah to go about his business. If Jesus keeps talking like this, the movement is sure to fizzle out as quickly as the latest video sensation on You Tube. Everyone knows that history is written by the victors and that the world is saved through the exercise of power. Jesus would be better to take a page from Steve Jobs's playbook and launch his campaign for Messiah in the way that Apple promotes a new iPad. Jesus could learn from how Rob Ford has ridden in on his high horse to clean up City Hall as the new sheriff in town.[7] Jesus should make his presence felt like the Allied Forces enforcing a no-fly zone in Libya. But rejection, suffering, and death? Come on! This is neither an effective nor relevant course of action, and it is certainly not becoming of God-in-the-flesh.

The mystery of the cross is the great scandal or stumbling block of the Christian faith. The resurrection has its detractors and the incarnation is hard to wrap our heads around, but by far the most offensive notion in Christianity is the assertion that we see God most clearly in the broken and disfigured body of the one who hangs like a common criminal upon the cross. The crucified Christ is the mystery at the center of the universe, before which all mortal flesh must keep silence.[8] This strange God is not the God we would have chosen for ourselves, if we had been the ones doing the choosing.[9] We'd much prefer a strong God, a powerful God, a successful God. We'd much rather have a Messiah who rides triumphantly into town and wins the day by being the biggest, the smartest, or the strongest. Perhaps that's why it seems that so much of today's most popular Christian music seems preoccupied with singing about how great and powerful God is, but makes scarce reference to Christ, much less Christ crucified.[10] This development would not have come as a surprise to the great Protestant Reformer John Calvin. Long ago he came to the conclusion that the human

---

Human One" when it is used as a title for Jesus.

7. This sermon was preached in the early days of Rob Ford's term as mayor of Toronto following his grassroots conservative campaign to clean-up City Hall and long before his antics became the staple of late-night comedy shows.

8. "Let All Mortal Flesh Keep Silence" is the title of a 19th century hymn by Gerard Moultrie, which is a paraphrase of the Eucharistic Liturgy of St. James which dates back to at least the fourth century.

9. Brueggemann, *Awed to Heaven*, 87.

10. Around the time of this sermon, I conducted a casual survey of the top twenty-five worship songs in Canada as listed by CCLI. Only eight of those songs made any type of reference to Christ crucified and for several of those eight the cross was only a peripheral matter which appeared to simply be mentioned in passing.

heart "is a perpetual factory of idols."[11] It is only in traveling with Jesus to the cross, through the season of Lent and through the seasons of our lives, that our idolatrous tendency to cast God in the image of our own aspirations is purged. It is only through looking in silence upon the figure of the broken body of our Lord hanging upon the cross that our eyes are opened to the disorienting reality that God saves the world, not through the exercise of sheer power, but through the exercise of suffering love.

Having been rebuked by Peter, Jesus turns around and returns the favor, rebuking Peter with the words, "Get behind me, Satan! You do not have in mind the concerns of God, but merely human concerns" (Mark 8:33). In Peter's rebuke, Jesus recognized the presence of the Tempter who, just as he had in the wilderness at the beginning of Jesus' ministry, and as he would again at the end of Jesus' ministry in the Garden of Gethsemane, was tempting Jesus to rely upon something other than the divine means of establishing the kingdom by way of the cross. Having resisted Satan's attempt to take advantage of Peter's partial understanding, Jesus summons the crowd and says, "Whoever wants to be my disciple must deny themselves and take up their cross and follow me" (Mark 8:34). Over the centuries, Christians have attempted to domesticate this saying by equating "denying oneself" with ascetic exercises like giving up chocolate for Lent and by interpreting Jesus' saying about taking up the cross to refer to all of the irritating and annoying situations we have to deal with in the course of daily life, from nagging in-laws to chronic health conditions. However, this doesn't seem to be what Jesus is talking about. The word that Jesus uses when he speaks of a follower "denying oneself" appears only four times in the Gospel of Mark; once in this passage and three times in chapter 14 in conjunction with Peter's denial of Christ.[12] The implication seems to be that the disciple must ultimately decide who they are living for: Jesus or themselves. The meaning of the command to "take up one's cross" would have been even plainer. The cross was the means by which Rome both executed and made an example out of those who got in their way. The command to "take up one's cross" means that being a follower of Jesus will necessarily bring one into confrontation with the principalities and powers who seek to rule our world through the power of the fear of death.[13] As one biblical commentator has put it, the sayings of Jesus at the end of chapter 8 "point to the fact that the crucial divide is not between those who acknowledge Jesus as the Messiah and those who do not, but between those disciples who are prepared to follow

---

11. Calvin, *Institutes*, 1.11.8.

12. Hooker, *Mark*, 208.

13. Myers, *Binding the Strong Man*, 246–47.

him on the way of suffering and those who are not."[14] As much as we may desire otherwise, we cannot have Christ without the cross, or be a Christian without being a disciple. As Dietrich Bonhoeffer famously framed the matter in his book, *The Cost of Discipleship*, "when Jesus calls a man, he bids him come and die."[15]

Bonhoeffer himself had discovered this reality in the years immediately leading up to his Christology lectures of 1933. During this period Bonhoeffer underwent what he later described as "a turning from the phraseological to the real."[16] Up to this point, Bonhoeffer had thrown himself into his work, amassing great personal accolades, including completing his doctorate at the unheard of age of twenty-one. But now he had come to recognize that the life of a theologian belonged to the church of Jesus Christ. No longer would he approach theology as a matter of mere intellectual curiosity or for the purpose of personal advantage. Bonhoeffer had been seized by Christ's call to discipleship.[17] In 1935, in a letter to his brother, Bonhoeffer incisively diagnosed the church situation of his time, writing, "The restoration of the church must surely depend on a new kind of monasticism, which has nothing in common with the old but a life of uncompromising discipleship, following Christ according to the Sermon on the Mount. I believe the time has come to gather people together and do this."[18] Bonhoeffer's prescription for the renewal of the church of his generation is just as applicable to the church of our day. All too often what passes for talk of church growth and renewal today, with its emphasis upon methods and programs and statistics, simply seems to be nothing more than a thinly veiled attempt to grow a successful organization while carefully avoiding the call to discipleship and carrying the cross. Bonhoeffer rightly saw that the future of the church in the modern Western world depends upon the church recovering, by the grace of God, a sense of its identity as a visible community of disciples on the way with Jesus. If the world were all of a sudden able to look upon Christian congregations and see not a group of individuals who have made a particular lifestyle choice or who share some type of religious preference,

14. Hooker, *Mark*, 208.

15. This reflects the dramatic phrasing of Reginald Fuller's original translation. The translation found in the more recent critical edition of *Discipleship* more closely reflects the austerity of the German: "Whenever Christ calls us, his call leads us to death." Bonhoeffer, *Discipleship*, 87n.11.

16. Bonhoeffer, *Letters and Papers* (2009), 358.

17. Bonhoeffer reflects upon this early period of his academic career and his subsequent "great liberation" in a letter sent in 1936 to his third cousin and theological colleague Elisabeth Zinn, found in *Theological Education at Finkenwalde*, 134–35.

18. Bonhoeffer, *London*, 285.

but rather a people called together by Christ, who bear in their bodies the marks of Jesus (Gal 6:17), there would be no telling how far or how quickly the Gospel might spread.

Bonhoeffer himself took up the challenge of "uncompromising discipleship" that he had posed in his letter to his brother. In 1935, he became the director of one of the preachers' seminaries of the Confessing Church, the Christian body which had objected to the Nazis' attempt to unify church and state. These seminaries were deemed to be illegal by the Nazis before they had even opened, yet for close to four years Bonhoeffer managed to fly under the radar of the Gestapo, directing the studies and spiritual lives of over one hundred future pastors. Bonhoeffer and his students shared life together in an experimental form of Christian community, embodying the new kind of monasticism he had previously recognized as being so desperately needed. Together they shared in morning prayer, in silent meditation, in confessing their sins to one another, in study, in meals and in recreation. Their "life together" was not simply for their own sake, or for the sake of their own intellectual or spiritual growth, but for the sake of Christ's body, the church, and the world which Christ loves.[19] The Gestapo sealed the doors of the seminary at Finkenwalde in September of 1937 and the path of Bonhoeffer's life branched off in a different direction. In 1939, just before war broke out, Bonhoeffer traveled to the United States in an attempt to avoid being called up for active duty in the German military. However, shortly after arriving he sensed that God was calling him to return to Germany. After all, how could he assist in the reconstruction of his country after the war, if he hid out in safety in the United States during the time of his people's greatest need?[20] So Bonhoeffer returned to Germany and became involved with a resistance group which operated under the cover of the German intelligence agency known as the *Abwehr*. As a member of this resistance group, Bonhoeffer participated in carrying out a plan called "Operation 7," which oversaw the smuggling of fourteen Jews out of Germany into Switzerland. When the Gestapo discovered financial irregularities involving money transfers to Switzerland, Bonhoeffer was arrested on suspicion of treason. He would spend the rest of his short life in prison.

In July of 1944, after having been imprisoned for more than fifteen months, Bonhoeffer penned a poem entitled "Christians and Pagans" that

19. Bonhoeffer's own theologically-informed reflections upon the life of the Finkenwalde community are found in his spiritual classic *Life Together*.

20. These sentiments are reflected in a letter Bonhoeffer wrote to the theologian Reinhold Niebuhr shortly before returning to Germany, found in *Theological Education Underground*, 210.

reflects many of the themes of our Scripture passage this morning. The poem reads:[21]

I

Men go to God when they are sore bestead,
Pray to him for succour, for his peace, for bread,
For mercy for them sick, sinning, or dead;
All men do so, Christian and unbelieving.

2

Men go to God when he is sore bestead,
Find him poor and scorned, without shelter or bread,
Whelmed under weight of the wicked, the weak, the dead;
Christians stand by God in his hour of grieving.

3

God goes to every man when sore bestead,
Feeds body and spirit with his bread;
For Christians, pagans alike he hangs dead,
And both alike forgiving.[22]

In the first stanza of the poem, Bonhoeffer identifies the common human tendency shared by both Christians and those of no faith at all to cry out to God in desperate times and situations. During his time in prison, Bonhoeffer had witnessed the most hardened and least religiously inclined of men calling out to God in sheer terror when the air raid siren sounded and the ground began to shake under the bombs that were falling upon Berlin.[23] In the second stanza, Bonhoeffer distinguishes Christians from pagans, by suggesting that what sets Christians apart is not only that they go to God in need, but they are also those who stand by God in God's own need. In a subsequent letter which continued with this theme, Bonhoeffer asserted that Christians are those who stay awake and keep watch with Christ in Gethsemane.[24] Bonhoeffer himself had been such a disciple. At a time

21. Reprinted with the permission of Scribner, a division of Simon & Schuster, Inc. from LETTERS AND PAPERS FROM PRISON, REVISED, ENLARGED ED. By Dietrich Bonhoeffer, translated from the German by R.H. Fuller, Frank Clark, et al. Copyright © 1953, 1967, 1971 by SCM Press Ltd. . All rights reserved.

22. Bonhoeffer, *Letters and Papers* (1997), 348–49.

23. Bonhoeffer, *Letters and Papers* (2009), 276.

24. Ibid., 486.

when the great majority of the church in Germany had fallen asleep, Bonhoeffer had remained alert. As a result of his consistent Christian witness he suffered many persecutions and hardships. First, he was removed from his teaching post at the University of Berlin. Then his seminary and Christian community at Finkenwalde was shutdown. Shortly after that, he was banned from speaking in public and prohibited from publishing any of his writings. He was further required to check in regularly with the police. The last two years of his life were spent in prison. From his prison cell he observed that it is through sharing "in God's suffering at the hands of a godless world" that one truly becomes a Christian and hence, a true human being.[25] This is a serious and demanding word. It is a word which would surely crush us, if it were the last word. But Bonhoeffer does not end his poem in this way, for he knows that the last word does not rest with us, but with God who has spoken the last word in Jesus Christ.

Our Scripture passage this morning comes to a similar conclusion. Six days after instructing the crowd in the demanding way of discipleship, Jesus takes Peter, James, and John with him up a high mountain. There he was transfigured before their eyes and his clothes became dazzling white. Elijah and Moses, two towering figures from Israel's history, appear alongside Jesus. Peter, not knowing what to say, and seemingly unable to recognize that this might be a time for saying nothing at all, blurts out, "Rabbi, it is good for us to be here. Let us put up three shelters—one for you, one for Moses and one for Elijah" (Mark 9:5). Peter still believes that it is possible to avoid the way of the cross, and in its place proposes to form a cult of adulation on the mountain. No sooner had Peter finished speaking than the group was enveloped by a cloud. A voice spoke from the cloud, saying, "This is my Son, whom I love" (Mark 9:7). The words spoken from the cloud echo the words pronounced over Jesus at his baptism, which in turn contain echoes of the second Psalm with its messianic promise, the servant songs of Isaiah 42 and 44, and perhaps even the sacrifice of Isaac where Abraham is instructed to offer his "beloved son" (Gen 22:2; my translation). Having identified Jesus as the Messiah, the one chosen to redeem Israel, God's beloved Son, the voice goes on to add a command to the disciples: "Listen to him!" (Mark 9:7). Or to paraphrase, "Quit your ceaseless chatter and abandon your own fallen aspirations of kingship and idolatrous notions of divinity, and listen to the words of my anointed one. The path that he is describing and is about to tread is, in fact, the path that I have chosen for him." As if to throw an exclamation upon this point, the celestial fireworks come to an end and suddenly, when the disciples looked around, they no longer saw anyone with them but Jesus.

25. Ibid., 480.

This is a real turning point in Mark's Gospel; from here on we will see no one except Jesus. Jesus healing. Jesus speaking. Jesus breaking bread. Jesus praying. Jesus bleeding. Jesus dying. Yet in framing the story of the transfiguration in this way—"Suddenly, when they looked around, they no longer saw anyone with them except Jesus" (Mark 9:8)—Mark is telling us that to see Jesus is to behold the glory of God. The same point is made by other New Testament authors in different ways. Paul tells the Colossians that Jesus "is the image of the invisible God" (1:15). In the Gospel of John, Jesus says, "Anyone who has seen me has seen the Father" (14:9). Here we are standing before the heart of the mystery—the Trinity—that stands at the center of the Christian faith. The Christian doctrine of the Trinity is actually shorthand for the Good News of the Gospel.[26] It tells us that in Jesus Christ we encounter God-in-the-flesh. There is no other mysterious God lurking in the background that we need to be wary of; there is only the God who demonstrates his love for us in the life, death, and resurrection of Jesus Christ. This is the reality toward which Mark is pointing us with his depiction of the transfiguration and his assertion: "When they looked around they no longer saw anyone with them except Jesus." Mark is telling us that as we follow Jesus down from the mountain on his way to Jerusalem and ultimately to the cross, we are in fact observing the way of God in the world. When we see Jesus welcoming the little children and compassionately laying his hands upon them, we are seeing the very welcoming embrace of God. When we behold Jesus bringing healing to the bodies and souls of the wounded, we are witnessing the very healing presence of God. When we look in upon Jesus breaking bread in the Upper Room with his disciples, we are witnessing God feeding his people "body and spirit with his bread." Jesus' journey to the cross is God's demonstration of the great lengths to which He will go to bring his children home safely. The broken body of Jesus on the cross is nothing other than the life of God being poured out for the life of the world. Or as the apostle Paul says, "in Christ God was reconciling the world to himself" (2 Cor 5:19, NRSV).

On the first Sunday after Easter in 1945, Dietrich Bonhoeffer found himself transported to Schönberg prison. His fellow prisoners requested that he lead a service of worship. Bonhoeffer preached on Isaiah 53:5, "By his wounds we are healed," and 1 Peter 1:3, "Praise be to the God and Father of our Lord Jesus Christ! In his great mercy he has given us new birth into a

---

26. When I was a teaching assistant for Professor Joseph Mangina and his systematic theology course at Wycliffe College, we determined that one of the best diagnostic questions to ask students in their oral examinations in systematic theology to determine if they were "getting it" was the question, "Why is the doctrine of the Trinity shorthand for the good news of the Gospel?"

living hope through the resurrection of Jesus Christ from the dead." At the conclusion of the service, two men appeared and summoned Bonhoeffer to come with them. A British prisoner-of-war who was present at the time remembers Bonhoeffer's final words, "This is the end—for me the beginning of life."[27] The next morning, April 9, 1945, while the artillery of the Allied forces thundered in the distance, Dietrich Bonhoeffer was hanged at the concentration camp at Flossenbürg. Bonhoeffer was someone who profoundly understood what it means to take up one's cross and follow after Jesus, but his serene confidence in the face of death was not the result of looking back upon a life well-lived. Rather, with the gallows looming before him, Bonhoeffer was able to utter his famous last words, because as in life, so in the face of death, he saw Jesus. As we make our own spiritual pilgrimage to Jerusalem this Lenten season, may we be silenced before the great and terrible mystery of the cross, by the love so amazing, so divine, it demands our souls, our lives, our all.[28] Let us not avert our eyes from the cruel spectacle of the crucifixion, for there upon the cross hangs the very life of the world, our Lord Jesus Christ. In his light, we see light (Ps 36:9).

27. Payne Best, *The Venlo Incident*, 200, quoted in Bethge, *Dietrich Bonhoeffer*, 927.

28. "Love so amazing, so divine, demands my soul, my life, my all," is a line from Isaac Watts's hymn, "When I Survey the Wondrous Cross" (1707),

13

Much Ado about Nothing?

Good Shepherd Community Church
Scarborough, Ontario
Sunday, March 24, 2013
Mark 11:1–11; Psalm 118
Palm Sunday

L et's face it, Palm Sunday is a rather strange Sunday. In fact, it may be the strangest Sunday of the year. Earlier this morning, we entered into worship with great celebration waving palm branches and singing, "Hosanna!" Yet, in a few moments, we will leave this place under the shadow of the cross having joined our voices with the mob crying, "Crucify him!" It is a most unusual day. The story of the triumphal entry itself is a rather unusual story. Our familiarity with the story can cause us to overlook its strangeness. According to Mark's account, it almost seems as if the whole thing was "much ado about nothing." Here we have this big production involving Jesus riding triumphantly into the city as king to the shouts and acclamation of the adoring throngs. When he finally arrives at the Temple, he simply looks around and then decides to pack it in for the night, leading his disciples right back out of the city. Talk about an anti-climactic conclusion to the day's events! To try to put it in perspective, imagine this scene with me: The lights dim and a hush falls over the thousands of fans gathered in the arena. Suddenly the opening chords of "Eye of the Tiger" blast from the stadium speakers and everyone rises to their feet as Rocky Balboa emerges from behind the curtains to make his way to the ring for his heavyweight prize fight. He is surrounded by a small entourage and the fans along the barriers reach out to touch their hero as he passes by. His robe glitters in the spotlight as he strides with determination toward the ring. One of his entourage goes ahead of him and holds the ropes open so that he can climb into the ring. Having entered the ring, Rocky surveys the cheering crowd, stares into the eyes of his opponent, and then as the music fades out, he turns, exits the ring, and walks quietly back to the dressing room.

Such is the strange conclusion to Mark's account of the triumphal entry, but if we are truly attentive to the text we will notice that mixed messages are communicated throughout the entire passage.[1] The whole series of events seems to be shrouded in a certain level of ambiguity. The careful reader of Mark's Gospel will notice that the account of the triumphal entry is deeply ironic; just a few verses earlier Jesus himself had predicted how the Jewish authorities and the Roman occupation force would conspire to put him to death (10:33–34).

Let's return to the beginning of the passage and take a closer look. In verse one, we read that the unlikely parade began at the Mount of Olives. This is not simply a passing detail. Since at least the days of the prophet Zechariah, the Mount of Olives had been identified in Jewish end-time expectations as the site where the LORD would appear to fight the final battle against the enemies of Israel (Zech 14:2–5). Then we have the seemingly bizarre account of Jesus sending two of his disciples to requisition the colt. How did Jesus know that his disciples, upon entering the village, would find this particular colt in that particular spot? Is it the result of divine foreknowledge? Or had Jesus simply made prior arrangements? Mark doesn't tell us. What *is* significant is that the colt is requisitioned at Jesus' initiative. Having walked everywhere through the duration of his ministry, Jesus, of his own accord, will now ride into Jerusalem.[2] Clearly there is some type of message that Jesus is intending to communicate through this course of action.

What might this message be? The first thing to note is that it was a mark of nobility in ancient Israel to ride upon a donkey. When David and Bathsheba conspired to ensure that Solomon would follow David as king over Israel, David had Solomon ride upon his mule to the coronation (1 Kgs 1:32–40). When the patriarch Jacob blessed his twelve sons before his death, he pronounced the following Messianic-sounding blessing upon the tribe of Judah: "The scepter will not depart from Judah, nor the ruler's staff from between his feet, until he to whom it belongs shall come and the obedience of the nations shall be his. He will tether his donkey to a vine, his colt to the

1. Myers suggests that the whole episode "resembling carefully choreographed street-theatre, is designed to give intentionally conflicting messianic signals" (*Binding the Strong Man*, 294).

2. Hooker, *Mark*, 257.

choicest branch; he will wash his garments in wine, his robes in the blood of grapes" (Gen 49:10–11). The fact that the disciples were sent for a colt that had never been ridden further underscores the Messianic claim inherent in Jesus' entry into Jerusalem. According to Jewish tradition, it was inappropriate for anyone else to ride the king's mount.[3] Jesus' self-identification as the true king of Israel is further emphasized by the additional instructions he gives to the disciples. If anyone asks them why they are taking the donkey, they are to reply, "The Lord needs it" (Mark 11:3). Now the significance of this response isn't entirely obvious to twenty-first century readers. In fact it looks like a rather unsatisfactory answer and might even suggest to us that the disciples were engaging in some type of hypnosis or Jedi mind trick. But what's really going on here is the exercise of the royal right of impressment.[4] Like a police officer in the movies who commandeers a vehicle from a civilian for his own use, the king in ancient Israel had the right to commandeer property and animals into his service as he had need. In this way, Jesus' impressing of the donkey into his service is as much a sign of his kingship as is his riding of it into the city.

It's becoming easy to see why Jesus' followers and the crowd could get so excited. Here was the long-awaited king of Israel riding into the capital city to set things right. Presumably this would involve driving out the Romans and all who conspired with them within the Temple hierarchy. But already at this point in the passage, before the parade has even begun, some dissonant notes have been sounded. Perhaps things are not as simply straightforward as they seem. After all, what kind of king has to borrow a donkey? Or for that matter, drawing upon the other Gospels, what kind of king has no place to lay his head (Luke 9:58)? The answer, of course, is the only kind of king who can be of any help to us; a king who comes weak and vulnerable, a God who draws near under the veil of sinful flesh, and in so doing, creates the time and space necessary for faith and repentance. The Church Father Augustine famously remarked, "God created us without us: but he did not will to save us without us."[5] Jesus came as a king in need of a donkey, and his need encounters us in the form of the gracious invitation to serve alongside him as his co-workers. We are invited to enter into the joy of the kingdom and live under the royal rule of him in whose service alone there is perfect freedom.[6] At any moment we may be encountered

3. Hooker, *Mark*, 258.

4. L.A. Losie, "The Triumphal Entry," in Green et al., *Dictionary of Jesus and the Gospels*, 859.

5. Augustine, *Sermo* 169.11.13, quoted in *Catechism of the Catholic Church* 8.1847.

6. A gloss on the phrase "whose service is perfect freedom" from "A Collect for Peace," in *The Book of Common Prayer*, 57.

by the gracious summons, "The Lord needs it." Upon hearing this inviting command (or commanding invitation), we must be prepared to gladly relinquish our time, our talent, and our treasure. This is why there is no such thing as private property for Christians. There is personal property, but it is never private. All that we have, we hold in trust for the Master who at any moment may address us with the words, "The Lord needs it."

Once the disciples returned with the colt, it was time to start the parade. The disciples threw their cloaks upon the donkey, creating a makeshift throne for Jesus to sit upon, and with that, the entourage was on its way. As the procession made its way toward Jerusalem, a crowd began to gather, and many threw their cloaks upon the road before the coming king, just as their ancestors, hundreds of years earlier, had spread their cloaks before Jehu when he was anointed and proclaimed king over Israel (2 Kgs 9:13). Others brought leafy branches from the fields and spread them before Jesus as he approached. Those running ahead and those following behind cried out in a loud voice, "Hosanna! Blessed is he who comes in the name of the Lord! Blessed is the coming kingdom of our father David! Hosanna in the highest!" (Mark 11:9–10). The first part of their cheer is taken from Psalm 118. Psalm 118 turns up again and again throughout the depiction of Holy Week in the Gospels. Jesus himself cites the psalm in the context of his dispute with the religious authorities, saying, "The stone the builders rejected has become the cornerstone; the Lord has done this, and it is marvelous in our eyes" (Mark 12:10–11). Psalm 118 was also most likely one of the psalms Jesus and the disciples sang following their celebration of the Passover and Jesus' institution of the Lord's Supper.[7]

Psalm 118 is part of a set of psalms known as *Hallel* psalms which are songs of praise celebrating God's mighty act of delivering his people in the exodus. Faithful Jews recited these psalms on many different occasions in a great variety of contexts. The pilgrimage to Jerusalem to observe the Feast of Dedication, also known as Hanukkah, was one such context in which Psalm 118 was recited.[8] At Hanukkah, the Jews celebrated the rededication of the Temple in the second century BC, following the unlikely triumph of Judas Maccabeus and his small band of guerilla fighters over the great imperial power of the day, the Seleucid dynasty.[9] Under the leadership of Antiochus Epiphanes, the Seleucids, by the strength of their massive military might, had captured Jerusalem. Antiochus then proceeded to outlaw the practice

7. Witherington, *Mark*, 376.

8. Hooker, *Mark*, 256.

9. 2 Maccabees 4:1—10:9 traces the developments surrounding Jerusalem's fall to Antiochus IV Epiphanes up to the purification of the Temple following the successful revolt led by Judas Maccabeus.

of Judaism and defiled the Temple by erecting an altar to Zeus upon which he sacrificed pigs—truly a desolating sacrilege![10] The actions of Antiochus Epiphanes sparked a grass-roots revolt among the Jews. Judas Maccabeus was able to channel this general resentment into a carefully coordinated campaign of guerilla strikes against the much stronger Seleucid forces which resulted in a string of surprising victories. Eventually, under Judas's leadership, the Seleucids were repulsed from Jerusalem, and the Temple was cleansed and rededicated to the one true God. For his military genius and ferocity in battle, Judas was given the name "The Hammer."[11] As pilgrims made their way to Jerusalem each year to celebrate Hanukkah, in honour of "The Hammer's" unlikely victory over the occupying imperial power of his day, they would take up palm branches and shout aloud songs of praise, including Psalm 118.[12]

With this in mind, we can begin to imagine some of the hopes and aspirations that may have been present among the crowd which took up palms and heralded Jesus' entry into Jerusalem. Was this a new "Hammer" on his way to Jerusalem to smash the iron grip with which the Romans held Israel, and to follow that up by cleansing the Temple? Or perhaps this was one whose status even exceeded that of "The Hammer!" The acclamations of the crowd in referring to David, the most esteemed warrior and greatest military conqueror in the history of Israel, seem to suggest that they were thinking along these lines. After all, as the saying goes, had not Saul "slain his thousands, and David his tens of thousands" (1 Sam 18:7, 21:11, 29:5)? The fact that the Passover, the celebration of God's most decisive deliverance of his people from their enemies, was near, would have further amplified the revolutionary hopes and aspirations of the people. Would this be the moment that God would finally act to redeem his people from their oppressors?

What the enthusiastic crowd heralding Jesus' entry into Jerusalem failed to recognize was that not only did the people of Israel stand in need of redemption from the enemies which ruled over their land, their captive hearts also needed to be set free. Such a redemption could not come through the triumph of a great military leader, but only through the faithfulness of the one who had come "to give his life as a ransom for many" (Mark 10:45). The people were correct in recognizing Jesus as the true king riding into Jerusalem, but the kingdom was not coming in the way they expected. For

10. An allusion to Daniel 9:27, 11:31, 12:11.

11. This seems to me the most likely explanation of the name "Maccabeus," but there is scholarly debate surrounding its origins. Uriel Rappaport and Paul L. Redditt, "Maccabeus," in Freedman, *Anchor Bible Dictionary*, 4:454.

12. James C. VanderKam, "Dedication, Feast of," in Freedman, *Anchor Bible Dictionary*, 2:124.

those with eyes to see, the signs were already present. After all, this king was not mounted upon a warhorse or riding in a chariot, rather he came "lowly and riding on a donkey" (Zech 9:9). The tension between the crowd's expectations and Jesus' understanding of his mission is poignantly displayed in a memorable scene from Andrew Lloyd Webber's musical *Jesus Christ Superstar*. As Jesus is making his way toward Jerusalem in Norman Jewison's Hollywood adaptation of the musical, he is surrounded by a crowd of frenetic followers dancing and yelling their devotion. Simon the Zealot steps to the forefront and urges Jesus to mount a proper revolution. "You'll get the power and the glory," he says, "for ever and ever and ever." After a moment of silence, Jesus turns and sings the haunting lines: "Neither you, Simon, nor the fifty thousand, nor the Romans, nor the Jews, nor Judas, nor the Twelve, nor the priests, nor the scribes, nor doomed Jerusalem itself—*understand what power is! Understand what glory is!* Understand at all."[13]

Palm Sunday is a day when we who have been on the way with Jesus are forced to admit that all too often we fail to understand what power is. More often than not we fail to understand what glory is. We too get Jesus wrong and in so doing we get our lives wrong. Conversely, we also get our lives wrong and as a result cannot help but get Jesus wrong. Perhaps then, the most significant tradition arising in association with Palm Sunday doesn't occur on Palm Sunday at all, but rather at the beginning of Lent in the following year, when the palms from the previous Palm Sunday are collected and burned to provide the ashes for Ash Wednesday. The sign of the ashes marks the beginning of Lent, a season of penitence. We find ourselves this morning at the climax of that penitential season, but we also find ourselves at this point in the midst of a broader season of penitence in the life of our congregation. In recent years, God has been disabusing us of the notion that we could be a people who sing "Hosanna!" without crying "Have mercy on us!" He is freeing us from any illusions that we could be a people who wave palms without also wearing ashes. He is liberating us from the idea that congregational success can be understood in any other terms than that of the faithfulness of the one who "for the sake of the joy that was set before him endured the cross, disregarding its shame, and has taken his seat at the right hand of the throne of God" (Heb 12:2, NRSV).

Now there may be days ahead, when we are gathered together, that we are overwhelmed with longing that our time of worship would look and feel something more like the scene that unfolded as the crowd gathered around Jesus on that first Palm Sunday. The feeling is understandable, but the Lord is calling us to something deeper, something much more profound. Our

---

13. *Jesus Christ Superstar*, directed by Norman Jewison (Universal Pictures, 1973).

king who rode into Jerusalem upon a donkey reveals to us that the ultimate criterion of success is the cross. This is the reality the apostle Paul spoke of when he wrote, "For the message of the cross is foolishness to those who are perishing, but to us who are being saved it is the power of God" (1 Cor 1:18). Rather than the boisterous crowd which lined the streets of Jerusalem on that first Palm Sunday, perhaps the life we are being called to as a congregation will more closely resemble the small group of women, who alongside the beloved disciple, found themselves huddled at the foot of the cross. Such a community of the cross, a community stripped of all its pretensions and defenses, cannot help but be characterized by radical vulnerability. This radical vulnerability is manifested in the way members of the community bear one another's burdens and share one another's joys and sorrows out of the recognition that their lives have been inseparably entwined with one another in the body of the one who bore the cross. It is demonstrated in the hospitality that the community shows in welcoming and responding to the needs of its neighbours, in the recognition that the face of the Crucified One is beheld in the faces of the least, the last and the lost. It is evident in a posture of radical attentiveness to the Spirit's leading, in the recognition that truth is not a possession under our control, but rather is the person of the living Lord Jesus Christ, who unfailingly encounters us along the way.

I had the opportunity this past week to watch the recent film adaptation of *The Hobbit*. I was struck by a scene that occurs well into the movie when the company of adventurers arrives at Rivendell, the enchanted domain of the elves. Gandalf the Grey, the wizard who has initiated the quest, is called into the presence of Lady Galadriel, the mightiest and fairest of all the elves. Galadriel inquires of Gandalf why he has enlisted into his company of questers the pint-sized hobbit, Bilbo Baggins, who had never before left his home, much less wielded a sword or fought in a battle. Reflecting the profoundly Christian imagination of *The Hobbit*'s author, J.R.R. Tolkien, Gandalf replies, "I don't know. Saruman believes that it is only great power that can hold evil in check. But that is not what I've found. I've found that it is the small things, everyday deeds of ordinary folk that keeps the darkness at bay: simple acts of kindness and love. Why Bilbo Baggins? Perhaps because I am afraid and he gives me courage." [14]

Like the disciples who followed Jesus on the way to Jerusalem, we too are often astonished and afraid (Mark 10:32). But God has recognized our need and has given us one another so that through simple acts of kindness and love, we may strengthen and encourage one another for the adventure

14. *The Hobbit: An Unexpected Journey*, directed by Peter Jackson (Metro-Goldwin-Mayer, 2012).

that has been set before us. We do not blaze our own trail, but rather follow in the footsteps of the one who on this day triumphantly entered Jerusalem, "lowly and riding on a donkey" (Zech 9:9). We set our eyes on the one who on Palm Sunday loosed the previously-bound colt and a few days later freely turned over his body to be bound, so that we who were bound may be free. He is our champion, the one who has triumphed over the forces of darkness, even death itself, through the power of a love which not even the grave could contain.

So, "Ride on King Jesus, ride on. No one can a-hinder thee."[15]

---

15. This is a refrain from a traditional Negro Spiritual, "Ride On, King Jesus," that was sung by the choir immediately preceding the sermon.

14

Provisions for Pilgrims

Good Shepherd Community Church

Scarborough, Ontario

Thursday, April 5, 2012

Matthew 26:26–29; Luke 22:39–46; John 13:1–17

Maundy Thursday

This evening marks the beginning of what the Christian church has traditionally referred to as the *Triduum Sacrum* or the Great Three Days.
The Great Three Days is the climax of Holy Week, the celebration of the
one great event which is Christ's Passover from death to life. The Great
Three Days begins with Maundy Thursday and encompasses Good Friday,
Holy Saturday, and Easter or Resurrection Sunday. Now to us this actually
sounds like four days, but the Jews of antiquity understood the day to begin
at sundown. Hence, the evening of Maundy Thursday is actually the beginning of Good Friday. The last evening of Jesus' life was filled with profound
moments, ranging from the tender scene in the Upper Room when Jesus
washed the feet of his friends, to the camaraderie around the table as Jesus
shared the Passover meal that he so eagerly desired to eat with his disciples,
to the agony in the garden when drops of blood fell like sweat from his
forehead, to the shattering of the evening tranquility by the light of torches
held high by the approaching mob, to the bitter sting of betrayal sealed with
a kiss. The accounts of Jesus' final evening presented to us in the Gospels
make for gripping reading. As we attend to these stories, we are not only
drawn in by the drama of the event, but we also come to realize that in
the midst of everything that is unfolding, Jesus Christ is making provisions
for his pilgrim people. He will be returning to the Father, but not without

providing for his people who will continue on in pilgrimage in the time between his ascension and coming again in glory.

On this the final night of his life, Jesus made a threefold provision for his pilgrim people: with the basin, at the table, in the garden. What better inheritance could be given to a people on the move than a refreshing and cleansing bath for tired and weary feet? What better provision could be made for a people on the way than food for the journey in the form of a moveable feast? What could be more valuable to a people on pilgrimage than direction and guidance for traversing the unknown terrain that lay ahead? What an extravagant expression of love, that our Savior would make such a provision for us in the very face of his own impending death!

This love is not without effect. As we sang a moment ago, "My song is love unknown, my Savior's love to me. Love to the loveless shown, that they might lovely be."[1] In God's gracious economy, the practices which Christ has provided for us of washing feet, breaking bread, and prayer are tools in the hands of the Holy Spirit by which the Spirit fashions a humble, thankful, and watchful people.

With the basin, God's people are schooled in the humility necessary to serve in Christ's upside-down kingdom.[2] The practice of foot-washing challenges our deeply held goals and aspirations by replacing popular conceptions of success with a vision of radical downward mobility. On another occasion Jesus told his disciples, "Whoever wants to become great among you must be your servant, and whoever wants to be first must be slave of all" (Mark 10:43–44). If this is not challenging enough, the practice of foot-washing delivers one further assault upon our prideful, self-sufficiency; not only are we called to wash others' feet, we also must learn to allow others to wash our feet.[3] This was Peter's struggle. The conversation that unfolds between Peter and Jesus following Peter's initial refusal to have his feet washed suggests that there is more to having one's feet washed than simply allowing oneself to be served by another. Jesus' references to a bath and a person being clean suggest that beneath the surface there may lie an underground stream connecting foot-washing and forgiveness. Just as it is easier to wash feet than to have one's feet washed, in a similar way it is much easier to forgive than it is to be forgiven. However, through the practice of foot-washing or, more accurately, having our feet washed, we receive training in being

1. Samuel Crossman, "My Song is Love Unknown" (1664).

2. Reflecting on the practice of foot-washing, Jean Vanier writes, "It is always very moving for me when someone with disabilities washes my feet or when I see a person wash the feet of their mother or father. It is the world turned upside down" (*Drawn into the Mystery*, 228).

3. Hauerwas and Coles, *Christianity, Democracy and the Radical Ordinary*, 208–28.

a forgiven people, who in turn are freed to offer to one another the gift of humble service, whose pinnacle is forgiveness. Those pilgrims who have bathed in the waters of baptism are clean, but until they reach the Promised Land they will need to wash each other's feet.

At the table, we are formed into a thankful people as we are treated to a meal we didn't work for, or for that matter, couldn't even imagine. Like the manna that was provided for Israel in the wilderness (Exod 16), at the Lord's Table we receive sustenance for the journey that lies before us. The bread and the cup sustain us not only by providing nourishment in the present, but also by pointing us toward the feast to come. At the table, God's pilgrims are provided with a foretaste of life in the Promised Land, a land flowing with milk and honey. In our Thanksgiving meal, elements from the created order—grain and grapes—in anticipation of God's great restoration of all things, are liberated from their bondage to decay to bear witness to the glory of God.[4] There is only one way to receive the redemption signified in the bread and the cup, and it is the same way that we are to receive every good and perfect gift that comes from the Lord, which includes our very lives themselves—that is, with thanksgiving.

In the garden, Jesus invited his disciples to keep watch and to pray with him. Prayer is necessary, if we are to be an alert and watchful people. One of the greatest threats to pilgrims on the way is the danger of sleep-walking through life. "The world is charged with the grandeur of God," the poet Gerard Manley Hopkins tells us, but the one who has fallen asleep is oblivious.[5] Not only is the person sleep-walking through life unaware of the many good gifts they have been given, they are also liable to wander from the path unawares or be swept up by the currents of the prevailing culture leading to death and destruction. Prayer orients the pilgrim to the true reality of things. Apart from prayer, there is the danger that the pilgrims will be caught up in the world's web of falsehood and deceit. "Pray that you will not fall into temptation," Jesus instructed his disciples (Luke 22:40). Instead, they fell asleep. The Gospels suggest that the failure of the disciples' to stand by Jesus in the time of his passion was first and foremost a failure to pray.

The washing of feet, the breaking of bread, and the ministry of prayer are each gifts from the Lord through which the Spirit makes us holy. These practices do not function in a magical or mechanical way. We cannot crudely manipulate them in order to achieve the spiritual benefit of our choosing. Rather, they serve as a means for helping us to locate our story in Jesus' story and to recognize that our lives are taken up in his. Each of these provisions

4. Bonhoeffer, *Christ the Center*, 65.
5. Gerard Manley Hopkins, "God's Grandeur," in Harter, *Hearts on Fire*, 10.

point beyond themselves to the reality of what Jesus ultimately provides for pilgrims . . . himself!

Let's return to the basin. Although there are hints throughout the Gospel of John that the Evangelist had some knowledge of the Lord's Supper, he does not include an account of the Supper in his Gospel. Instead, in its place, he includes the account of another prophetic sign-action—the foot-washing. What Jesus enacts in deed in John 13 in rising from the table, removing his outer garment, wrapping a towel around his waist, and bending down to wash the disciples' feet, the church proclaims of him in words in Philippians 2: "Who, being in very nature God, did not consider equality with God something to be used to his own advantage; rather, he made himself nothing by taking the very nature of a servant, being made in human likeness. And being found in appearance as a man, he humbled himself by becoming obedient to death—even death on a cross" (2:6–8)! The basin anticipates the cross. The one who removes his outer garment in the upper room, will, in a matter of hours, have his outer garment removed just prior to his crucifixion (John 19:23–24). The next time we will see him wrapped in cloths will be when his lifeless body is laid in the tomb (John 19:40). In other words, Jesus gives his life to make us clean.

At the table, we share communion with the one who is the bread of life (John 6:35). On the night that he was betrayed, in the tradition of the great prophets of Israel, who were often called upon to enact God's coming judgment and salvation through concrete prophetic actions, Jesus broke the bread and said, "'Take and eat; this is my body.' Then he took a cup, and when he had given thanks, he gave it to them, saying, 'Drink from it, all of you. This is my blood of the covenant, which is poured out for many for the forgiveness of sins" (Matt 26:26–28). In doing so, Jesus graphically represented to the disciples his approaching crucifixion, where his blood would be poured out and his body would be given over to death on the cross. But notice that there is more going on here than simply one man predicting his death. In the act of identifying the bread and the cup with his body and blood, Jesus is saying that his life given over to death will become a source of life and nourishment—food and drink—for his disciples. His blood is the blood of the covenant welcoming all sinners, Jews and Gentiles alike, into communion with God.

In the garden, the one who taught his disciples to pray "your will be done, on earth as it is in heaven" (Matt 6:10) faithfully committed himself to the plans and purposes of the Father, praying, "Father, if you are willing, take this cup from me; yet not my will, but yours be done" (Luke 22:42). In committing himself to the Father's will and, by doing so, fulfilling all righteousness, Christ reveals himself to be the true and faithful High Priest. On his lips, the command to watch and pray is not an unbearable burden, but rather is the blessed invitation to share in the prayer of the one who lives to intercede for us. Through the gift of prayer we are drawn up into the very life of the triune God, graciously enabled to call upon God as our Father as we are joined to our brother Jesus Christ through the bond of the Holy Spirit.

So then let us tonight enter into the mystery of our salvation in Christ, as we join him with the basin, at the table, and in the garden.

15

A Tale of Two Jesuses

Good Shepherd Community Church

Scarborough, Ontario

Friday, April 6, 2007

Matthew 27:11–26; Isaiah 52:13—53:12

Good Friday

"It was the best of times, it was the worst of times."[1] These words—among the most famous in all of English literature—mark the beginning of Charles Dickens's celebrated historical novel, *A Tale of Two Cities*. These words could also be used to describe this day on which we are gathered. Good Friday is indeed "the best of times," for on this day our salvation was won, but it is also "the worst of times," for that salvation was won at the cost of our dear Savior's blood.

It has been said that the most appropriate sermon that one can give in response to the events of Good Friday is to sit in stunned silence. Reverent awe and silence is perhaps the most appropriate response when confronted with the profound mystery of God-in-the-flesh dying for us on a cross outside Jerusalem. Yet this morning I have been given the task of reflecting upon this most profound of mysteries and it would seem that the most appropriate way to do so is to simply attend to the story.

First century Jerusalem at the time of Jesus' arrest, trial, and crucifixion was in many ways surprisingly similar to eighteenth century Paris as described by Charles Dickens in *A Tale of Two Cities*. Dickens's Paris was a ticking time bomb waiting to explode. The downtrodden common people

1. Dickens, *Tale of Two Cities*, 1.

116

were ready to rise up against the French monarchy and aristocracy that had ruled over and oppressed them. Revolution was in the air.

Revolution was also in the air during that fateful week in Jerusalem close to two thousand years ago. Israel was an occupied territory under the control of the Roman Empire, the superpower of the first century. Now there were some among the Jewish aristocracy, particularly among the chief priests and Sadducees, who had been able to make the Roman occupation work to their advantage, but most of the Jews longed for the day when the Roman occupation would be over and Israel would be free. The events described in this morning's passage took place at the time of the Feast of Passover. Every year at Passover, faithful Jews from throughout Israel would converge upon Jerusalem in remembrance of Israel's deliverance from slavery in Egypt. With the large crowds gathering in Jerusalem to commemorate the liberation of their people, it was obviously a nerve-wracking time to be the commander of an occupying force. All it would take was one crazed Zealot thinking that he had been divinely chosen to bring about a new exodus and all hell could break loose. So Pontius Pilate, the Roman Emperor's hand-picked choice to be the governor of Judea, made his way from his palace at Caesarea Maritima to Jerusalem to provide a strong imperial deterrent and to ensure order during the feast.[2]

The similarities between Dickens's novel and our Scripture passage this morning are not limited simply to matters of setting. Central to the plot development of A Tale of Two Cities is the physical similarity between the two characters Charles Darnay and Sydney Carton. The story reaches its climax when Darnay is sentenced to death. While he is awaiting his appointment with the guillotine, his look-alike Sydney Carton meets him in prison, drugs him, and arranges for him to be transported away. Then the unsuspecting officials, who can't tell the difference between the two men, put Carton to death in Darnay's place.

Now what we have in our Scripture passage is not a case of two men sharing a similar appearance, but rather it is a case of two men who share the same name. What we have is A Tale of Two Jesuses.[3] Before the restless crowd that had assembled, Pilate paraded two men who had both been ar-

2. Senior, *Matthew*, 320.

3. Not all ancient manuscripts of the Gospel of Matthew include the name "Jesus" in connection with Barabbas; hence, the name does not appear in certain English translations of the Bible (eg. NASB, KJV). On the basis of the appearance of "Jesus Barabbas" within certain important ancient manuscripts and the writings of the Church Fathers, in addition to the shape of the story itself within Matthew's Gospel, I am inclined to side with those Bible translators who opt for the inclusion of the name "Jesus Barabbas" (eg. NRSV, MSG). The most recent version of the NIV has changed its stance, now opting to include the name "Jesus" alongside of "Barabbas" where it was previously omitted.

rested as rebels and were facing similar charges of sedition or insurrection.[4] The first man was named Jesus Barabbas, which in Aramaic literally means "son of the father." Pilate introduced the second as "Jesus who is called the Messiah" (Matt 27:22), whom we know as *the* Son of the Father.[5] You can see how it could be more than a little confusing. Essentially, the question that Pilate put to the crowd was this, "Which Jesus do you want?"

Now we don't know a great deal about this figure that Matthew identifies as Jesus Barabbas. He simply strolls out of the shadows into the spotlight at this climactic moment in the drama of salvation and then, having played his part, once again promptly vanishes into the mists of ancient history. In fact, the only things we know about Barabbas are what have been recorded for us in the four Gospels. John describes Barabbas as a "bandit" or a "robber" (18:40, NRSV, KJV). Mark and Luke both tell us that Barabbas was among a group of rebels who had committed murder during an insurrection or uprising (Mark 15:7; Luke 23:19). It appears then that Barabbas was a radical revolutionary who made a living out of assassinating key political leaders. According to the logic of Barabbas and others like him, the Romans and any members of the Jewish ruling class who were perceived to be in league with the Romans would have to die so that the people could be free.[6] Pilate knew just what to do with men like Barabbas. Force must be met with force, violence with violence, an eye for an eye, and a tooth for a tooth. Insurrectionists must be brought to their knees by the piercing talons of the Roman eagle. Those who attempt to rise up against the powers must be lifted up in humiliation upon a cross for all to see. The fact that three crosses had been prepared seems to suggest that Pilate had already issued the verdict upon Barabbas.[7] Barabbas was a dead man walking. He had been condemned to die.

Jesus, called Messiah, on other hand, was confounding to Pilate. Pilate didn't know what to do with him. While the Romans and Zealots and Sadducees and priests were all busy crashing their helmets together at the line of scrimmage, this Jesus Messiah had marched onto the football field of first century Palestine dressed in an argyle sweater carrying a 3-iron in his hand. In other words, Jesus wasn't playing the same game as Pilate, or Barabbas, or the chief priests and the elders. That's why in response to Pilate's question, "Are you the king of the Jews?" Jesus responds with the ambiguous "You

---

4. Brown, *Crucified Christ*, 10.

5. Samuel Wells brings to the fore the parallels between the two men placed before the crowd in *Power and Passion*, 68.

6. Ibid., 69.

7. D.A Carson, "Matthew," in Gaebelein, *Matthew, Mark, Luke*, 569.

have said so" (Matt 27:11). Jesus is the king of the Jews, but not in a way that a power-broker like Pilate could ever understand.[8] Jesus met force with humility and violence with nonresistance. To those who said "Eye for eye, and tooth for tooth," he responded, "Love your enemies and pray for those who persecute you" (Matt 5:38, 44). Jesus opted out of the human power struggles that characterized the reign of death and instead heralded the arrival of God's life-giving rule. He unmasked the lies and falsehood upon which the systems of power and oppression are based with the light of the truth of God's present and coming kingdom. When we recognize this, we come to see that the issue is not that Barabbas is a revolutionary and Jesus is not. Rather, Jesus Barabbas and Jesus the one called Messiah are both revolutionaries. However, from our Lord's perspective Barabbas is not nearly revolutionary enough. Barabbas, as a true son of his fathers, still believed that what mattered was who the government was. He believed that the exercise of sheer power was the key to shaping reality. Whereas Barabbas put others to death in the hopes of freeing his people, Jesus recognized "that he must die so that others may be free."[9] Jesus Christ is the real revolutionary, "because he promises a totally new empire—not the rule of Caesar but the kingdom of God; a completely new form of rule—not being served but serving; a vastly different manner of ushering in a new regime—not the horse of war but the donkey of peace; and a unique mode of transformation—not revolution but resurrection."[10] Jesus was a far greater threat to the Romans, to the chief priests, and to the elders than Barabbas could ever be. For them the issue was simple: Jesus had to die.

Like the end of a Roman gladiator contest, which generally took place between condemned criminals, Pilate paraded out the two men so that the crowd could choose who would die and who would live. "Which one do you want me to release to you: Jesus Barabbas, or Jesus who is called the Messiah" (Matt 27:17)? Now the name *Jesus* is derived from the Aramaic *Yeshua*, which in turn is from the Hebrew *Joshua* which literally means "the LORD saves." So the choice placed before the crowd is actually a choice between ways of salvation. It's a question continually placed before us. In whom do we trust? Do we place our trust in ourselves and what we hope we can control through our own devices and exercising of power—like Barabbas? Or do we radically place our trust in God and follow Jesus who is called Messiah, setting aside the idols of productivity and effectiveness in the name of faithfulness and humility, looking to God alone for our vindication?

8. Matera, *Passion Narratives*, 107.

9. Wells, *Power and Passion*, 70.

10. Ibid., 70.

It shouldn't surprise us that the mob chose Barabbas. It probably wouldn't have taken much work to convince them to ask for Barabbas. Just as present day suicide bombers can simultaneously be regarded as terrorists by one group of people and heroic martyrs by another, the notorious Barabbas, who was being held as a Roman prisoner, would have, in the eyes of many of the common people, been a national hero.[11] We can't be too hard on them, for we too often opt for Barabbas. Our preference for Barabbas and his political theology is on display whenever we wistfully remark that all would be well if we could just get the right people—"our people"—into power. Then we could clean up society and rid ourselves of those—insert your favorite scapegoat group here—who are taking our society to hell in a hand-basket. That's Barabbas talk. Also, whenever the name of Jesus is called upon to endorse our own individual or corporate goals or agenda without simultaneously calling us to renewal and repentance, then there's a good chance that the Jesus who is being called upon is not Jesus the Messiah, but Jesus Barabbas.

The mob that had gathered on that fateful day in Jerusalem made their choice. They opted for Barabbas and called for Jesus' crucifixion. After Pilate's Oscar-worthy hand-washing performance, the crowd cried out, "His blood is on us and our children" (Matt 27:25)! This has to be one of the most terrifying lines in all of Scripture, partly because of what it says, but even more so because of the way it was been ripped out of its context and used as a legitimation by Christians throughout the centuries for the harassment, persecution, and murder of our Jewish brothers and sisters. This use of Scripture is nothing less than Satanic and must be denounced as such.

So how then are we to understand this shocking statement, "His blood is on us and our children"? There is a sense that the Gospel of Matthew understands Jesus' death as being one more instance in the long history of rejection of the prophetic messengers sent by God to Israel. Jesus himself, in the days leading up to his execution, describes this history of rejection in the following manner: "Therefore I am sending you prophets and sages and teachers. Some of them you will kill and crucify; others you will flog in your synagogues and pursue from town to town. And so upon you will come all the righteous blood that has been shed on earth, from the blood of righteous Abel to the blood of Zechariah son of Berekiah, whom you murdered between the temple and the altar. Truly I tell you, all this will come on this generation" (Matt 23:34–36). Matthew understands the fulfillment of this "blood curse" to be the destruction of Jerusalem, which occurred some

11. D.A. Carson, "Matthew," in Gaebelein, *Matthew, Mark, Luke,* 569.

thirty years after Jesus' death, at the hands of the Romans in response to Israel's insistence upon the Barabbas way of salvation by the sword.[12]

Although Matthew connects the rejection of Jesus by his people in 33 AD with the destruction of the Jerusalem Temple in 70 AD, it would by no means be correct for us to baldly state that the Jews killed Jesus. Matthew would not have us do that. Instead, Matthew draws upon the Greek word *paradidōmi*, meaning "to give or hand over," to trace out a series of transactions that take place over the final hours of Jesus' life.[13] Over the course of this series of events Jesus is passed along from one person or group of people to another like a hot potato or an unwanted Christmas present. The sequence begins with Judas betraying or "handing over" Jesus to the chief priests and elders (Matt 26:14–16, 26:45). After their sham of a trial, the chief priests and elders hand Jesus over to Pilate (Matt 27:2). And finally, with a dramatic washing of his hands, Pilate hands Jesus over to be crucified (Matt 27:26). It's not entirely clear to whom Pilate hands Jesus over. It can't really be the mob, since only the Romans possess the legal right to crucify someone. And it doesn't really make sense to say that Pilate handed Jesus over to the Roman soldiers, since technically he was already in their possession. In the end, it almost seems as if Jesus dies of neglect, being handed over to the abyss of death, because no one wanted to take responsibility for him or to have anything to do with him.[14] A theatrical hand-washing performance worthy of Lady MacBeth is not enough to get the blood off of Pilate's hands, or for that matter, the hands of the Roman soldiers who nailed him to the cross, the disciple who sold him for thirty pieces of silver, the crowd who cried out for his death, or the chief priests and elders who coordinated the action from behind the scenes. Everyone seems to be implicated in the death of Jesus and that everyone extends beyond the lead actors and bit players of first century Palestine to each one of us. Matthew has written his Gospel in such a way that we cannot help but see ourselves fleeing with the disciples, denying our Lord with Peter, betraying him with Judas, jealously conspiring with the chief priests and elders, and washing our hands of responsibility with Pilate. Who killed Jesus? We all killed Jesus. His blood is on us and our children.

If we were to stop here, there would certainly be nothing particularly good about Good Friday. For here we stand under the judgment of God, already condemned, his blood is on us and our children. But if we go back and

12. R.A. Guelich, "Destruction of Jerusalem," in Joel B. Green et al., *Dictionary of Jesus and the Gospels*, 172–76.

13. Danker, *Greek-English Lexicon*, s.v. παραδίδωμι, 761–62.

14. Milbank, *Being Reconciled*, 82.

trace this pattern of "handing over" or "giving over" through the Old Testament Scriptures, we uncover another dynamic at work amid the ugliness of the human betrayals and politics of Good Friday. In the Greek translation of the Old Testament, the word *paradidōmi* is largely reserved for the activity of God. After bringing Israel up out of slavery in Egypt, it is God who "gives over" the land of Canaan with all of its kings and inhabitants to Israel (Exod 23:31; Num 21:34; Deut 1:21, 2:33, 7:23–24, 32:30; Josh 2:24, 10:8, 24:11; Judg 1:4). As the story of God's dealings with Israel continues, the narrative takes a dramatic shift when, according to the words of the prophets, the LORD "hands over" his people Israel to foreign kings and empires, sending them into exile on account of their sin (Jer 21:10, 22:25, 32:28–29, 34:2; Ezek 7:21, 11:9, 16:27, 23:28). This "handing over" is intensified and reaches its culmination in the figure of the Suffering Servant who appears in the prophecy of Isaiah.[15] Twice in the climactic Servant Song, the word *paradidōmi* is used to describe God's active "handing over" of his Servant, once in Isaiah 53:6, where it tells us that the LORD "gave over" the Servant "to" or "for" our sins and once in 53:12 where we are told that the Servant's life is "given over" to death. Matthew gives several other clues that he wants us to have the figure of the Suffering Servant in mind as we read his account of Christ's trial and crucifixion. Jesus' silence before Pilate resonates with Isaiah's poetic description of the Servant: "He was oppressed and afflicted, yet he did not open his mouth" (53:7). Pilate's subsequent amazement reminds the alert reader of how the Servant will amaze the nations and how "kings will shut their mouths because of him" (Isa 52:15).[16] In the death and crucifixion of Jesus of Nazareth, we are meant to see the Suffering Servant of the LORD: the one who is "handed over" by God on behalf of the many; the innocent one who quite literally takes the place of the murderer Barabbas upon the cross; the righteous one who stands in the place of sinful humanity before God, bearing away the sins of the world upon the cross, and reconciling God and humanity.

We must be sure that we do not mistake this Suffering Servant for some innocent bystander who is left to suffer at the hands of a capricious God with an anger management problem. This Suffering Servant is Jesus of Nazareth who is the Word made flesh. He is Immanuel—"God with us" (Matt 1:23). He is, as the Nicene Creed states, "God from God, Light from

15. The figure of the Servant takes on special prominence in chapters 40–55 of the book of Isaiah.

16. In the Greek translation of the Old Testament (known as the Septuagint or LXX), Isaiah 52:15 reads, "In this way many nations will be *amazed* by him . . ." drawing upon the same Greek word that Matthew uses to describe Pilate's amazement at Jesus.

Light, true God from true God." There is one other important "handing over" in the Gospel of Matthew that at this point we need to consider. Before the monumental events of Holy Week and before his triumphal entry into Jerusalem, Jesus tells all those who will listen, "All things have been 'handed over' to me by my Father" (Matt 11:27; my translation). What we see then, amid the rejection, humiliation, suffering, and death of Jesus of Nazareth is God giving himself away for us. We see God taking the full burden of sin upon himself, entering into the alienation and isolation of our doomed existence, simply because he would not have us lost.

When the Holy Spirit opens our eyes and hearts to recognize that the tears Jesus' weeps over Jerusalem are God's own tears, to perceive that it is God in the flesh who is nailed to the tree outside the city walls, and to realize that the blood that pours from his hands, his feet and his side is the very blood of God, then we are also enabled to recognize that the saying, "His blood is on us and our children!" is not only our judgment, but it is also our salvation. The blood of Jesus is the blood of the covenant which is poured out for the forgiveness of sins.[17] For this reason there is "power,

---

17. In the great drama of God's saving dealings with Israel, the sprinkling of people with blood is a sign of their inclusion within the covenant people. In one of the defining moments in the history of Israel, after leading the Hebrew people out of Egypt and across the Red Sea to freedom, the LORD formalized his relationship to Israel through entering into covenant with them at Mount Sinai (Exod 24). In the climactic confirmation of the covenant, sacrifices were made and the blood was collected in bowls. Half the blood was poured upon the altar and then the Book of the Covenant was read to the people, to which they responded, "We will do everything the LORD has said; we will obey" (Exod 24:7). Then Moses took the remaining blood and sprinkled it upon the people, sealing the covenant with this action and the accompanying words, "This is the blood of the covenant that the LORD has made with you in accordance with all these words" (Exod 24:8). We hear similar words of covenantal confirmation in the mouth of Jesus at the Last Supper when he says to his disciples, "This is my blood of the covenant, which is poured out for many for the forgiveness of sins" (Matt 26:28). However this scene in the Upper Room depicting the confirmation of a new covenant seemingly remains incomplete, for Matthew does not record the people voicing their assent to the terms and conditions of the covenant, nor are the words of institution followed by a sprinkling of the covenantal people with blood. Allusions to these covenantal elements do not appear until Jesus is presented by Pilate to the people and they cry out, "His blood is on us and our children." It is God's own enemies, the very ones who rejected Jesus Christ, who are sprinkled with his blood and welcomed into covenant with him through the forgiveness of sin! As the apostle Paul writes, "But God demonstrates his own love for us in this: While we were still sinners, Christ died for us" (Rom 5:8) and "if, while we were God's enemies, we were reconciled to him through the death of his Son, how much more, having been reconciled, shall we be saved through his life!" (Rom 5:10). As the apostle Peter writes in his first epistle, we "have been chosen according to the foreknowledge of God the Father, through the sanctifying work of the Spirit, to be obedient to Jesus Christ and sprinkled with his blood" (1 Pet 1:2).

power, wonder-working power in the blood of the Lamb."[18] Power to make the foulest offender clean; power to move the hardest heart to repentance; power to set us apart for new life with God in Christ. The great Reformer John Calvin was fond of saying, "When the sermon is preached, the blood of Jesus drips on the congregation."[19] May that blood drip down upon us this morning and in the weeks to come as we gather together and hear the Word proclaimed. May we all be sprinkled by the blood of the Lamb. His blood is on us and our children!

18. Lewis E. Jones, "There is Power in the Blood" (1899).

19. Shepherd, *Our Evangelical Faith*, 75.

16

"Early on the First Day of the Week . . . "

Nashville Road Community Church

Kleinburg, Ontario

Sunday, March 31, 2013

John 20:1–18

Easter Sunday

It is both a great privilege and a daunting responsibility to be with you here today at Nashville Road Community Church, entrusted with the task of proclaiming the resurrection of our Lord Jesus Christ. It is a great privilege because this day stands above all others as the day we rejoice that "Death has been swallowed up in victory" (1 Cor 15:54). On this day, we rejoice that our Lord has risen triumphant over the grave. On the other hand, what could one possibly say about such an earth-shattering and momentous event that, by its very nature, stretches the human mind and the English language to its limits? This is the daunting challenge.

It is perhaps for this reason that I am drawn to a story told by an old pastor describing the best Easter sermon that he ever preached. As the preacher entered the pulpit on that particular Easter morning, an expectant hush fell over those who had assembled. After silently surveying the congregation which he had come to love and cherish, he called out in a loud voice, "Alleluia, Christ is risen! Let us worship the risen Lord!" After saying this he stepped away from the pulpit, indicating that his sermon was complete. As he did so, the congregation erupted in joyous celebration and song.[1]

---

1. Robert E. Webber recounts a similar experience from the perspective of a congregant in *Worship is a Verb*, 167.

This morning I hope to say a little more than that preacher who simply proclaimed, "Alleluia, Christ is risen!" but I don't intend to say anything different. My intention this morning is simply to follow along with John as he describes this new and wonderful thing that God has done. John begins his account as follows, "Early on the first day of the week, while it was still dark, Mary Magdalene went to the tomb" (20:1). Mary Magdalene had been enshrouded in darkness since the Friday past, when Jesus of Nazareth, her teacher and friend, was put to death on a Roman cross atop a hill outside Jerusalem. He was the one who had brought healing into her life. He had freed her from the demons which had haunted her (Mark 16:9; Luke 8:2), but now he was gone. Since that time Mary had found herself immersed in grief, drowning in torrents of despair. The world that she, along with the other followers of Jesus, had known had been thrown into chaos. Not only had they lost their teacher and friend, they had lost the leader of their movement; the one who they thought would restore Israel before the sight of God and the nations. Their hopes and dreams had been laid to rest in the cold, dark tomb alongside the body of their master.

Engulfed in this darkness, Mary made her way to the grave site early on the first day of the week. John doesn't tell us why Mary went to the tomb. Perhaps she came to anoint the body, although, John does tell us that Nicodemus and Joseph of Arimathea had already done that (19:38–42). Maybe she came to grieve. Perhaps she simply wanted to be near the place where the body of her loved one had been laid. So she came to the tomb, the place where Jesus had spent the seventh day, the Sabbath, at rest. It's fitting then that she came to the tomb in the darkness of the early morning, not only because of the darkness that flooded her own heart, but because for parts of three days, Jesus Christ had lain in the tomb—the light of the world swallowed up by the darkness of death.

Of course, here in this first verse there is already a hint of what is to come. You'll recall that John began his telling of the Jesus story at the beginning of his Gospel with the words "In the beginning" (1:1). These opening words direct our attention and imagination back to the beginning of God's work of creation as it is depicted in the opening chapters of the first book of the Bible. Here, at the climactic moment of the story, John once again draws upon imagery from the beginning of the book of Genesis. What is going to happen next is so amazing, so mind-blowing, that the only event to which it can be compared is the act of creation itself. The darkness of the early morning as Mary made her way to the tomb is reminiscent of the darkness of the first day of creation. At that time, the book of Genesis tells us that "the earth was formless and empty, darkness was over the surface of the deep, and the Spirit of God was hovering over the waters. And God said, 'Let there be light'" (1:2–3). As we move back to the Gospel of John, we see that early in the morning on the first day of the week the Spirit of God was once again hovering over the face of the earth. It was the dawning of the new creation. Into the darkness God would once again speak the words, "Let there be light!"

Mary arrives at the tomb and finds that the stone has been rolled away. For Mary, this discovery is a further kick in the teeth. In the midst of the darkness which enshrouds her heart and mind, this can only mean one thing—someone has taken Jesus' body away. So she goes running to Simon Peter and the beloved disciple and says to them, "They have taken the Lord out of the tomb, and we don't know where they have put him" (John 20:2). Peter and the beloved disciple jump to their feet and race for the tomb. Peter gets out of the blocks quickly, but he's eventually overtaken by the other disciple, who is the first to arrive at the tomb. He bends over and looks in, but he doesn't enter. Peter is the next to arrive on the scene and, in classic Petrine fashion, he barges right into the tomb. When Peter enters the tomb he sees the strips of linen in which Jesus had been wrapped, lying on the ledge where Jesus' body had lain. The burial cloth that had been around Jesus' head is rolled up and sitting by itself apart from the linen. Eventually the other disciple also enters the tomb and sees the linen strips and the rolled up facecloth. Peter leaves the tomb baffled, but a spark is ignited within the other disciple and he begins to realize what has happened. It dawns on him that no grave robber would take the time to remove the burial wrappings. No thief would take the time to roll up the facecloth. The beloved disciple starts to see that there is a far greater and more mysterious power at work here than tomb raiders.[2]

Perhaps the beloved disciple's thoughts were taken back to Bethany where he had seen Jesus summon the dead man Lazarus out from the tomb (John 11:1–44). As readers of John's Gospel, that's where our thoughts are directed, as that is where we first encountered strips of linen and a facecloth similar to those which are described as being left in the tomb where Jesus' body had been buried. When we hear of a burial facecloth, our first inclination is probably to think of a little cloth square that we might use to wash our face, but what John is describing here is a cloth that would have been wrapped around the head of the deceased, so that his mouth would not fall open.[3] When Lazarus is called forth from the tomb, he emerges still wrapped up in his grave clothes. I've always imagined Lazarus staggering forwards into the daylight with his arms extended in front of him in mum-

2. Keener, *Gospel of John*, 2:1182; Vanier, *Drawn into the Mystery*, 335.
3. Brown, *John (XIII-XXI)*, 986.

my-like fashion, but this may simply be the symptom of having watched too many zombie movies as a child. There is significance, though, to the fact that Lazarus emerges from the tomb still dressed in his grave clothes, for although Lazarus has been raised, he will yet face death.[4] Although Lazarus was brought back to life, he would once again die and return to the grave. In fact, as a result of being raised, Lazarus became "Number Two," right behind Jesus, on the chief priests' hit list (John 12:10).

Jesus, on the other hand, has left his grave clothes behind. Lazarus needed to be unwrapped from his grave clothes, but the cloth that had been around Jesus' head had been rolled up and set aside by the one who has been raised to new life, never to die again.[5] Jesus has left his grave clothes behind because "death hath no more dominion over him" (Rom 6:9, KJV). A burial shroud is of no use to the "risen conquering Son," for in the resurrection of Christ we witness "the undoing of death."[6]

John, the fifth-century bishop of Constantinople, whose eloquent preaching earned him the surname Chrysostom, which literally means "the golden-mouthed," proclaimed this Easter reality with such passion and anointing that his Easter homily became permanently embedded in the Easter liturgy of the Eastern churches.[7] I couldn't imagine returning to Nashville Road next Easter to discover that you were reciting parts of my sermon as part of your Easter worship, let alone entertain the thought that it would still be recited 1500 years later! Yet this is exactly what happened with Chrysostom's Easter sermon. Chrysostom's words continue to resonate with the truth and power of the Gospel. Listen to this small excerpt from his Easter message:

> Let no one fear death, for the Death of our Savior has set us free.
>
> He has destroyed it by enduring it.
>
> He destroyed Hell when he descended into it.
>
> He put it into an uproar even as it tasted of His flesh.
>
> Isaiah foretold this when he said,
>
> "You, O Hell, have been troubled by encountering Him below."
>
> Hell was in an uproar because it was done away with.
>
> It was in an uproar because it was mocked.

4. Newbigin, *Light Has Come*, 263.

5. Wright, *John for Everyone*, 2:143.

6. "Risen conquering son" is a phrase from Edmund L Budry's Easter hymn, "Thine is the Glory!" (1904). The phrase "the undoing of death" is the title of a collection of Holy Week and Easter sermons by Fleming Rutledge.

7. For a brief introduction to the life and preaching of John Chrysostom, see Edwards, *History of Preaching*, 72–84.

It was in an uproar, for it is destroyed.

It is in an uproar, for it is annihilated.

It is in an uproar, for it is now made captive.

Hell took a body, and discovered God.

It took earth, and encountered Heaven.

It took what it saw, and was overcome by what it did not see.

O death, where is thy sting?

O Hell, where is thy victory?

Christ is Risen, and you, o death, are annihilated!

Christ is Risen, and the evil ones are cast down!

Christ is Risen, and the angels rejoice!

Christ is Risen, and life is liberated!

Christ is Risen, and the tomb is emptied of its dead;

for Christ having risen from the dead,

is become the first-fruits of those who have fallen asleep.

To Him be Glory and Power forever and ever. Amen![8]

This would be a wonderful place to end the sermon, but I can't bear the thought of leaving Mary standing alone, weeping outside the tomb. So let's return to her. After Peter and the beloved disciple have gone their way, Mary continues her frantic search for Jesus. She bends down and looks into the tomb and sees two figures dressed in white. She calls out to them, "They have taken my Lord away and I don't know where they have put him" (John 20:13). Immersed in the darkness of the depths of despair, she does not yet see or understand. She turns around and sees a man whom she takes to be the gardener and cries out, "Sir, if you have carried him away, tell me where you have put him, and I will get him" (John 20:15). A question arises at this point, namely: Why does John include this seemingly extraneous detail about Mary thinking that Jesus was the gardener? My suspicion is that John is making a subtle, but important, theological point.[9] Once again, this point goes back to the opening chapters of Genesis—this time to the creation of the first human being and God's placing him within a garden to work and tend the earth. In order to see this, we will need to overcome our tendency to read this story as a case of mistaken identity. What I mean is that we tend to read the story like this: Mary thought the man standing before her was

8. John Chrysostom (ca. 400 AD), quoted in Brad Jersak, "Nonviolent Identification and the Victory of Christ," in Jersak and Hardin, *Stricken by God?*, 52–53.

9. N.T. Wright shares my suspicion and unpacks it in a similar, but not quite identical, way to how I have approached it here. Wright, *John for Everyone*, 2:146.

the gardener, but she was mistaken. It turns out that it was not actually the gardener Mary was speaking to, but rather Jesus himself. However, rather than a case of mistaken identity, it may be better to think of this as a case of revelation of identity. For what Mary is soon to discover is not that the man standing before her is not the gardener, but rather that the gardener is Jesus. For this encounter occurs on the morning of the first day of the week, the dawning of the new creation, and this one standing before her is, in the words of Colossians, "the firstborn from among the dead" and "the image of the invisible God" (1:18, 15). He is the second Adam, the faithful human covenant partner, who exercises the true vocation of humanity and through his obedience even unto death, overcomes the disobedience of the entire human race. At the same time he is Emmanuel, the very presence of the covenanting God-with-us in the flesh, who, in bearing our humanity into the presence of the Father, opens the way for the coming of God's Spirit to dwell with his people.

It won't be until Jesus pronounces her name that Mary's eyes will be opened to this wonderful reality. Until then she will continue to be the whirlwind of motion and activity which she has been throughout the passage. We have heard of her coming to the tomb, running to Simon and the other disciple, bending over and looking into the tomb, spinning around, calling out, questioning—all part of a desperate search to find her Lord. Mary's frantic searching in many ways resembles each of our own spiritual quests. We are all seekers, searching to fill the God-shaped hole that stands in the center of our being. In the words of the famous prayer of the Church Father Augustine, "Thou hast made us for Thyself and our hearts are restless till they rest in Thee."[10] We have been created in the image of the living God for relationship with him, and apart from him our hearts are restless. We strive to quench this thirst or fulfill this longing in various misplaced and misdirected ways, because like Mary, we do not even recognize what or who it is that we are looking for. Some people immerse themselves in their careers; others convince themselves that if they could just find the right partner or start a family everything would be alright. Some turn to the world of consumer goods, attracted by the latest gadget, entertainment device, or sport utility vehicle. Others seek to fill the void at the center of their souls with things that end up placing them on the news or in jail. It's important to notice in our Scripture passage this morning that, in spite of all her searching, in the end it is Jesus who finds Mary and calls her by name.[11] Our spiritual quest will ultimately reach its goal, but not because we are

10. Augustine, *Confessions*, 1.1.

11. Vanier, *Drawn into the Mystery*, 336.

expert seekers who know how to navigate their way to God. Far from it. Our spiritual quest will ultimately reach its goal because the Good Shepherd has entered into the darkness to seek and save the lost. He calls each of his sheep by name and leads them on into the light of life (John 10:3).

After hearing the Lord call her name, Mary's eyes are opened and she recognizes her teacher standing before her. She reaches out and clings to Jesus, but he says to her, "Do not hold on to me, for I have not yet ascended to the Father" (John 20:17). Mary must learn that from now on, there will be a new way for the disciples of Jesus to follow their Master. She cannot hold on to Jesus or try to keep him to herself, for this new way of relating to the Lord will not be a private affair. Nor will the relationship involve the bodily presence of the Lord or include disciples physically following after him through the rocky hills of Galilee. Mary must let Jesus go, for he is on his way to the Father; then he will pour out his Holy Spirit so that he can be present with and dwell in the midst of his new creation people wherever they may be found. In the Gospel of John, the resurrection cannot be separated from the cross or from Jesus' return to the Father. Jesus' ascension prepares the way for his return to dwell with his people in the power of the Holy Spirit so that they may share in the eternal life of God.

"Do not hold on to me, for I have not yet returned to the Father. Go instead to my brothers and tell them, 'I am ascending to my Father and your Father, to my God and your God'" (John 20:17). Rather than clinging to Jesus, Mary is commissioned to be the apostle to the apostles. She is appointed to take the news of the resurrection and the message of the risen Lord to the very ones who abandoned him and denied him in his darkest hour. Jesus does not send a message of vengeance—an ominous "I'll be back!" Instead, Jesus commissions Mary to proclaim to his people a word of grace: "I am returning to my Father and your Father, to my God and your God." Something definitive has happened. Up to this point in the Gospel of John, we have only heard Jesus speak of "the Father" or "my Father," but now he says, "I am returning to my Father and *your* Father."[12] Something has changed. In his death and resurrection, Jesus has opened up a way where before there was no way. Jesus has become the firstborn of many brothers and sisters, who have been given the Spirit as a pledge of their adoption. All who believe in him have been given "the right to become children of God—children born not of natural descent, nor of human decision or a husband's will, but born of God" (John 1:12–13).

Mary Magdalene had the privilege of being the first to proclaim this Easter message. She is the first Easter preacher and she begins her message

---

12. Newbigin, *The Light Has Come*, 266; Wright, *John for Everyone*, 2:145.

by saying to the disciples, "I have seen the Lord!" (John 20:18). In his Gospel, John doesn't actually tell us how this first Easter message was received, although Luke suggests that Mary may have been laughed out of the pulpit by the as-yet-to-believe apostles (24:9–11). However, it doesn't matter how that first Easter sermon was received by the apostles, because the story of Mary's encounter with the risen Lord has not been recorded for their benefit. The apostles would have their own encounter with the risen Lord in due time. The story of Mary's meeting with the risen Lord is recorded for our sake, so that "we may believe that Jesus is the Messiah, the Son of God, and that by believing we may have life in his name" (John 20:31).[13] So hear the good news of the Gospel, "Christ the Lord is risen today!"[14] He is risen for those who are mourning like Mary. He is risen for those who are puzzled like Peter. He is risen for those who are huddled together behind locked doors like the beat-up and beleaguered community of disciples on that first Easter Sunday. He is even risen for those like Thomas who do not yet believe, but one day soon, upon encountering the Living One, will fall to their knees before him and declare, "My Lord and my God!" (John 20:28). He is risen for all who are stumbling in the darkness and for all who find themselves journeying through the valley of the shadow of death. He is risen for you and for me. So hear the good news of Easter and believe: "Alleluia, Christ is risen!"

13. I have changed the pronouns in the verse from the second person plural to the first person plural.

14. Charles Wesley, "Christ the Lord is Risen Today" (1739).

17

An Unlikely Candidate for Sermonic Success

Good Shepherd Community Church

Scarborough, Ontario

Sunday, May 24, 2015

Acts 2:1–41; Exodus 19:1–9, 16–19

Pentecost Sunday

It shouldn't have worked. We've just heard Peter's famous sermon from the Day of Pentecost. It was the first Christian sermon ever preached. By the end of it there were three thousand people clamouring to join the emerging Jesus movement, but all I find myself thinking is: "It really shouldn't have worked!" It was a sermon delivered by the wrong person, to an ill-defined audience, in the midst of a difficult context. To top it all off, the text of the sermon itself is enough to give contemporary homileticians hangovers. This speech was a most unlikely candidate for sermonic success.

Let's start with the preacher. The renowned nineteenth-century professor and preacher Horace Bushnell once remarked that "it takes just four talents to make a great preacher; namely,—a talent of high scholarship; a metaphysical and theologic thinking talent; style or a talent for expression; and a talent of manner and voice for speaking."[1] Peter had none of these things going for him. He had not graduated from one of the most prestigious Torah schools. In fact, he hadn't graduated from any school. There were no initials he could place after his name on his business card. It simply

---

1. Bushnell, *Building Eras in Religion*, 185, quoted in Lischer, *Company of Preachers*, 85.

read Simon, Son of Jonah. Full stop. No PhD, no MDiv, no BA, not even a Galilean secondary school diploma. The latter probably wouldn't have been much help, as every refined and sophisticated person in Jerusalem knew that Galileans were provincial and uncultured. They were not to be taken seriously. This judgment was reinforced by the strange way Galileans talked, as they struggled to pronounce certain letters and swallowed other syllables.[2] Perhaps Peter's time with Jesus over the course of his ministry could make up for some of these deficiencies. Now there certainly is something to this line of thinking, but it must be noted that it wasn't all smooth sailing for Peter. He had traveled a rocky road on the way to his date with his Pentecostal destiny. It is true that at Caesarea Philippi Peter had been the first to confess Jesus to be the long-awaited Messiah, but soon after he revealed he had no idea what he was talking about when he attempted to stand in the way of Jesus' journey to the cross (Matt 16:13–28). The last time we heard Peter speak in public, he was surrounded by a handful of servants huddled around a fire in the courtyard of the high priest. His words on that occasion were memorable for all the wrong reasons (Luke 22:54–62). "Woman, I don't know him." "Man, I am not one of his disciples." "Jesus who? I don't know what you're talking about." This was a most unlikely candidate to proclaim perhaps the most important sermon in the history of the church.

The context wasn't very conducive for sermonic success either. Now, don't get me wrong. It was Jerusalem—Mount Zion, the great city on a hill which had once sheltered the splendor of Solomon, the site of the Temple of the LORD. Where else could a sermon of such magnitude be preached? But Jerusalem didn't exactly have the best track record when it came to the reception of sermons. Jesus himself had summed up the situation not long before when he proclaimed, "Jerusalem, Jerusalem, you who kill the prophets and stone those sent to you" (Luke 13:34)! Jesus was executed not too long afterwards. So the prospects of sermonic success for one of Jesus' disciples preaching in Jerusalem were not great, to put it mildly. Beyond that, the author of Acts doesn't even tell us where in Jerusalem the sermon was preached. Great speeches normally require a dramatic setting.[3] Think of Martin Luther King Jr. boldly declaring his dream from the steps of the Lincoln Memorial surrounded by two-hundred and fifty-thousand marchers. Or Winston Churchill defiantly announcing before the British House of Commons that in the face of the encroaching Nazi juggernaut, "We shall never surrender." I'm not going to go so far as to say that the context made

2. Stott, *Acts*, 65.

3. Scholars surmise that the sermon must have been preached in the Temple precincts as this was the only place in Jerusalem that could have accommodated a crowd of the size mentioned in the passage. Witherington, *Acts of the Apostles*, 132.

either of these speeches, but I suspect they would not have had nearly the same effect if they were delivered in your living room or mine. Yet we are not told where Peter's speech takes place. We only know the disciples were all gathered together in "one place" when they heard the sound like wind and saw the tongues like fire (Acts 2:1). Surely if this sermon was to be of any historical importance it would have to take place in a setting significant enough to warrant mentioning.

The crowd that had assembled was not the most promising audience either. Now the book of Acts does tell us that they were devout Jews, so this was a huge plus. It meant that they knew their Scriptures and they were religiously sincere. Some of them would have traveled great distances to be in Jerusalem for the festival, and they would have been open, in theory anyway, to the notion of God showing up. We cannot underestimate the significance of these factors. However, they were also an incredibly diverse collection of people from all over the world who spoke a variety of languages: "Parthians, Medes and Elamites; residents of Mesopotamia, Judea and Cappadocia, Pontus and Asia, Phrygia and Pamphylia, Egypt and the parts of Libya near Cyrene; visitors from Rome (both Jews and converts to Judaism); Cretans and Arabs" (Acts 2:9–11). Such radical diversity is a significant obstacle if you're looking to start a burgeoning movement. Ask any sociologist and he or she will tell you that the quickest way to gain traction in a movement and grow any type of group is to aim for homogeneity. As one scholar puts it, "human beings show an overwhelming predisposition to bind together with 'their own kind.'"[4] An entire church growth movement was founded upon this "homogenous unit principle."[5] Essentially, it said that it you're looking to grow your church, the best way to do this is to target a demographic group and cater everything to garnering that group's attention. The "homogenous unit principle" has been widely and rightly criticized, but it's amazing how many churches who repudiate the principle in theory continue to operate by it in practice, even if it's only at an implicit level. The confessional divides which have previously separated one denomination from another now seem to pale in comparison to the ever-widening gap between the young and the old, the rich and the poor, and all of the various cultural and ethnic groups within the church in Canada. But Peter seemed to have missed the memo about how to quickly grow a popular movement by appealing to people who look, dress, and sound like one another. He may have caught fish back in Galilee, but he certainly didn't have any instincts for selling them!

4. Kraft, *Culture, Communication, and Christianity*, 61.

5. The Lausanne Committee for World Evangelization had a special consultation in 1977 to discuss the relation of the homogenous unit principle to the church's evangelistic commission. See "Lausanne Occasional Paper 1."

When all of these mitigating factors are considered, it becomes apparent that Peter is going to have to exhibit some true homiletical heroism if he is going to salvage this sermon. His opening words are less than promising: "Fellow Jews and all of you who live in Jerusalem, let me explain this to you; listen carefully to what I say" (Acts 2:14). Essentially Peter begins the most important speech of his life sounding like a Sunday school teacher trying to capture the attention of a group of rambunctious five year-olds. "Listen up!" is certainly not the most rhetorically sophisticated way to begin a sermon. Furthermore, Peter runs the risk of sounding authoritarian by beginning with an imperative and we all know there's nothing people hate more than being told what to think or what to do. Perhaps Peter hadn't read the homiletical textbooks that make it clear that truly stimulating preaching is all about induction and indirection. You can't beat people over the head with truth claims; instead, you have to let the hearers organically discover the truth for themselves. A preacher must learn to preach "as one without authority."[6] If that's not bad enough, he follows up his questionable opening line with what appears to be a terribly lame joke. "These people are not drunk, as you suppose. It's only nine in the morning" (Acts 2:15). If it's not a joke, then the line is perhaps even more pitiable. From there, Peter jumps right into some wild end-time prophecy from the Old Testament. Sounding much like a crazed homeless man standing on a street corner with a placard strapped to his chest, Peter tells the crowd that the wind, the fire, and the tongues are all signs that the end of the world is upon them. After his brief foray into the book of Joel, Peter returns to the recent past. "People of Israel. Remember that Jesus fellow? The rabbi from Nazareth? You know, the one who went around casting out demons, healing the sick, raising the dead, and proclaiming the kingdom of God? Oh come on, you must remember him! He's the one you handed over a little over a month ago to those godless Romans to be crucified. Remember him? Well, I bet you thought you'd heard the last of him when they took him down from the cross and laid him in the tomb, but it was all part of God's plan and now he's back. God has raised him from the dead!"

This is a huge claim. At this point we might expect any speaker worth his salt to marshal his best proofs to support this astounding claim. What we get from Peter is a convoluted reading of Psalm 16 that would make many modern historians role over in their grave. After all, these scholars would

---

6. *As One Without Authority* is the title of Fred Craddock's famous work, which made a significant contribution to the inductive turn in twentieth-century homiletics. The tongue-in-cheek criticisms raised in this paragraph apply more directly to the popular reception of the inductive method than to Craddock's more nuanced articulation of his position.

argue, a passage can only mean what the original author intended it to mean and there's no way that David, writing a thousand years earlier, could possibly have had Jesus in mind! Peter then follows it up by pointing out the grave of a beloved national hero and reminding his listeners that their hero continues to lie sealed within the tomb where he has lain dead for close to a millennium. "Yes, your beloved David is dead, but our Jesus has been raised from the dead and we Galileans, whom you suppose to be drunk, are the witnesses." Peter's evidence seems far from overwhelming, but he apparently thinks it's enough to build on, so he continues. "This peasant teacher who was cruelly crucified as a common criminal has now ascended to the right hand of the Father and shares in God's rule of the universe. From there he has poured out the Holy Spirit, inaugurating God's new age of light and life and love." Moving toward his conclusion Peter then lays out the bottom line, saying, "If there's one thing you should take home from my sermon this morning it is this: God has made the man *you* crucified both *Lord* and *Messiah*!" Having laid the rhetorical smack down, we can almost imagine Peter dropping his microphone and exiting stage right.

It's astonishing that Peter could preach such a sermon. It's perhaps even more astonishing that he could get away with preaching such a sermon and that he didn't end up getting stoned to death. Telling your audience that they murdered the Author of Life is certainly no way to win friends and influence people. There are so many external issues surrounding the sermon and what appear to be so many rhetorical missteps within that there is no way it should have worked. All things considered, there is absolutely no earthly reason why this sermon should have been successful. But then again that's the very crux of the matter, isn't it? There is no *earthly reason* why it should have been successful!

The author of the book of Acts gives his readers a clue that something is up right at the beginning of his account of the Day of Pentecost. In the first verse of the passage, Luke begins by writing, "When the Day of Pentecost had fully come" or "In the fulfillment of the Day of Pentecost."[7] Unfortunately most of our English translations fail to pick up on the subtleties of Luke's language at this point and offer a rather non-descript translation, like the NIV: "When the day of Pentecost came." But the verb Luke uses in this verse is a word that speaks of fulfillment. It is eschatological language—end-times speech—which signifies that the deep realities to which the Feast of Pentecost pointed were coming to fruition on that very day. In order to have a better sense of what's going on in this passage, we therefore need to have some understanding of the place of the Feast of Pentecost in the life

---

7. Witherington, *Acts*, 132n7; Pelikan, *Acts*, 48–49.

of Israel. Pentecost was the second of three major festivals celebrated by the people of Israel. It was also known as the Feast of Weeks. Both names reflect the celebration's relationship to the previous festival, Passover; *Weeks* because it occurs seven weeks after Passover and *Pentecost* because it takes place fifty days after Passover. In its very name we see that there is an inseparable connection between Pentecost and Passover. The Bible doesn't tell us nearly as much about Pentecost as it does about Passover and the other major festival, Tabernacles. However, the Old Testament does tell us that the Feast of Weeks was originally a harvest festival associated with presenting the firstfruits of the wheat or grain harvest to the LORD (Exod 23:16, 34:22; Lev 23:15–16; Num 28:26; Deut 16:9–10). When the Day of Pentecost had fully come, it was time for the great ingathering to begin. Jesus had previously exhorted his disciples, saying, "Open your eyes and look at the fields! They are ripe for the harvest" (John 4:35). With the coming of the Holy Spirit, who is the firstfruits of the new world on its way, it was time to bring in "not the sheaves of grain but the firstfruits of souls that are consecrated to the Lord."[8]

This Pentecostal picture is further enriched by the fact that by Jesus' time, the Feast of Pentecost had come to be associated with the giving of the Law at Mount Sinai and God's entering into covenant with his people. The Israelites arrival at Sinai was reckoned to have occurred fifty days after the exodus, when the LORD, with "a mighty hand and outstretched arm" (Ps 136:12), had delivered his people from slavery in Egypt. After leading them through the waters of the sea and through the wilderness by a pillar of cloud by day and fire by night, the LORD brought them to Sinai, where fire and smoke descended upon the mountain, the earth shook, a trumpet sounded, and the people trembled in fear. This was the sensational backdrop for an even more astounding development—the creator of the universe was about to bind himself to a rag-tag bunch of former slaves and claim them as his very own people. They were presented with the Torah, a set of laws and instructions to govern their life together as God's treasured possession. The Torah announced a way of living before God which would set God's people apart from all the nations of the earth as "a kingdom of priests and a holy nation" (Exod 19:6). Reflecting back upon the events at Sinai, Jewish interpreters would later claim that the Law of God was carried by angels to the people below on tongues of fire and that it was announced in the seventy languages of the nations of the world.[9] The fire and the wind and the tongues on the day of the fulfilled

8. Bede, *Acts of the Apostles*, 2.41, quoted in Martin and Smith, *Acts*, 36.

9. Bruce D. Chilton, "Festivals and Holy Days: Jewish," in Evans and Porter, *Dictionary of New Testament Background*, 374; Brown, *Once-and-Coming Spirit*, 10; Witherington, *Acts*, 131.

Pentecost points to the giving of a new covenant and the gathering together of a renewed Israel. While Moses had to ascend the mountain to receive the Law on tablets of stone, when the day of Pentecost came in its fullness, the Holy Spirit came down and inscribed the law of the new covenant upon tablets of flesh. Through the mouth of the prophet Jeremiah, the LORD had declared, "This is the covenant I will make with the people of Israel after that time. . . . I will put my law in their minds and write it on their hearts. I will be their God and they will be my people" (Jer 31:33). A similar vision had been revealed to the prophet Ezekiel, "I will give you a new heart and put a new spirit in you; I will remove from you your heart of stone and give you a heart of flesh. And I will put my Spirit in you and move you to follow my decrees and be careful to keep my laws" (Ezek 36:26–27).

Perhaps it shouldn't be surprising that Luke tells us that when the crowd heard Peter's sermon they were "cut to the heart" (Acts 2:37). On the day of the fulfillment of the Day of Pentecost, the Holy Spirit was wielding the scalpel of the Word in order to perform spiritual surgery. Today approximately 3,500 heart transplants are performed annually throughout the world.[10] The Holy Spirit nearly matched that number on a single day. However, this mass of cardiac surgeries was not frivolous or unnecessary. If the patients were to be saved, the work that God had done for us in Christ, quite apart from us, would have to also be worked in us. Just as Passover and Pentecost are inseparable in the Old Testament, so they are inseparable in the New. Just as Pentecost is semantically inseparable from Passover, so it is also theologically inseparable as well. The original exodus from Egypt freed the Hebrews from the slavery of their past, but it was the covenant at Sinai that opened up their future to a life as God's beloved people. Passover is incomplete without Pentecost. In a similar way, in his great Passover from death to life, Jesus has triumphed over the great oppressors Sin, Death, and the Devil. Our sin has been atoned for. In the words of the letter to the Colossians, Jesus has "canceled the charge of our legal indebtedness, which stood against us and condemned us; he has taken it away, nailing it to the cross" (Col 2:14). In the words of the old Gospel song, "The old account was settled long ago."[11] Perhaps we can do no better than Jesus' own confident proclamation from the cross: "It is finished" (John 19:30). There is nothing for us to add to Christ's perfect and sufficient work—"It is finished." However, on this day of Pentecost we are reminded that although it is true and right to say, "It is finished!" we must also go on to add, "but it's not over." "'It is finished.' But it is not over."[12] The one who has

---

10. Gillinov and Nissen, *Heart 411*, 501.

11. Frank M. Graham, "The Old Account Settled Long Ago" (1902).

12. Neuhaus, *Death on a Friday Afternoon*, 205, 225, quoted in Hauerwas,

definitively dealt with our past has also opened up for us a future of sharing life with God through the pouring out of the Holy Spirit. It is the Holy Spirit who conveys God's very life to us by weaving our lives into the life of Jesus. It is the same Holy Spirit, whose power raised Jesus Christ from the dead, which breathed upon those assembled on the Day of Pentecost in Jerusalem, animating the corporate body of Christ with the breath of life. It is the same Spirit who continues to be present where even two or three are gathered in the name of Jesus. Where the Spirit of the Lord is, there is life. Where the Spirit of the Lord is, there is freedom. Where the Spirit of the Lord is, there is a future because the presence of the Lord and Giver of Life is the very presence of God's future. "There's a new world coming / it's already here / there's a new world on its way."[13]

Because Peter recognized that Pentecost had come in its fullness and this very Spirit had been poured out upon all flesh, he was set free to become a true Gospel preacher. In verse forty, Luke admits that he has only given us the Coles Notes version of what Peter said on this particular day. However, in light of what Luke has recorded and in the face of the testimony of Scripture as a whole, with a pinch of sanctified imagination mixed in for good measure, I think we can expand upon Peter's response to the earnest questioning of the people in the following way: "Yes, it's true, you killed him. But don't think that we're any better. In the hour of trial these guys all fled and I even denied him three times. In one way or another all of us here, and in fact the entire human race, are implicated in Jesus' death. But the grave could not contain him. Death could not hold him down. The gates of hell could not stand against him. He is risen! But he has not come back bearing the sword of vengeance, rather he is 'risen with healing in his wings!'[14] Therefore repent—change your minds about Jesus—acknowledge his Lordship, take his yoke upon you for his yoke is easy and his burden is light. Sin at its root is nothing but unbelief, but Jesus has made an end to sin, so there's really nothing left to stop you from believing the good news. God doesn't believe in your disbelief. Our ancestors knew that the way to the Promised Land is through the Sea, so be baptized in Jesus' name and know that just as the Egyptians were swallowed up in the waters, your sins have been swallowed up in the oceanic depths of the love

---

Cross-shattered Christ, 88.

13. This is the refrain from a song that was well-known to some of the members of the congregation. Bryan Moyer Suderman, "New World Coming," *Detectives of Divinity: Songs of Faith for Small and Tall* (SmallTall Music, 2011). Suderman is a Canadian singer-songwriter shaped by the Anabaptist tradition, who is passionate about empowering the whole people of God, both young and old alike, to participate in the adventure of worship and discipleship (www.smalltallministries.com).

14. Charles Wesley, "Hark! The Herald Angels Sing" (1739).

shared from all eternity between the Father and the Son in the Holy Spirit. When you emerge from the waters, you will find that you have been made part of a new people—'a chosen people, a royal priesthood, a holy nation, God's special possession, that you may declare the praises of him who called you out of darkness into his wonderful light' (1 Pet 2:9). You will discover that you are a brick, a living stone, in a great Temple that the Lord is constructing as a dwelling for his very own Spirit (1 Pet 2:5). This spiritual house will spread out over the entire world renewing the face of the creation. The Spirit will give you power to be witnesses in word and deed to the life-giving reign of Jesus (Acts 1:8). The Spirit will set you free from fear and hate and suspicion to love God 'with all your heart and with all your soul and with all your mind and with all your strength' and to 'love your neighbour as yourself' (Mark 12:30–31). The Spirit will breathe the life of the risen Christ into your mortal bodies so that you will be a generative people reflecting the eternally generative life of the triune God. This is a sure and certain promise because our Lord Jesus Christ, risen from the grave, now sits at the right hand of the Father. He himself has assured us that if we as human parents know how to give good gifts to our children, then we can be certain that our heavenly Father will give the Holy Spirit to all who ask him (Luke 11:13). This promise is for those both near and far, in space and in time. It is for the inhabitants of Jerusalem and for those dwelling in the farthest corners of the earth. It is for the young and old and for generations not yet born. This world is passing away and one day the foundations of the earth will be laid bare, but the glory of the Lord endures forever (2 Pet 3:10, Ps 104:31). So, call upon the name of the Lord Jesus and allow yourselves to be saved from this corrupt generation."[15]

What more could I say? Peter has said it all. And so my sermon, a sermon about a sermon that began with tongue firmly planted in cheek, now comes to a close with a tongue loosed to declare God's praise. Who could have imagined that such a sermon would work? Maybe it didn't, but if it did then we can only thank God that the Spirit who came in roaring wind and tongues of fire on that first Pentecost, loosening the tongues of the disciples to proclaim the wonders of God in every language, transforming a cowardly fisherman into a courageous proclaimer of the truth, and uniting people from every tongue and tribe in the one body of the Messiah Jesus—we can only thank God that *that* Spirit—continues, just as the Lord has promised, to be present among God's people today and until the end of the age. Praise be to the Father, and to the Son, and to the Holy Spirit. Amen.

---

15. Many English translations offer a Pelagian-sounding translation of Acts 2:40—"Save yourselves from this corrupt generation"—but in Greek the verb (*sōzō*) appears in the passive voice.

Part III

Occasional Preaching

18

Thoughtfully Following through the Waters

Good Shepherd Community Church

Scarborough, Ontario

Sunday, February 7, 2010

Exodus 14:1–31

The Baptisms of Nikki Robinson & Cathy Xu

Following is not an easy thing.[1] The people of God have always struggled with following. The first human beings were given just one command to follow, but they could not do it. Instead, out of their own aspirations to be like God, they decided to blaze their own trail. The history of the people of Israel is the tale of one prolonged struggle between God and his wayward people. It began in the wilderness where the people first started to mumble and grumble against the LORD. It continued in the Promised Land, where the people suffered from a type of spiritual amnesia, forgetting who they were and what God had done for them. Engulfed in this spiritual fog, they began to create their own religious and moral practices according to their own whims and desires. This struggle with following continues right into the pages of the New Testament. The apostles are depicted as constantly misunderstanding Jesus. In the crucible of the events of Good Friday they all turn tail and run, abandoning Jesus to the cross. The struggle even con-

---

1. In addition to being a baptismal sermon, this sermon was situated within a series of sermons exegeting the congregation's new mission statement: "Good Shepherd Community Church exists to invite ordinary people to encounter Christ and thoughtfully follow him in the world." For this particular sermon, I had been assigned the phrase "thoughtfully following him."

tinues after Pentecost, as in Paul's letters we see the apostle again and again addressing wayward churches that have set out in their own direction, calling them to return to the source of their life in the Lord Jesus Christ. The theological term that we use for this refusal to follow the Lord, this failure to acknowledge that God is God, is sin.

The difficulty of following has been a perennial challenge for the church. However, there is a further challenge we face in light of our mission statement, which encourages us to "thoughtfully follow" Jesus. We are faced with the challenge of being thoughtful followers in an increasingly thoughtless culture. How do we "thoughtfully follow" Jesus, in the midst of a culture that reduces life to a collection of sound-bites, Twitter feeds, and text messages? Not too long ago, I came across an article on the Internet that drew upon research suggesting that our very ability to work through and give sustained attention to lengthy, complex arguments is being eroded by our constant exposure to the simple and superficial level of thought and conversation which dominates the Internet, e-mail, Facebook, and Twitter. I would tell you more about the article, but I got distracted and surfed to a different website before I could finish reading it!

The church, both local and universal, cannot allow the thoughtlessness that pervades our surrounding culture to seep any further into its life together, for thoughtlessness quickly leads to forgetfulness and forgetfulness to unfaithfulness. The Christian life cannot be reduced to a collection of catchphrases, sound bites, or pithy slogans. As Christians, we cannot settle into a way of life that is a mile wide, but only a quarter of an inch deep, for we believe that we have been called by the living God who has woven himself in deep and profound ways into the fabric of the story of our lives. Or, to say it better, we have been taken up and woven into God's story—immersed in the depths of the love that is shared by the Father, the Son, and the Holy Spirit.

So this morning I want us to direct our attention to one of the central stories of Scripture: the story of the exodus. The exodus stands at the heart of the faith of our Jewish ancestors. Without knowledge of this story, our understanding of Jesus' life and work cannot help but be superficial and incomplete. After the people of Israel had been held in slavery for four hundred years, the LORD worked mighty signs way down in Egypt's land, which convinced old Pharaoh to let God's people go.[2] The LORD then led the people out of Egypt, going before them in a pillar of cloud by day and a pillar of fire by night. The people of Israel did not know where they were

---

2. There are several allusions in this sentence to the African-American spiritual, "Go Down, Moses."

going. Each day they had to depend upon the LORD and follow him as he led the way through the wilderness. However, as is often the case, the LORD did not lead his people in the most direct route. Eventually the people of Israel arrived at the edge of the Sea and were instructed to encamp there in the shadow of Baal Zephon. As the Israelites begin to set up camp—Behold!—off in the distance, dust rising in the desert.[3] This was no natural sandstorm; it was the dust rising from the wheels of Pharaoh's chariots as they rumbled across the desert in hot pursuit. The people of Israel were trapped. With the Sea on one side of them and the full military force of the superpower of their time quickly closing in upon them from the other side, the people of Israel found themselves at a dead end. They had exhausted all of their resources. With no way forward and no way to retreat, the people began to grumble. It is the first of many grumblings recorded in the book of Exodus. "Is it because the cemeteries were all full in Egypt that you brought us out here to die in the desert, Moses? We told you that we should have stayed in Egypt." When confronted with fear and uncertainty, the Israelites, like all of us, were tempted to fall back upon familiar patterns of living and behaviour. Here we see that it is one thing to get God's people out Egypt, it is quite another to get Egypt out of God's people. Trapped between the Sea and the sword, the Hebrews longed to return to their old way of life in Egypt.

However, God had something else in mind for his people. His prophet Moses stepped forward and addressed the people, "Do not fear. Quit your squirming and abandon your futile plans. God is about to make a way where there is no way."[4] This speech stands at the center of our passage this morning. It is the only time Moses speaks in the entire chapter and it stands right at the climactic moment when the gathering storm clouds are at their very darkest. In preparing for this morning, I took the time to work through this entire passage, translating it from the Hebrew. Now that may not seem to be the most efficient use of time, but if I hadn't done so I probably would have missed the jewel hidden in the middle of the speech. Here at the center of this morning's passage, Moses quite literally says, "Do not be afraid. Stand firm and see the salvation of the LORD which he will do for you this day" (Exod 14:13; my translation). What jumped off the page at me, as I was working my way through it in Hebrew, was the word translated as salva-

---

3. My inclusion of the word "Behold!" is an attempt to give voice to the Hebrew particle *hinneh* ('lo!' or 'behold'), which remains untranslated in most English Bible translations of this passage.

4. "Making a way out of no way" is a saying with deep roots in African American preaching and spirituality, although its origins are not entirely certain. For a brief investigation into the history of its usage and, more particularly, Martin Luther King's employment of the phrase, see Mieder, *"Making a Way Out of No Way,"* 181–86.

tion; for the word translated as salvation is a construct of the Hebrew word *yeshua*.

As Christians, standing on the other side of the cross and empty tomb, we know that God's salvation *is* named *Yeshua*, or in English, Jesus. It shouldn't surprise us that we would find Jesus in the midst of this mess, standing with his people who are in disarray and distress as they find themselves out of luck and out of possibilities. In fact, that's exactly the type of place where we would expect to find him, shining light into the midst of darkness, bringing life out of death, hope out of despair, healing the wounded, binding up the broken-hearted, opening the eyes of the blind, and setting the captives free. To suggest that Jesus is at the center of the exodus might sound rather strange, but it really shouldn't surprise us, for if we read the Gospels carefully we will also see that the exodus is the context for Jesus' life.

The opening chapters of the Gospel of Matthew are steeped with exodus imagery. Allusions to this central event in the history of Israel abound in these verses. If you read Exodus 1–20 back to back with the first five chapters of the Gospel of Matthew, you cannot help but be struck by the deep interconnections. The Gospel of Luke contains many similar elements, including a depiction of the Transfiguration in which the disciples witness Jesus standing upon the mountain, shining like lightning, talking with Moses and Elijah. The content of this conversation, Luke tells us, is nothing other than Jesus' upcoming "exodus" which was about to take place at Jerusalem (9:31).[5]

The Gospel writers understand that God's deliverance of his people Israel in the exodus is a pattern or anticipation of God's ultimate act of deliverance in the life, death, and resurrection of the Messiah of Israel, Jesus Christ. The same power that raised Jesus from the dead is the power that created for God's people a way where there was no way. The same power that brought the world into being in the beginning when the Spirit of God hovered over the waters, dividing the dry land from the Sea, is the power that was on display as the wind piled up the waters so that the people of Israel could pass through the Sea on dry ground with a wall of water on either side. Israel's journey through the waters is a journey from death into life. It is a complete break from their old way of life in Egypt and deliverance by the hand of God from the power of Pharaoh which held them captive.

---

5. English translations often obscure this connection by translating the Greek word *exodon* with the English word departure. Longman, *How to Read Exodus*, 152–53. Although Brevard Childs argues, "The connection is only possible by means of an illegitimate semantic transfer" (*Exodus*, 233).

This morning we baptized Cathy Xu. Cathy knows about this kind of thing. Just as the LORD performed mighty signs in Egypt in anticipation of the exodus, Cathy has shared with us about the dramatic signs that the Lord has performed in her own life, including answered prayer and longed-for healing. Cathy also knows something about leaving Egypt behind. I remember several months ago being invited over to Cathy's house along with several other elders and leaders from the congregation in order to pray with Cathy. She asked us to help her remove the various items connected with ancestral Buddhism that she had inherited from her family. Cathy, those of us who were there that day were so proud of you for taking such a bold step in breaking with that particular aspect of your past in response to the Holy Spirit's leading. In some ways that day was a natural prelude to the events of this morning, for the apostle Paul describes baptism as being a break with the power of Sin which seeks to hold us captive. In baptism, we are buried with Christ, united with him in his death. As the apostle Paul writes, "For we know that our old self was crucified with him so that the body ruled by sin might be done away with, that we should no longer be slaves to sin" (Rom 6:6). As a result, every baptism, including the two baptisms we have witnessed this morning, stand as a sign that the powers of darkness are living on borrowed time.

Returning to our Scripture passage, as the people of Israel made their way through the waters, the Egyptians took up pursuit and entered into the Sea after them. However, the Egyptian chariot wheels began to get bogged down in the mud and the seaweed and their progress dragged to a halt. The cutting-edge military technology, in which the Egyptians had placed their trust, had failed them and they cried out, "Let's get away from the Israelites! The LORD is fighting for them against Egypt" (14:25). It is only within this chapter in the book of Exodus that the Egyptians began to refer to those they were pursuing not as Hebrews, but by the name of Israel.[6] The fleeing Hebrews entered the waters as a disparate collection of slaves; they emerged from the water as a people.[7]

There is a clue a few chapters earlier in the book of Exodus that alerts us to the fact that lying behind the miraculous signs and wonders performed by the LORD in Egypt is God's desire to form a people for himself. At the beginning of chapter 10 we read that the LORD said to Moses, "Go to Pharaoh, for I have hardened his heart and the hearts of his officials so that I may perform these signs of mine among them that you may tell your children and grandchildren how I dealt harshly with the Egyptians

6. Propp, *Exodus 1–18*, 492.
7. Childs, *Exodus*, 237.

and how I performed my signs among them, and that you may know that I am the LORD" (vv. 1–2). As one commentator reflecting upon this passage suggests, the drama of the exodus plagues and the miraculous deliverance of Israel from Egypt takes place so that grandparents will have something to say to their grandchildren.[8] God's people live from the remembrance of God's mighty works of salvation and this living memory is carried by grandparents who are entrusted with sharing the stories of what God has done with their grandchildren. Now within the church, this relationship between grandparents and grandchildren cannot be reduced to the merely biological level. In Christ we have been made part of a large family and given many grandparents and many grandchildren. Nikki, you have been given many grandfathers and grandmothers in the faith, men and women who have surrounded you here at Good Shepherd since you were a child, praying for you and sharing with you the story of Jesus in word and deed. People like Joan and Les Howell, Don and May Marshall, Vi Lucas, Jean Miller, and Jessie Geddes, just to name a few. Of course, at the head of the list is your own biological grandmother, Evelyn. From the earliest days of Good Shepherd, your grandmother has been bringing you here to worship, seeking to live the story of Jesus before you, and, behind the scenes, faithfully praying for you. Today is a very proud day for her, but it is also a proud day for your entire Good Shepherd family, because your baptism is sign to us of God's faithfulness in raising up faithful witnesses like your grandmother to share the good news of what God has done with the next generation. It is also a sign to us of God's work in your own life, allowing you to receive that testimony, and entrusting you with your own position of responsibility within God's family to speak and live the Gospel for the benefit of others.

The word *responsibility* from that last sentence is a crucial one. It is essential that we come to understand the freedom to which we are called in Christ. Our North American culture's understanding of freedom is very different from the Bible's understanding of freedom. As the Israelites pass through the waters of the Sea in our passage this morning, they wash off slavery and emerge as a free people.[9] Now, the Israelites are not set free in the sense that they are now liberated, autonomous individuals, each of whom is free to follow their heart's desire as long as they don't harm anyone else. This cultural definition of freedom is in fact what the Bible understands to be slavery, or what the apostle Paul calls being "in Adam." The Scottish author and pastor, George MacDonald, accurately assessed the situation when he

---

8. Walter Bruggemann, "Antidote to Amnesia," in Fleer and Bland, *Reclaiming the Imagination*, 9.

9. Propp, *Exodus*, 562.

claimed that "the one principle of hell is—'I am my own.'"[10] Freedom in the Bible is always both freedom *from* and freedom *for*. The Israelites are freed from Egypt, so that they may be free to love and serve the LORD. Remember, the people who crossed through the waters of the Sea were on their way to Sinai, where they would receive the covenant and the law, binding them to God as his specially chosen people. At Sinai, the LORD spoke to his people saying, "Although the whole earth is mine, you will be for me a kingdom of priests and a holy nation" (Exod 19:5–6). The apostle Peter draws upon this language in his first letter to the churches scattered throughout the Roman Empire, writing, "you are a chosen people, a royal priesthood, a holy nation, God's special possession, that you may declare the praises of him who called you out of darkness into his wonderful light" (1 Pet 2:9). We enter the waters of baptism as individuals, but we come out from the water as part of a people loved and claimed by the Lord. We are no longer our own, but this is a good thing. In the words of the famous first question and answer of the Heidelberg Catechism, "What is your only comfort in life and in death? That I belong—body and soul, in life and in death—*not to myself* but to my faithful Savior Jesus Christ."[11]

Christ has claimed us as his own. In the waters of baptism we are ordained into the priesthood of all believers.[12] We have been claimed by God to love and serve him as part of his peculiar people—the firstfruit of the new creation called church. In baptism, we are each ordained into ministry. Through the work of the Holy Spirit we are enabled to be priests for one another. We are granted the privilege of being Christ to one another as we speak the truth of the Gospel to one another, as we forgive one another our sins, and as we exercise the unique gifts that the Spirit gives to each believer for the building up of Christ's body the church.

As I was thinking about this aspect of baptism—as our ordination into the priesthood of all believers—I was led to reflect upon my own ordination to the particular ministry of Word and Sacrament. In his message that evening, Paul Johansen pointed us to the story of the baptism of Jesus. In that story, the Spirit of God once again hovered over the waters, and the chosen Son of Israel was led through them. As Jesus emerged from the waters, a voice came from heaven saying, "You are my Son, whom I love; with you I am well pleased" (Luke 3:22). In our baptism, we are united with Christ, and the words that the Father pronounced over Jesus are now spoken over

10. George MacDonald, "Kingship" in *Unspoken Sermons: Third Series*, 40.

11. *Heidelberg Catechism*, question and answer 1 [italics mine].

12. Martin Luther, "To the Christian Nobility of the German Nation Concerning the Reform of the Christian Estate (1520)," trans. Charles M. Jacobs, in *Christian in Society I*, 127–31.

us, "You are my beloved child, with you I am well pleased." It is this love that is the source of each of our ministries within the priesthood of all believers and it is the knowledge of this love that will sustain us through the most difficult of times.

Karl Barth, perhaps the greatest theologian of the twentieth century, understood this profound reality. Near the end of his life he crossed the ocean and came to North America for the first time to deliver a series of lectures. After a particularly impressive lecture, a student stood up to ask him a question: "Dr. Barth, what is the greatest thought that has ever passed through your mind?" The aging professor paused for a long time, obviously reflecting deeply and thoughtfully upon his answer. Then he said with great simplicity, "Jesus loves me! This I know. For the Bible tells me so."[13]

The Christian life—the life of thoughtfully following Jesus—is a life of constantly returning to our baptisms to hear afresh the voice of the Lord proclaiming our true identity over us, "You are my beloved child; with whom I am well pleased."[14] The Christian life is also a continual returning to our baptism because the old Adam is a good swimmer. We need to be drowning our old selfish selves daily, but the water in which the old Adam is drowned is the very depths of the love of God.

Baptism is not a passport to some type of utopian or idyllic existence; rather, it is the entrance into a tooth-and-nail struggle against Sin, Death, and the Devil. However, victory is assured, for we have the "right man on our side, the man of God's own choosing."[15] It was this man, the Lord Jesus Christ, who allowed the great Protestant Reformer Martin Luther to emerge victorious when Satan came against him while he was locked up in Wartburg Castle. At that time, Luther was a fugitive on the run, a bounty had been placed upon his head, and some of his closest friends had taken him and locked him up for his own protection in the tower of an old castle. There Luther spent day after day praying over, translating and reflecting upon the Scriptures. In the midst of his isolation and loneliness, the devil came against Luther with terrifying power tempting him to doubt and despair. In the face of these assaults Luther stood firm and drove out the devil by hurling his ink well at him and crying out "Get away from me Satan. I am baptized!"[16]

---

13. Martin Rumscheidt, epilogue to Barth, *Fragments Grave and Gay*, quoted in Mangina, *Karl Barth*, 9.

14. This is a central theme in the writings of Henri Nouwen. See, for example, *Life of the Beloved* and *Return of the Prodigal Son*.

15. Martin Luther, "A Mighty Fortress" (1529).

16. The story of Luther throwing the inkwell at the devil has been widely circulated, although scholars continue to debate its origins and historicity. Luther himself once wrote, "The only way to drive away the Devil is through faith in Christ, by saying: 'I

So Nikki and Cathy, in the days ahead when Satan comes against you, as he will, and you are tempted to doubt and despair, remember this day. Remember your baptism. Remember that you have been claimed by the triune God of grace. The name of the Father, Son, and Holy Spirit has been pronounced over you. You have been given a name that the world cannot give you and that the Devil can never take away. It is the name *Christian.* So as you go forward from this day to face the world with all of its complexities and life with all of its uncertainties, do not forget this central fact: you are not your own, but belong body and soul, in life and in death to your faithful Savior Jesus Christ. Nikki and Cathy, I say to you and to all of the baptized who seek to thoughtfully follow their Lord in the world: Remember who you are—the beloved children of the Father, bought by the precious blood of Christ and sealed with the Holy Spirit until the day of redemption. With you, God is well pleased.

---

have been baptized, I am a Christian.'" Luther, *Luthers Werke*, vol. 6, no. 6830; 217, 26–27, quoted in Oberman, *Luther*, 105.

19

"You Have Saved the Best till Now"

Byron United Church

London, Ontario

Saturday, July 10, 2010

John 2:1–11

The Wedding of Beth Dean and Drew Crinklaw

A young pastor was officiating his first wedding. Although he was quite nervous, he managed to successfully navigate his way through almost the entire service. But then, just before the end, at the very moment when he was supposed to present the newly married couple to the congregation, his mind went blank. Everyone was looking at him, expecting him to say or do something, but he stood frozen like a deer in the headlights. After what seemed like an eternity, words of wisdom from his revered seminary professor came flooding into his mind, "If in doubt, read Scripture." So the young pastor clumsily reached for his Bible, desperately flung it open, and began to read aloud the first verse that his eyes fell upon: "Father, forgive them, for they do not know what they are doing" (Luke 23:34).[1]

Now I know that Beth struggles with preachers who mistakenly believe they are stand-up comedians, but the story I've just told isn't so much of a joke as it is a way to suggest to you, Beth and Drew, that I don't think you know what you're doing. The fact that you've invited me to preach should be evidence enough, but what's going to happen next will seal my case. In a few moments, you are going to stand up before this congregation in the presence of God and exchange vows, promising to love and care for one another, to be faithful to the other alone, to appreciate the other as a

---

1. I'm unable to recall the context in which I first came across this anecdote.

precious gift from God, and then you will each conclude by saying, "With the greatest joy, I enter this marriage with you, a commitment made in love, kept in faith and lived in hope as long as we both shall live." To top it all off, after that you will exchange rings symbolizing unbroken fidelity to the promises you have made.

Those are pretty outrageous gestures. How can you make such unconditional promises, when you don't even know what's going to happen tomorrow, much less five, ten or twenty years from now? After all, circumstances change, feelings change, people change—and sometimes very quickly. The nineteenth century English poet Samuel Rogers cynically observed, "It doesn't much matter whom one marries, for one is sure to find out the next morning that it was someone else."[2] Perhaps that's why the great Protestant Reformer Martin Luther insisted that there were two things in life that it takes great courage to enter into: marriage and jousting tournaments.[3]

Just as great crowds assembled to take in those frightful medieval jousts, so today a large congregation has gathered to witness the promises that you will exchange with one another. But the work of your friends and family who have assembled here today does not come to a close at the end of the service or at the close of the reception this evening. Rather, they have the important responsibility in the days ahead of upholding you in prayer, encouraging and supporting you through good times and bad, and, perhaps most importantly, holding you to the promises that you made when you didn't know what you were doing.[4]

You are not alone in this marriage. Each person here today bears responsibility for seeing that your marriage succeeds. However, this doesn't negate your own personal responsibility for the future health of your marriage. It will be highly significant how you respond to the various questions and challenges that will confront you in the days ahead, after the excitement of this day has passed—when the fancy suits and the elegant gowns have been packed up in the closet. What's going to happen then? What's going to happen when the newness of being husband and wife is replaced by the routine of married life? What are you going to do, Drew, when Beth's

2. Wood, *Preaching and Professing*, 224.

3. Ibid., 230.

4. Stanley Hauerwas has repeatedly highlighted how modern conceptions of freedom combined with rationalistic accounts of agency have threatened to make marriage and baptism unintelligible. We think that we have only made a free decision when we knew what we were doing, but one can never exhaustively know what they are doing when they enter into the covenant of marriage or onto the path of discipleship. The church, therefore, has the responsibility of holding the married couple to the promises they made when they didn't know what they were doing. Hauerwas, *Hauerwas Reader*, 514; and Hauerwas, *War and the American Difference*, 17.

wonderful, but weird little dog, Scruff, attacks your feet for the hundredth time as you are walking out the door? Or Beth, what are you going to do when you get up one morning and, as you're starting to make some coffee, you look out your kitchen window straight into the eyes of a deer hanging in the backyard?[5] What are the two of you going to do when the intoxication of romantic attraction wears off? What is going to sustain your marriage when the wine runs out?

That final question brings us to the Scripture passage we heard a few moments ago. Jesus and his disciples had been invited to a wedding, but in the midst of the celebration the bride and groom are confronted by the embarrassing predicament of having run out of wine. Now we don't come to this passage with the hope of finding tips for preserving marital bliss or uncovering some type of formula for building a successful marriage. Those things are simply not there to be found. For example, I'm not sure that it would be particularly helpful for me to suggest to you that when hosting a pancake dinner, you should always serve the best maple syrup first, and wait until the guests have entered into some type of sucrose-induced stupor before bringing out the lesser quality syrup.[6] It would be even less advisable for you, Drew, to respond to Beth when she approaches you some Saturday afternoon with the observation, "The grass sure is getting long!" by saying to her, "Woman, why do you involve me? . . . My hour has not yet come" (John 3:4).

So we turn our attention to this passage from the Gospel of John, not in order to discover tips and pointers for newlyweds, but rather to catch a glimpse into the true nature of things—to see our lives and our world as they truly are, caught up in the love that is shared between the Father and the Son in the Holy Spirit from all eternity. It shouldn't surprise us that Jesus would choose a wedding for the first of his miraculous signs. After all, the Scriptures make it quite clear that God loves a party and the Bible is full of weddings. In fact, the Scriptures begin with a garden wedding when the first man and the first woman are given to one another in marriage. Unfortunately, that marriage quickly went sour when the first couple forfeited their communion with God and one another by seeking to become like God. Their failure was not so much their desire to be like God; after all, in Christ we are called to be imitators of God—freely giving of ourselves to God and neighbour in love. Rather, the error of that first couple lay in the mistaken

5. The marriage between my sister and brother-in-law was, in some respects, a classic case of city girl marries country boy.

6. The groom's family had been in the maple syrup industry for close to two hundred years and operated a successful Sugar House at which they sold various maple syrup products and hosted large pancake dinners each spring.

conception that the way to become like God is to become self-sufficient. "Masculine domination and feminine deception" were the results of that ill-fated power play and marriage has been a battleground ever since.[7]

In light of this rather inauspicious beginning for the institution of marriage, it is perhaps somewhat surprising that the Scriptures also end with a wedding. In the book of Revelation, God gathers up his beloved children from the four corners of the earth to share in the great marriage feast of the Lamb (19:9). It's quite a contrast between the strife and dissension of that first marriage and the peace and harmony of the wedding to come. The gulf between the two appears to be unbridgeable, but between the first wedding that went bad and the final wedding that will be made good, Jesus ushers in his kingdom. At Cana he performs the first of his miraculous signs, changing the water into wine. The fact that the author goes so far as to tell us that this takes place on the third day—the day of the resurrection—indicates that this is more than just a good party trick. In fact, the great Hebrew prophets of old had long associated the coming day of the LORD with the abundant provision of the finest of wines (Hos 2:22; Joel 3:18; Amos 9:13–14). The changing of the water into wine points to the in-breaking of the kingdom of God into the midst of this world and reveals the true identity of Jesus as the one who rightly proclaims, "See, I am making all things new!" (Rev 21:5, NRSV)—even marriage!

However, the God who created us without us, will not save us without us.[8] Notice that Jesus involves the servants at the party, instructing them to go and fill the jars with water and, then, once they are full, to draw some of the water and take it to the chief steward. Now the text tells us that each jar held something in the neighborhood of one hundred liters and there were six jars, so that's approximately six hundred liters worth of water in total. I'm not sure how exactly the servants would have gone about filling up the water jugs, but rest assured, filling jars with six hundred liters worth of water in the days before there were backyard hoses would have been no small task. It likely would have been a particularly time-consuming, labour intensive, perhaps even monotonous task that involved numerous trips to the village well or cistern.

The work to which you are called in marriage is, in many ways, not that different from the work of drawing water and filling water jugs. It occurs amid the mundane, seemingly ordinary events of daily life shared between two people who have entered into covenant with one another as husband and wife. This means that a large part of marriage is simply about

7. Wood, *Preaching and Professing*, 224.
8. Augustine, *Sermo* 169.11.13, quoted in *Catechism of the Catholic Church* 8.1847.

showing up, about being present to one another, and taking the time to listen to each other. It involves taking to heart the apostle Paul's instructions to "Bear with each other and forgive one another if any of you has a grievance against someone" (Col 3:13). I must admit that none of this is particularly glamorous and it generally flies in the face of popular conceptions that understand marriage to be the culmination of a couple's love for one another—something like the cherry on top of the sundae or the star on the Christmas tree. Perhaps that's why so many marriages today end in disillusionment and despair. Marriage is not an extra-storey built upon "the house that love built." [9] Rather, marriage is a gift from the Lord, which provides a context in which those called to marriage are given the opportunity to learn what it means to truly love another person. Marriage is the foundation that makes love possible between husband and wife.[10] It is the sanctity and permanence of marriage that creates the freedom for spouses to be truly vulnerable with one another and enables us to love one another even when we are unlovable, which as it turns out, is quite often.

To love the unlovable is to enter into the realm of the divine. It is striking that the Gospel of John records only two conversations between Jesus and his mother. The first exchange takes place at the wedding at Cana where the water was changed into wine, the second at the cross where the wine of the divine love was poured out for the life of the world. There, at the cross, we see that forgiveness is the form God's faithfulness takes when it meets our sin. For this reason, the apostle Paul can speak of marriage as a reflection of God's faithfulness to his people. When husbands and wives remain committed to journeying together in love, bearing one another's burdens and forgiving one another, their marriage, in some mysterious way, mirrors the boundless love of Christ for his church (Eph 5:32). The water of daily faithfulness with its seemingly small acts of kindness, patience, and mercy, is taken up in the love of God and transformed into the new wine of the kingdom.

So in closing, I'd like to present you with a gift that is representative of my prayer for you—a prayer that I'm sure many others who have gathered here today will join with me in praying in the days ahead. It is our prayer that your marriage may be immersed in the divine wine of the kingdom,

9. "The house that love built" is an allusion to the dark and brooding title track of an album recorded by my brother's band. My brother was one of the groomsmen in the wedding party. The Shaky Gallows House Band, *The House That Love Built*, 2004.

10. In a sermon written from prison for the marriage of his niece Renate Schleicher to his best friend Eberhard Bethge, Dietrich Bonhoeffer wrote, "It is not your love that upholds marriage, but from now on it is marriage that upholds your love" (*Letters and Papers* (2009), 84).

which is the love that is shared for all eternity between the Father, the Son, and the Holy Spirit. We pray that whenever you open this bottle, whether it be a year from now, or five, ten or twenty years from now, that you will be able to give thanks to God for your marriage saying, "Everyone brings forth the choice wine first . . . but you have saved the best till now" (John 2:10)!

20

"We Have to Give Thanks to God"

Saturday, September 13, 2014

Good Shepherd Community Church

Scarborough, Ontario

Acts 9:36–43; Psalm 27:1–5

The Funeral of Jessie Elaine Geddes

It is a poignant scene. A very special woman has died. A woman dearly loved by her community. A woman of character recognized for her faithfulness, wisdom, and generosity. The body is lovingly prepared and set in a special place. The word is sent out and the mourners begin to assemble. Prominent among the mourners are many widows; the women who have been left alone and counted down-and-out in the eyes of the world, but who, through the care of this very special woman, have discovered that they are of boundless worth in the eyes of God. Some of them are even wearing the dresses that she has made, and perhaps, even specially embroidered for them.

I am, of course, speaking of the scene from the book of Acts that we heard a moment ago, but I could just as easily be speaking of the life of Jessie Elaine Geddes and our gathering here today in her memory. It really shouldn't surprise us that the stories of these two women of faith would bleed into one another: Tabitha (or Dorcas) whose name means "Gazelle" and Jessie whose name means "gift of the Lord." For the stories of the lives of both Tabitha and Jessie are both part of a much larger story, the story of a kingdom where things are not quite what they seem; a story of a world turned upside down and inside out by the unrelenting love of God in Christ Jesus. This story gives birth to a new community. A community in which, as one commentator has observed, "no one stays in his or her place. Common fishermen are preaching to the temple authorities, paralyzed old men are up and walking about changing lives, and a woman called Gazelle heads a welfare program among the poor in Joppa."[1] It takes a community like this to recognize that although today we are not surrounded by all the pomp and circumstance that accompanies a funeral for a head of state, the humble life of the disciple we remember today may, in God's economy, be just as, if not even more, significant than that of any world leader. For our Jessie is a daughter of the King.

I first met Jessie in 2004. I was a young pastoral intern here at Good Shepherd, when Paul Johansen, the senior pastor at the time, went on Sabbatical. In order to ensure that the ministry of pastoral care did not fall through the cracks in his absence, Paul partnered me with Jessie and assigned us the task of visiting the elderly and the shut-ins. It was a brilliant move on Paul's part. In this simple plan, he both arranged for my continuing pastoral education in the presence of a master and ensured that I would be held accountable for making the needed visits. I can still hear Jessie saying to me, "We have to get out and visit the old people." Even though she was eighty-four at the time, she clearly did not consider herself to be one of "the old people." I profited greatly from my summer of "Driving Miss Jessie" from one pastoral visit to another. I can still recall the look on some people's faces as the two of us—the little, old Guyanese woman and the striking, young pastor (okay, maybe I wasn't striking, but I was young)—walked through the doors and down the halls of retirement homes and care facilities. It wasn't the sort of team that people were used to seeing, but in God's upside-down kingdom, nothing could be more natural.

It wasn't long after that summer that Jessie had knee surgery and all of sudden I found myself visiting my former partner in the ministry of visitation. I was Jessie's pastor for six years. Over that period I developed a taste for mauby, sorrel and even ginger beer, but throughout the course of my many visits, I was never entirely clear as to who was really ministering to whom. I officially stopped being Jessie's pastor when I resigned from Good Shepherd in 2010, but long before that point she had already adopted me as a grandson. When I first came to Toronto from London, Ontario, I would never have imagined that I would inherit a Guyanese grandmother. Looking at the career and social trajectories of my friends from my university days, it still seems incredibly unlikely that such a thing would have happened. But it wasn't beyond the imagination of God.

It was this same imaginative God who took the woman named Gazelle and elevated her to a position of importance in his kingdom, caring for

---

1. Willimon, *Acts*, 84.

the widows of Joppa. The most important thing about Tabitha is revealed in the very first verse of our reading, where she is identified as a disciple. Everything else which follows—her reputation for "always doing good and helping the poor" (Acts 9:36) and her ministry caring for the most vulnerable in Joppa—all of these things flow from the fundamental reality that Tabitha was a disciple. In fact, this is the only time that the feminine form of the Greek word for "disciple" is used in the entire New Testament.[2] This clearly was a very special woman, a woman dearly and deeply loved by all whose lives were drawn into the sphere of her influence. This conclusion is supported in several subtle ways within the biblical text. We are told that Tabitha's body was washed and placed in an upper room. Now this was not a particularly unusual practice in the ancient world, but this is the only time the practice of washing the body is mentioned in the Bible. In this context, this expression of care and reverence for the deceased begins to make clear just how much Tabitha was loved within the community.[3] This reality is reinforced a few verses later when we encounter the scene of the weeping widows surrounding Peter and "showing him the robes and other clothing that Dorcas had made while she was still with them" (Acts 9:39). It's not entirely clear whether we are to imagine the widows holding up various pieces of clothing for display or whether they are pointing to the clothes that they are currently wearing.[4] In either case, the displaying of the garments seems to communicate two realities at the same time. On the one hand, it is eloquent testimony to the legacy of this woman of faith. On the other, it communicates the profound existential question which now confronts these widows, namely, "Who is going to care for us now? How can we go on without her?"

Today, we too, are confronted by these questions. The shadows seem a little longer, the autumn breeze a little cooler, the silence a little emptier, now that Jessie is gone. We too are left asking ourselves how we are to go on without our beloved mother, grandmother, and great-grandmother, our trusted friend and counsellor, our cherished sister in Christ? If Jessie were here, she would counsel us, perhaps even by referring to the closing verse of the twenty-seventh Psalm which was so dear to her heart, saying, "Wait for the LORD; be strong and take heart and wait for the LORD" (v. 14). Athanasius, a little bishop from Africa, who was derogatorily referred to as the "black dwarf" by his opponents, was one of the staunchest defenders of the Gospel in the fourth century. Five times Athanasius was exiled from his

2. Gaventa, *Acts of the Apostles*, 159.

3. Ibid., 160.

4. Witherington, *Acts*, 332.

home in Alexandria on account of his dogged determination to cling to the apostolic confession of the deity of Christ. Athanasius offered the following words of counsel, "If you experience the harsh and vehement attacks of the enemy, and they crowd against you, despising you as one who is not anointed, and on this account fight against you, do not succumb to these attacks but sing Psalm 27."[5] Looking back on Jessie's life, it makes sense to me that the twenty-seventh Psalm resonated with her in a special way. It takes a certain type of fortitude to set out in middle age to start a new life in a strange and distant country. It takes a certain type of confidence to set out by oneself leaving one's country, one's people, and one's father's household for a new land (Gen 12:1), trusting that God would provide for every need. It takes a certain type of humble strength to devote oneself to chasing children around as a caregiver at a time in life when many are retiring. It takes the type of person who has internalized the words of Psalm 27: "The Lord is my light and salvation—whom shall I fear? The Lord is the stronghold of my life—of whom shall I be afraid?" (v. 1). Jessie knew that those who fear God have nothing else to fear. Instead, all of life can be received with thanksgiving. "We have to thank God," was a recurring refrain that I heard Jessie utter many times in many contexts. It was even on Jessie's lips the last time I saw her. Here was a woman who had been hospitalized for several months, her leg had been amputated, and she was undoubtedly aware that she would never return to her apartment again. Yet throughout our conversation she kept repeating, "I have to give thanks to God."

Like Tabitha, Jessie made clothing. She went to school in Guyana to be a dress-maker and she loved to embroider, but the true legacy that Jessie has left behind is not to be found in any wardrobe or closet. Rather, you are Jessie's legacy. Jessie's legacy is the daughters she has taught to pray and love the Lord and give their lives in service. Here at Good Shepherd we have seen this firsthand over the past number of years as we've watched Maureen so devotedly care for her mom. Jessie's legacy is the grandchildren whom she has loved and sometimes even raised as her own. Jessie's legacy is the women in need and in crisis whom she took under her wing and guided with her counsel. Jessie's legacy is the children she cared for, now long grown-up, in whom she so richly invested. Jessie's legacy is the many people she has adopted as brothers and sisters, children and grandchildren in Christ. Look around and you'll see Jessie's legacy.

So today we give thanks to God for the life of Jessie Elaine Geddes. However, if we were to stop here we would be missing out on the most

5. Athanasius, "On the Interpretation of the Psalms," in Kannengiesser, *Early Christian Spirituality*, 67, quoted in Blaising and Hardin, *Psalms 1–50*, 204.

important part of the story. Yet this is what often happens in funerals today. In recent years, memorial services and celebrations of life have increasingly come to replace the traditional Christian service of death and resurrection. We do remember and give thanks for Jessie's life, but she herself would be the first to say, "That's not the end of the story." Our passage today does *not* end with the widows gathered together showing off the clothes Tabitha has made and sharing their memories. It continues with the apostle Peter turning toward Tabitha in the power of the Holy Spirit and in the name of Jesus Christ pronouncing the words, "*Tabitha, kumi!* Tabitha, arise!" These words echo the words Christ himself pronounced at the bedside of the daughter of the ruler of the synagogue, "*Talitha, kumi!* Little child, arise!" (Mark 5:41; my translation).[6] The raisings of both Tabitha and the synagogue ruler's daughter are anticipations of the resurrection of Christ himself—the Holy One who has tasted death and triumphed over the grave so that we might truly live. Because of his victory, "neither death nor life, neither angels nor demons, neither the present nor the future, nor any powers, neither height nor depth, nor anything else in all creation, will be able to separate us from the love of God that is in Christ Jesus our Lord" (Rom 8:38–39).

Jessie's story is only just beginning because her story has been taken up in the story of the Lord of Life. Our attempts to conceptualize the reality of the new heavens and the new earth are limited by the frailties of human language and the poverty of our imaginations. Often artists and novelists are far more successful than theologians in communicating something of the mysterious majesty of God's future. C.S. Lewis, at the conclusion of *The Chronicles of Narnia*, puts it like this: "But for them it was only the beginning of the real story. All their life in this world and all their adventures in Narnia had only been the cover and the title page: now at last they were beginning Chapter One of the Great Story which no one on earth has read: which goes on forever: in which every chapter is better than the one before."[7] The words of our Scripture passage this afternoon provide us with resources for envisioning the opening lines of this new chapter of Jessie's story. This chapter begins with the Lord of Life reaching down into death, and gently taking his faithful disciple by the hand, and, with the same voice that spoke the stars into being, uttering the words, "Miss Jess, my child, arise!" And for that, Jessie herself will tell us, "We have to give thanks to God."

---

6. Witherington, *Acts*, 332–33.

7. C.S. Lewis, *The Last Battle*, book 7, *The Chronicles of Narnia* (New York: Harper-Trophy, 1994), 228.

21

Mary and Martha, Lucia and Lazarus

Monday, October 6, 2014

Good Shepherd Community Church

Scarborough, Ontario

John 11:1–3, 17–44

The Funeral of Lucia Metella Robinson

Preaching at a funeral can be a difficult assignment. Sometimes the preacher must valiantly struggle to find something to say and to make some type of connection with the life of the deceased. The juxtaposition of the long and full life of Lucia Metella Robinson with the reading we have just heard from the Gospel of John ensures that I will have no such difficulties. In fact, my challenge is precisely the opposite; for with the life of Lucia and the story of the raising of Lazarus I have more material than I could ever hope to incorporate into a single sermon!

The story we've just heard from the Gospel of John is one of the most dramatic moments in all of Scripture. The raising of Lazarus is Jesus' seventh and climactic sign. It both reveals his true identity as the Lord of Life and sets in motion the events which will lead to his crucifixion and death. Surprisingly, we know very little about the man Jesus called forth from the tomb. Here's what we do know. We know that Lazarus was from the town of Bethany, which means "house of the poor."[1] We also know that he lived with his two sisters, Mary and Martha, perhaps suggesting that Lazarus had some kind of disability and relied upon the care of his sisters.[2] These details suggest that in the eyes of the world, Lazarus was a man of little to no sig-

---

1. Wright, *John for Everyone*, 2:4.
2. Vanier, *Drawn into the Mystery*, 195–96.

nificance; one of "the sick, the sad, and the sorry."[3] However, we are told one additional detail that makes all the difference in the world—Lazarus was loved by Jesus. So as Lazarus lay dying, his sisters sent word to Jesus, "Lord, the one you love is sick" (John 11:3). The fourth century Church Father St. Augustine pondered the nature of the message sent by the sisters. Augustine observed, "They did not say, 'Come,' for the intimation was all that was needed for one who loved. They did not venture to say, 'Come and heal him,' nor did they venture to say, 'Command there, and it shall be done.' . . . These women said nothing like this, but only, 'Lord, behold, he whom you love is ill'—as if to say: It is enough that you know. For you are not one that loves and then abandons."[4]

The sisters knew Jesus well. They knew that he is not one that loves and then abandons. We actually know more about the two sisters, Martha and Mary, than we do about Lazarus. The Gospel of Luke introduces us to the two sisters (10:38–42). On that occasion they had welcomed Jesus to their house for a festive meal. While Martha was toiling away in the kitchen, elbow-deep in stuffing the Thanksgiving turkey, Mary had taken a seat at Jesus' feet and was intently listening to all that he had to say. Sitting at Jesus' feet was highly significant. In first century Judaism, to sit at the feet of a master meant that you were one of his disciples. Women were not permitted to sit at the feet of a rabbi.[5] So this was a big deal. But big sister Martha, who had been left to fend for herself in the kitchen, was not particularly impressed. Exasperated she took the matter to Jesus and urged him to instruct Mary to stop neglecting her responsibilities and to get down to work. But Jesus surprised her with his response, saying, "Martha, Martha, . . . you are worried and upset about many things, but few things are needed—or indeed only one. Mary has chosen what is better, and it will not be taken away from her" (Luke 10:41–42).

Lucia knew this story well. If you were Lucia's pastor—as I once was—you knew that you could drop in at any time. However, she generally preferred some warning so that she could prepare a large meal. For Lucia, feeding her pastors was the equivalent to entertaining angels. On one occasion, another pastor and I had joined Lucia for lunch. After gorging ourselves on various island delicacies and other offerings, we had pushed back our chairs and were contentedly relaxing around the table. However, Lucia had already left her spot and was now frantically taking dishes back

3. "The sick, the sad, and the sorry" was a refrain that Lucia would commonly include within her intercessory prayers.

4. Augustine, *Tractates on the Gospel of John*, 49.5, quoted in Elowsky, *John 11–21*, 3.

5. Jeffrey, *Luke*, 152.

and forth from the dining room table to the kitchen. One of us called out to Lucia, "Martha, Martha, come and sit down." Without missing a beat, Lucia replied, "I've always liked Martha!" before continuing to shuttle the dishes back to the kitchen.

It makes sense to me that Lucia would like Martha. Like Martha, Lucia was a strong woman. A woman who did not bear responsibility lightly. A woman who was quick to take action when she recognized a need. A woman to be reckoned with. I'm sure her children and grandchildren could corroborate these observations with many stories and recollections. But this Martha-like energy and commitment was also on display in her deep involvement with churches in Jamaica, New York, and Toronto. Those of us here at Good Shepherd would never have gotten the chance to meet Lucia if she had not, in Martha-like fashion, picked up and moved from New York to Toronto when she perceived that her family here was in need.

In our passage from the Gospel of John, Martha continues to display some of the same traits that were on display in the earlier story from Luke. Martha takes the initiative of coming out to meet Jesus, while Mary remained at home. She remains the industrious go-getter. Later, she makes the very practical observation that after four days the tomb will stink (John 11:39). This Martha-like combination of level-headedness and industriousness can take one a long way in life. Lucia has sought to instill a certain work-ethic and sense of responsibility among those within her sphere of influence, particularly her children and grandchildren. Perhaps one of her proudest nights was the evening many of us gathered at the Milliken Community Center to celebrate her ninetieth birthday. Lucia was positively beaming, not only because she was the center of attention, but also because she was surrounded by a very fine looking collection of children and grandchildren who had gone on to distinguish themselves personally and professionally in so many different ways. While she delighted in your hard-work and your triumphs, she would also be the first to tell you in the midst of your success that you must not lose sight of what it's all about. Or as she put in her own words that night, "Grow in grace and God will keep you strong."

It's important for us to recognize that although Lucia may have had the hands of Martha, she also had the heart of Mary. Lucia's Martha-like resolve and energy sprang forth from her Mary-like devotion. In the life of faith, activism and contemplation are inseparable sisters. Lucia was not only a strong woman of action; she was a devoted woman of prayer. In fact, we could say Lucia was a woman of action, because she was a woman of prayer. This was reflected in her deep love for the Psalms, several of which we've heard today. The Psalms have been called the "Prayerbook of the Bible."[6] But to our supposedly enlightened, but actually spiritually superficial age, the Psalms can be both startling and off-putting on account of their sheer earthiness. In addition, the utter transparency and vulnerability of the Psalmists on display in the Psalter can leave us shifting uncomfortably in our pews. But the Psalms have been the great school of prayer for God's people for thousands of years. In learning to pray the Psalms we learn to pray with Jesus who himself prayed and lived the Psalter. Lucia's own faith was formed through her immersion in the school of prayer which is the Psalms. As a result she could speak quite openly and freely about her own missteps and mistakes. She could also speak quite matter-of-factly about her various ailments, sometimes leaving prim and proper listeners squirming on account of the detailed nature of her accounts. Prayer was an essential discipline for Lucia. Somewhere along the line that discipline became a habit and Lucia became not only one who prayed, but someone who was prayerful. Many of you have probably heard the stories emerging from the Wexford Retirement Home over the past year of Lucia praying for all of her fellow residents and all of the people who worked on her floor. The first time I went to Lucia's house, I remember a fellow pastor saying to me, "Make sure you get Lucia to pray for you. You haven't really been prayed for until Lucia has prayed for you."

This isn't the stole I normally wear for funerals. This is the stole I was presented with on the night I was ordained to the ministry of Word and Sacrament. On that night, as she did on many other occasions, Lucia prayed for me. It was a special privilege to be prayed for by Lucia. At times she may have even had the gift of praying in tongues. Of course, I can't be certain, because once Lucia got on a roll and her Jamaican accent kicked into overdrive, it was all I could do to keep up with what she was saying. This is no great secret. Lucia herself knew that I didn't always understand everything she was saying, but she loved me anyway.

Jesus loved Martha and Mary and their brother Lazarus. The full extent of his love for them is increasingly on display as our passage from the Gospel of John continues with the arrival of Mary upon the scene. The narrator tells us that, "When Jesus saw her weeping, and the Jews who had come along with her also weeping, he was deeply moved in spirit and troubled. 'Where have you laid him?' he asked. 'Come and see, Lord,' they replied. Jesus wept" (John 11:33–35). Although verbally austere, these few words open up a breathtaking vista for considering the profound mystery of our existence. The terse phrase, "Jesus wept," presents us with a window into the

---

6. Bonhoeffer, *Prayerbook*.

heart of the human condition. At the tomb of his dear friend, in the face of joy marred by grief and despair, in the presence of community fractured by separation, confronted by life interrupted by death, Jesus wept. "Why did Christ weep?" Augustine asks, "Why did Christ weep, except to teach us to weep."[7] In the days ahead, as Lucia's absence looms large over everything, know that your tears do not fall to the ground alone, but are mingled with the tears of our weeping Lord.[8]

The phrase "Jesus wept" also allows us to peer into the bottomless depths of God's love for his beloved. Jesus wept knowing that his skirmish with death at the tomb of Lazarus would set in motion the events that would lead to his final showdown with death upon a cruel Roman cross (John 11:45–57). In calling Lazarus, the one he loves, from the tomb, Jesus seals his own fate. The voice of the eternal Word pierced the silence of the tomb, calling Lazarus forth into life, but because of this, the eternal Word himself would lay silenced, sealed within the cold, dark tomb.[9] The short verse, "Jesus wept," allows us to peer into the mystery of our salvation in the person of Jesus Christ. "The love which moves the sun and the other stars" has condescended to us in our weakness and borne the burden of our frail and sin-marred existence.[10] God has come to our side of the equation, so that in him our lives might balance with the sum of his undying love. He who is the resurrection and the life, has tasted death, so that we might live. As the great hymn-writer Charles Wesley, put it,

> 'Tis mystery all! Th'Immortal dies!
> Who can explore His strange Design?
> In vain the first-born seraph tries
> To sound the depths of love divine.[11]

---

7. Augustine, *Tractates on the Gospel of John*, 49.19, quoted in Elowsky, *John 11–21*, 21.

8. In his profound personal reflections following the death of his wife, Joy David-man, C.S. Lewis penned the poignant sentence, "Her absence is like the sky, spread over everything" (*Grief Observed*, 11).

9. Many commentators have reflected upon the "transparent irony" (Carson) and "dramatic paradox" (Brown) of how Jesus' raising of a dead man to life in the Gospel of John leads directly to his own death. Carson, *John*, 405; Brown, *John (XIII-XXI)*, 429.

10. "The love which moves the sun and the [other] stars" is a line found within the Italian poet Dante Alighieri's (1265–1321) famous work, *The Divine Comedy* (Canto XXXIII). I was first introduced to the line through the writings of Stanley Hauerwas, where it frequently appears.

11. Charles Wesley, "And Can It Be, That I Should Gain?" (1738).

We are swimming in oceans of love, immersed in the mystery of the God who is love. We technologically adept children of the scientific age don't do well with mystery. We much prefer puzzles. Puzzles are to be solved. Mysteries must be inhabited. Lucia understood this. She once told me a story from her days in New York. As she was walking along the street by herself, she heard a voice say to her, "Lucia, hold on to your purse." At the very moment that she tucked her purse firmly under her arm, a man ran up behind her snatching at the purse as he raced by. I must admit, I wasn't sure what to make of this story the first time I heard it. The prevention of the theft of Lucia's purse seemed somewhat trivial in light of all of the pressing needs in the world. It seemed hard to imagine that Lucia's purse would even rank on a list of God's most urgent action items when there is war in the Middle East, outbreaks in Africa, and homelessness in Toronto. Yet this is the type of God we've got: a God who invites us to pray, "give us today our daily bread" (Matt 6:11); a God who has initiated a mustard-seed revolution which involved bringing back to life an unknown, poor, disabled man. Perhaps just as shocking as the raising of Lazarus are the words Jesus addressed to Martha, "I am the resurrection and the life" (John 11:25). The resurrection and the life is a person! The ultimate reality which all of us must finally reckon with is personal. How could it be otherwise if God truly is love?

Our passage this morning assures us that there is no end to love. The calling of Lazarus from the tomb is surely meant to serve as an anticipation of the fate of all who die in Christ. The day of the Lord does not end with mourning, but with the one who is the resurrection and the life calling each of his sheep by name and leading them into life eternal. Perhaps then we are not only to see glimpses of Lucia in the figures of Mary and Martha, but maybe we are ultimately to see Lucia in the figure of Lazarus. The name Lazarus is a short form of the name Eleazar which means "God helps" or "God has helped."[12] In death, Lucia remains dependent upon the grace of the "God who helps." Just as in life she joined the psalmist in placing her trust in the Lord for deliverance from her enemies, in death she continues to rely upon the Lord's deliverance from the last and greatest enemy. Like Mary and Martha, in our grief we call out to Jesus, saying, "Lord, the one you love is sick. Lord, the one you love has died." It is enough. As Lucia herself knew well, her Lord is not one who loves and then abandons.

12. R.W. Paschal, Jr., "Lazarus" in Green et al., *Dictionary of Jesus and the Gospels*, 461.

22

The Monuments Men

White Oak Cemetery
Westminster Township, Ontario
Sunday, June 22, 2014
Psalm 25; Revelation 7:9–17
51st Annual Memorial Service

A t a crucial moment in the recent film, *The Monuments Men*, Lt. Frank Strokes, played by George Clooney, addresses his rag-tag Army platoon composed of museum directors, curators, architects, and art historians, saying, "You can wipe out an entire generation, you can burn their homes to the ground, and somehow they'll still find their way back. But if you destroy their history, you destroy their achievements and it's as if they never existed. That's what Hitler wants and that's exactly what we are fighting for."[1] *The Monuments Men* tells the forgotten story of the Monuments, Fine Arts and Archives program: a group of men and women who left their careers in art, academia and museums during the latter part of the Second World War in order to protect, preserve and restore the great art treasures of Western Civilization from pillaging and destruction at the hands of the Nazis. It sounds like a rather strange assignment, sending middle-aged art connoisseurs on a treasure hunt while the young men of a generation were dying in the trenches, the great cities of Europe were being reduced to rubble, and smoke was continuing to rise from the furnaces of Dachau and Auschwitz. Yet these Monuments Men recognized that Western civilization found itself in the precarious position of potentially winning the war, but losing its soul. The Monuments Men knew that the great paintings and sculptures of

---

1. *The Monuments Men*, directed by George Clooney (Columbia Pictures, 2014).

Europe were the embodied memory of a civilization. If these cultural artifacts were to be irretrievably lost, part of the memory, and hence, identity,
of a people would be lost with them.

This afternoon I would like to suggest that you also are engaged in a
similar type of work. You are contemporary "Monuments Men and Women"
engaged in an equally strange, yet vitally necessary task. With the rise of the
Internet Age, we find ourselves living in the perpetual present. Yesterday's
viral video is old news. Like a supernova, today's newsmakers flame out in
a glorious burst of light and then are relegated to the darkness of oblivion
along with the dancing baby, the Friday song, Tebowing, and the Harlem
Shake. Memory has been replaced by a sheer glut of information, which
is never more than a click away, but there is no sense as to how this raging
torrent of data comes together into any type of coherent whole. We are also
witnesses to the effacing of place. In cyber-space one can simultaneously be
everywhere and yet nowhere at all. This phenomenon is not limited to the
Internet, for when one is seated comfortably in one's booth at McDonald's, it
is nearly impossible to tell if one is in London, Beijing, or Berlin. Crusading
global capitalism seeks to convince us that we are all autonomous units of
consumer desire, free to construct our own identities on the basis of our
own arbitrary consumer preferences. Yet in the face of these obtrusive realities, here you are gathering in an obsolete church building to remember
that you are not story-less people. By gathering today, you, in some way,
recognize that you are rooted in the soil and in the history of your ancestors.
I hope you realize what a wonderfully peculiar thing it is that you are doing!

In some ways, our gathering here today is reminiscent of a Texas tradition known as Graveyard Day, which is depicted with endearing insight by
William Humphrey in his novel, *The Ordways*.[2] The book traces the history of the Ordway family over several generations as it moves to Texas and
struggles to thrive and flourish in the rugged land on the edge of the prairies.
Graveyard Day is the name given to the annual event when the community
gathers at the cemetery to clean and re-mound the graves of their ancestors.
On Graveyard Day, "Texans learned who they were by learning who their
ancestors were."[3] The following passage from the novel explains:

> With each [plot] was associated some story, which, as his or
> her mound was raked, the weeds cleared away and the fallen
> stone set upright, was once again retold. Yearly repetition did
> not dull these tales; on the contrary, we looked forward to

2. I am indebted to the account of the novel provided by Stanley Hauerwas in *Christian Existence Today*, 25–45.

3. Hauerwas, *Christian Existence Today*, 32.

them as, seated in the concert hall with program in hand, one anticipates the opening notes of a favorite piece of music, and we would have been disappointed if, for instance, the tending of Great-uncle Hugh's grave had not elicited from my grandfather the story, known to us all by heart, of Uncle Hugh and the lady's corncobs. . . . on a day in March 1858, [Hugh] had once been among the guests at a supper party, back in Tennessee. The menu included roasting ears, and to the problem of what to do with the unsightly cobs, the hostess had worked out this delicate solution: the white-gloved Negro butler . . . would go around the table with a big silver platter . . . and collect them from the guests between servings. From right to left he went, and as our Uncle Hugh happened to be seated on his hostess's left, by the time it got to him the platter was piled high. As he had done with the dishes of food all evening, the butler stood with his platter at Uncle Hugh's elbow. Noticing him at last, Uncle Hugh inspected his soggy offering, and in his broadest back-country accent said, "No, thank you just the same, don't believe I'll have any."[4]

The story of Uncle Hugh could be of a piece with some of the stories emerging from the history of White Oak Church. For example, in some of the archival material that was passed on to me I read of the dedication service for the laying of the foundation stone of the Christian Education Hall in 1956. Now, there's nothing particularly unusual about such a dedication service in and of itself. To this day religious and even secular organizations continue to have ground-breaking and dedication ceremonies. The surprise comes a moment later when the archivist matter-of-factly writes, "Rev. Gordon Hume, pastor, officiated from his car due to a case of the mumps."[5] Now that would have been a dedication service to remember!

Although I have been granted access to some of the historical documents pertaining to the life of the White Oak congregation, I must admit that I am an outsider who has come late to the party. The stories of the Beggs, the Boyces, the Crinklaws, the Daubeneys, the Jacksons, the Joneses, the Mannings, the Mennills, the Shores and all of the other families represented just outside these doors must live on through you. In fact, it is these stories that help to provide some type of anchor in a world where we are threatened to be cast adrift by the story that we have no story. However, the stories of our ancestors are not able to do all of the heavy lifting that we

4. Humphrey, *The Ordways*, 19–21, quoted in Hauerwas, *Christian Existence Today*, 33.

5. The document I received from the church archives is simply entitled "White Oak United Church." It appears to be from 1967.

need them to do, if they are going to help us shape our future in a healthy way. This is so because every family has secrets and every person is shaped by stories that cannot be told—stories of hurt and betrayal and wrongs that cannot be made right. In their very unspokenness, these stories continue to hold us captive, fating our future in real and tangible ways. Reflecting upon the novel *The Ordways*, the theologian Stanley Hauerwas, himself a Texan, comments upon this dilemma, observing that

> the story of Texas is a story of overcoming hardship, but such a story requires us to forget parts of our past that must become part of us if we are to be whole. We Texans have little ability to know how to admit our failures, and cruelty, and our tragedies. We thus make a virtue out of some of our worst sins—like the sign that hung over Greenville for years: "Welcome to Greenville: The Blackest Land, the Whitest People."[6]

Our stories, and the stories of our ancestors, must be set within a larger story that gives us the resources to truthfully face our past, if we are to find a way forward while claiming our histories as our own. The fact that you have gathered here today in a historic church building for a service of worship suggests that you understand something of this reality. Hauerwas suggests that if our stories have been taken up in the larger story of "a God who is capable of forgiveness—indeed, whose very nature is forgiveness . . . [then] we have no reason to seek to hide from others and ourselves in the sinfulness of our fathers and our own history."[7] A similar conviction seems to have been operating among the Session of White Oak United Church when they submitted their annual report in 1967. Listen to what they wrote: "We acknowledge the goodness of a kind Providence in supporting us and our work during the past year. We go forward into the new year with the assurance that nothing can separate us from His love. As we now give an account of our stewardship as a Session, we implore his forgiveness for our failures and sins, and pray that He might bring some blessings from our faltering efforts."[8] There are profound echoes here of the words of the psalmist we read a few moments ago: "Remember, O LORD, your great mercy and love, for they are of old. Remember not the sins of my youth and my rebellious ways; according to your love remember me, for you are good, O LORD" (25:6–7). Only people who recognize that they have been grasped by God's mercy and taken up into a larger story where their memories have been transformingly embraced by God's memory are free to speak like the psalm-

6. Hauerwas, *Christian Existence Today*, 37.

7. Ibid., 41.

8. "White Oak United Church" (1967).

ist and the Session of White Oak United Church. It is the mercy of God which opens the future by liberating us from the crushing burden of having to author our own stories. It is the redemptive love of God that transforms our history so that we can receive it back again, not as a burden but as a legacy.

While the Nazis were busy pillaging the cultural treasures of Europe, the German pastor Dietrich Bonhoeffer sat in an austere seven-by-ten-foot cell, awaiting trial on account of his involvement in a plot to smuggle fourteen Jews out of Germany into Switzerland. As Bonhoeffer faced his first Christmas in prison, he was filled with longing for days gone by. His thoughts turned to festive meals shared with family, to evenings spent gathered around the piano with friends, and to the relatively short time he had spent with his new fiancée before being imprisoned. He sought solace in Scripture and in the hymns of the church, particularly those of the German hymn-writer Paul Gerhardt. He was particularly taken by a verse from one of Gerhardt's hymns where the risen Christ declares, "Calm your hearts, dear friends; / whatever plagues you, / whatever fails you, / I will restore it all."[9] In a letter to his close friend, Eberhard Bethge, Bonhoeffer reflects upon the meaning of this verse: "What does it mean, 'I will restore it all'? [It means that] nothing is lost; in Christ all things are taken up, preserved, albeit in transfigured form, transparent, clear, liberated from the torment of self-serving demands. Christ brings all this back, indeed, as God intended, without being distorted by sin."[10]

If we are to remember rightly, it must be situated within the context of the remembering of Christ, who allows nothing that is beautiful, true, or good to be lost. He purifies his people, their history and their memories, and restores all things. This is why it's so significant that you are gathered here today to remember in the context of worship. In worship, we not only remember the past in giving thanks for what God has done for us in Christ, in forgiving our sins, raising the dead, and making a way where there was no way, we also, somewhat counter-intuitively, remember God's future. This reality is dramatically depicted in the images of the Ghent altarpiece. During the Second World War, in an attempt to keep the altarpiece out of the hands of the Nazis, the canon of the cathedral in Ghent arranged for the work to be smuggled out of the city under the cover of darkness in a junk-truck. The plan ultimately failed as the altarpiece was eventually seized by the Nazis in France. It was only recovered at the end of the War when the Monuments

9. *Evangelisches Gesangbuch*, no. 36, "Fröhlich soll mein Herze springen," quoted in Bonhoeffer, *Letters and Papers* (2009), 229.

10. Bonhoeffer, *Letters and Papers* (2009), 229–30.

Men discovered it alongside ten thousand other cultural artifacts hidden deep within a salt mine in Austria. The Ghent altarpiece, also known as "The Adoration of the Mystic Lamb," goes back to the early fifteenth century and is regarded as the world's first oil-painting.[11] The main panel of the altarpiece dramatically depicts the scene from Revelation, which we heard a few moments ago. At the center of the painting, surrounded by angels, and, beyond them, a vast multitude of men and women from across the ages, there is a lamb standing upon an altar looking as if it had been slain. The banner on the front of the table, reads, "Behold the Lamb of God who takes away the sins of the world." This central panel would only have been visible on Sundays when the outer wings or doors of the altarpiece were opened when the community gathered for worship. From its position in front of the sanctuary, the altarpiece would have served for the worshipping congregation as a looking glass into the true nature of reality. As God's people engage in the work of worship, they not only remember the past and the future, but in the very act of remembering, they discover themselves to be participants in the worship of the saints who are gathered around the throne, having been bathed in the blood of the lamb who takes away the sins of the world. In worship, the Christian community remembers both the past sacrifice of Christ, which, in taking away the sins of the world, opens up their future, and the triumphant lamb whose coming will restore their past. Through this remembering they rediscover in the present, in the very midst of this dreary and anguished world, a creation "charged with the grandeur of God."[12]

In other words, it's all about remembering: remembering the God who remembers us, while remembering our sins no more. God's remembrance simply is salvation. Such a salvation calls for a new type of "Monuments Men and Women," who, through their remembering, become living monuments to the truth of the remembering God in the very midst of a world bent on forgetting. George Clooney may have done more than he realized when he placed the Ghent Altarpiece at the center of his film, but his instincts were good. Our past and our future, and therefore our present, are all bound up with the Lamb.

11. The altarpiece was recently restored and as part of that project the panels were photographed in high-definition and subjected to infrared and x-rays, with the result that the altarpiece can now be viewed online in exquisite detail. See "Closer to Van Eyck: Rediscovering the Ghent Altarpiece," http://closertovaneyck.kikirpa.be/#intro.

12. Hopkins, "God's Grandeur," in Harter, *Hearts on Fire*, 10.

Part IV

Preaching to Pastors

23

Bodybuilding

Tyndale Seminary In-Ministry Program Chapel

Toronto, Ontario

Thursday, November 22, 2012

Ephesians 4:1–16

The other day while I was out running a few errands I came across a store that was displaying a large table full of puzzles. For some reason or other, our culture has decided that puzzles make wonderful Christmas gifts. Now I don't have anything against puzzles, but I'm not sure I understand their connection with Christmas. Nonetheless, in inviting me to come and preach today on the fourth chapter of Ephesians, you have presented me with the gift of a puzzle. In preparing to be with you, I have found myself confronted with a seemingly disparate collection of fragments. Like a person sitting before a table covered in puzzle pieces, I have found myself asking, "How does it all fit together?" First, there is the challenge of coming cold into your cohort. Over the past several months you have been building relationships, growing in knowledge, and learning new skills. I will have the opportunity to join you in your journey next year, but right now I am the newcomer, the outsider.[1] How do I fit in? On top of that, I find myself jumping mid-stream into a sermon series on Ephesians that began before I was with you and will continue in the weeks after I'm gone. How does my sermon fit in with the messages that you have already heard and the ones that are still to come?

---

1. The In-Ministry program allows students who are serving in a full-time capacity as pastors and ministry leaders to complete an MDiv degree. During the first semester of the program, the professors who will be teaching at some point in the program are invited to come and preach to the cohort. The courses I have taught have occurred in the second and third years of the program.

Turning to the letter of Ephesians itself, the presence in verse one of the little Greek word *oun* ("therefore") naturally raises the question of how this passage fits within the larger context of the letter. What is the "therefore" there for? It's not even entirely clear how the passage itself fits together! Those who dare to closely examine the Greek find themselves confronted with an exegetical train wreck. For starters, verses eleven to sixteen are actually only one elaborate, elongated sentence. Then there is the utilization of unusual, perhaps even Gnostic, vocabulary.[2] There is, what appears on the surface to be, a misquoting of the Old Testament (Eph 4:8; cf. Ps 68:18). Metaphors from the realms of anatomy, construction, and marriage are mixed together with seemingly reckless abandon and major interpretive disagreements in the history of biblical interpretation are found throughout. You know you're in for it when a leading New Testament scholar commenting on one of the verses writes, "In the original language the diction and syntax of this verse are 'rather incomprehensible.'"[3] When all of these various pieces were spread out in front of me, I found myself confronted with a rather formidable puzzle. How does it all fit or hold together?

Our passage from the letter to the Ephesians challenges us to reformulate the question. Rather than asking, How does it all hold together?, it suggests to us that the better question is, In whom does it all hold together? This question is thrust upon us by the hymn-like pronouncement standing at the center of our passage. "There is one body and one Spirit, just as you were called to one hope when you were called; one Lord, one faith, one baptism; one God and Father of all, who is over all and through all and in all" (Eph 4:4–6). The sevenfold repetition of the adjective "one" in these three verses and the tripartite structure of the confession have led many scholars to conclude that Paul, at this point, is drawing upon an early Christian creed.[4] The contents of this creed-like confession stand at the heart of the Christian faith. If this confession is true, as Christians of all times and places have affirmed, then there are definite implications for preaching. If everything holds together in the one—the one God of Israel: the Father who has sent his Son in the power of the Holy Spirit; the Son who has taken on flesh and has triumphed over death and ascended to the right hand of the Father pouring out his Spirit upon all flesh; the Holy Spirit who builds up the body of the Lord Jesus Christ unto the glory of the Father—then we as preachers do not need to be hermeneutical heroes, bravely bridging the gap between an ancient text and our present day communities. If what Paul is

2. Yoder Neufeld, *Ephesians*, 26.

3. Schlier, *Epheser*, 208, quoted in Barth, *Ephesians* 4–6.

4. Stott, *Ephesians*, 150; Yoder Neufeld, *Ephesians*, 173.

saying is true, the gap has already been bridged by the risen Lord who is continually present to his church in the power of the Holy Spirit. The same God who led the Israelites out of Egypt, the same Lord who walked the dusty streets of Galilee calling disciples to follow him, the same Spirit who was building a temple out of the living stones of the believers in Ephesus, continues to be at work in the midst of his people. This means that it is not up to us as preachers to make everything fit together. Rather, we are simply called to discover the connections that already exist between the text and our lives, between the church in Ephesus and our congregations in Toronto, between what has already occurred and what is yet to come, because everything holds together in the one God.

He is the one who speaks. He is the one who calls. On the basis of this reality, Paul is able to address the Ephesians at the beginning of our passage by saying, "As a prisoner for the Lord, then, I urge you to live a life worthy of the calling you have received" (4:1). It is from the Latin translation of the word "calling"—*vocatio*—that we get our English word vocation. In contemporary English, vocation is frequently equated with one's career or occupation. For example, you might hear someone say, "I am an architect by vocation," or "she really found her calling when she went into nursing." From a Christian perspective these are somewhat confused uses of the words "vocation" and "calling."[5] Now our professions certainly are one field or forum in which we live out our calling as Christians, but they cannot simply be equated with our calling in and of itself. In the New Testament the word "calling" or "vocation" never appears in the plural.[6] There are not multiple callings or vocations, but rather only one calling that is shared by all Christians. There is one calling, because there is "one Lord, one faith, one baptism." Picking up on the prevalent themes of Ephesians, we could describe our vocation by saying that we are "called to be church."[7] In using the word *church*, I am not talking about institutions and organizations that offer a variety of goods and services to omnivorous religious consumers. Nor am I speaking of a group of individuals who decide to come together on account of their agreement on a set of propositions. Rather, what I have in mind in using the word *church*, following the lead of the apostle Paul, is a gathered community—a people, whose life together demonstrates the triumph of the love of Christ over all the forces and powers which seek to divide, denigrate, and destroy.

5. For a discussion of "vocation" and "calling" with an eye toward the context of Ephesians, see Barth, *Broken Wall*, 211–14.

6. Barth, *Ephesians*, 454.

7. Robinson and Wall, *Called to Be Church.*

This is why Paul was so concerned that the Ephesians make every effort within their power to "keep the unity of the Spirit through the bond of peace" (4:3). The key to maintaining this unity is found in the development and exercise of particular virtues and ways of relating to one another. Paul describes these as humility, gentleness, patience, and bearing with one another in love (Eph 4:2). These attributes would hardly have been considered praiseworthy in the ancient Greco-Roman world. In fact, humility was looked upon by cultured Hellenists as being the despised character trait of slaves.[8] I would suggest that humility, gentleness, patience and bearing others in love are equally as foreign in our present day culture. If you have any doubts about this, then I think there is a good chance that you've never driven a car in Toronto![9] Although the virtues Paul describes are counter-cultural, the apostle did not simply pull them out of a hat. Rather, it appears that he has heeded the voice of the one who came preaching peace, saying, "Take my yoke upon you and learn from me, for I am gentle and humble in heart, and you will find rest for your souls" (Matt 11:29). The apostle Paul can call Christians to bear one another in love, for they are a people who have been called and claimed by the one who has borne their sins upon the cross. In urging the Ephesians to walk with all humility and gentleness, with patience, bearing one another in love, Paul is not simply pushing some abstract set of moral principles; rather, he is calling the body to be conformed to the image of its head, the Lord Jesus Christ.

This Pauline theme of conformation to Christ features prominently in the writings of the German pastor and theologian Dietrich Bonhoeffer. Bonhoeffer writes, "*The church is the place where Jesus Christ's taking form is proclaimed and where it happens.*"[10] Bonhoeffer did recognize that in speaking like this there was the danger that he could be misunderstood as advocating some type of human-driven moral self-improvement program. So in the closing pages of his well-known book *Discipleship* he wrote:

> To be conformed to the image of Jesus Christ is not an ideal
> of realizing some kind of similarity with Christ which we are
> asked to attain. It is not we who change ourselves into the image
> of God. Rather, it is the very image of God, the form of Christ,
> which seeks to take shape within us. It is Christ's own form
> which seeks to manifest itself in us. Christ does not cease work-
> ing in us until he has changed us into Christ's own image. Our

---

8. Stott, *Ephesians*, 148; Yoder Neufeld, *Ephesians*, 172.

9. Toronto perennially ranks among the most congested cities in North America and boasts some of the longest commute times among major cities in the world.

10. Bonhoeffer, *Ethics*, 102 [italics original].

goal is to be shaped into the entire *form* of the *incarnate*, the *crucified*, and the *transfigured one*.[11]

Bonhoeffer's comments resonate with the logic of the apostle Paul in our passage. We have been called by Christ and the call of Christ renders us responsible. However, being responsible is never a matter of being left to our own devices. Christ forever remains the Lord over his church. The church remains the field of Christ's life-giving reign and activity. The body lives only in and from the head.

This is particularly evident in verse seven, which reads, "But to each one of us grace has been given as Christ apportioned it." Following this verse, Paul goes on to refer to Psalm 68, a psalm which celebrates the eschatological triumph of God over all of his enemies. The psalm presents images of a great victory parade which includes both the exhibition of the defeated powers and rulers and the corresponding celebration of God's people. The fact that Paul takes this psalm describing the triumph of the God of Israel and makes Jesus the subject of the ascent and the distribution of gifts says something important about Paul's understanding of the identity of Jesus Christ. The christological implications are further reinforced by Paul's gloss on the passage which follows. Here Paul writes, "He who descended is the same one who ascended far above all the heavens, so that he might fill all things" (4:10, NRSV). Every good Jew would have known that there is only one who fills all things.[12] God himself had said as much through his prophet Jeremiah: "'Who can hide in secret places so that I cannot see them?' declares the LORD. 'Do not I fill heaven and earth?' declares the LORD" (23:24). The implications of the claim that Christ fills all things are now plainly apparent; if the one who has given his life for us is one with the God of Israel, then there can be no thwarting his plans, purposes, and provision for his church.[13] The fact that Christ is ascended far above all the heavens, above all things, means that in each and every circumstance Christ gives his church every good gift that they need to be faithful to their calling.

Our passage goes on to describe one particular type of gift that Christ gives to his church. The list in verse eleven is not nearly as well known as the more familiar lists of spiritual gifts found in 1 Corinthians 12 and Romans 12. In those passages Paul appears to be describing special Spirit-given talents and abilities, but here in Ephesians the gift that Christ gives to

11. Bonhoeffer, *Discipleship*, 284–85.

12. Gerhard Delling, "πληρόω," in Kittel and Freidrich, *Theological Dictionary of the New Testament*, 6:288–90.

13. Gerhard Delling, "πληρόω" in Kittel and Freidrich, *Theological Dictionary of the New Testament*, 291–92.

his church is people. More specifically, Christ gives to his church apostles, prophets, evangelists, and teaching pastors or shepherding teachers. The absence of the definite article before the word *didaskolos* ("teacher") when all of the other items in the list are preceded by definite articles suggests that what Paul has in mind with the words shepherd and teacher is one office.[14] This exegetical insight is of particular importance for this group. Presumably many of you are or will be pastors, which means that in a certain sense you are a gift that God has given to the church. Now it's important that you understand this in the right way. I'm sure we've all met pastors who think and act like they are God's gift to the church. Maybe even some of them are your colleagues! Please note, to be a pastor is to be a servant of the Word. Notice that all of the offices listed in verse eleven are speaking roles. Apostles, prophets, evangelists, and shepherding teachers all share in the commonality of being servants of the Word.[15]

The church is built up through the ministry of the Word which is the proclamation of the Gospel. There is an interesting contrast between the apostles, prophets, evangelists and teaching shepherds in verse eleven who are charged with equipping or training the body and the proponents of false doctrine in verse fourteen, who, through trickery and cunning, seek to lead the young in faith astray.[16] Those charged with equipping the saints must rely on the efficacy of the Word alone. The schemers, however, have at their disposal, if we translate the Greek quite literally, "the methods of deception." This tension between Word and methods leads to one of the fundamental decisions that each and every pastor must face. The question is whether I, in my ministry as a pastor, will rely upon the Word of God to equip the saints for the work of ministry so that the body of Christ may be built up or whether I will make recourse to the plethora of methods and church growth strategies which are so readily available both online and upon the shelves of every Christian bookstore. Now the problem is not that the methods and church growth strategies don't work. In fact, many of them appear to work all too well. The problem is that it's not at all clear that what they grow is, in fact, church.

This choice between reliance upon the Word or resorting to methods is a choice that every thoughtful pastor and reflective congregation will face. Of course, many churches and pastors will simply be unthinkingly dragged along in the current of the latest fashions and fads. This is what Paul feared might happen to the Ephesians and why he warned them that they must

14. Barth, *Ephesians*, 438.
15. Yoder Neufeld, *Ephesians*, 179.
16. Barth, *Ephesians*, 443.

grow up or else risk being tossed about by the waves like a ship during a storm at sea or being blown over like a toddler in a strong wind.[17] I can particularly relate to the latter image because I have a two year old daughter who whenever she is hit by a gust of wind cries out, "It's windy out! Pick up me!" There is an additional layer of complexity to the church's situation, for although my daughter has the wherewithal to recognize that she is in danger of being blown over, in some situations a congregation might not even have the capacity to recognize that it is being carried along by the prevailing winds of the times. This is why, if I may put a plug in for my own discipline, the practice of theology is so important. It is through the practice of theology that the church is enabled to test its life and its proclamation against the testimony of Scripture. A congregation or a pastor that neglects or despises theology will sooner or later be swept away by the raging tides and swirling winds of false doctrine. The practice of theology is essential to the life of the church, if it is to indeed grow up in every way into him who is the head.

The growth and maturation of the body is intimately connected with the work of the apostles, prophets, evangelists, and teaching shepherds who have been commissioned "to equip the saints for the work of ministry, for building up the body of Christ" (Eph 4:12, NRSV). Once again we face another crucial exegetical decision. This time we have to decide where the commas go. Some older translations of the Bible inserted two commas into the sentence with the result that the work of ministry and the building up of the body became the sole responsibility of a clerical elite. Against this breaking up of the sentence it seems better to read "for building up the body of Christ" as a dependent clause.[18] In other words it is the task of pastors to equip the members of the congregation for the work of ministry, so that through the ministry of each and every member the body of Christ may be built up. This means that although there might only be a single pastor in a congregation, every member is a minister. Not only does this fit well with our democratic sensibilities—which can sometimes actually lead us astray—but it is also more in keeping with what Paul says at the end of this passage about the body building itself up in love as each part does its work.

When properly understood, Paul's conception of the church as the body of Christ is one of the most terrifying thoughts emerging from the pages of Scripture, because it means there is no escaping the fact that we are all in this together. Paul's comments about the body of Christ, both here in Ephesians and in his other letters, place before us the inconvenient truth

17. Yoder Neufeld, *Ephesians*, 186.

18. I am in agreement here with the exegetical conclusions of Barth, *Ephesians*, 477–84; Stott, *Ephesians*, 166–68; and Yoder Neufeld, *Ephesians*, 181–83.

that our salvation is bound up with the weird and wonderful, sometimes inspiring, other times outright infuriating, group of people called church. As much as this grates against our modern individualistic sensibilities, it is a reality that cannot be avoided if we are committed to engaging with the Scriptures with any level of integrity; for the corporate nature of salvation is found not only in Paul, but throughout the pages of both the Old and New Testaments.

My undergraduate degree in kinesiology has helped me to appreciate what Paul says about the corporate and corporeal reality of the church. Through my hours in the anatomy lab and days in the athletic trainers' room I came to an understanding of the intricate interconnectedness of the human body. For example, if one leg is as little as a quarter of an inch shorter than the other it can cause a chain reaction of consequences that run throughout the entire body. For starters, the discrepancy in length between the two legs will cause the pelvis to tilt. This rotation of the pelvis will then create additional tension on the iliotibial band on the side of the longer leg and additional pressure on the knee joint of the shorter leg. But it doesn't end with the lower body. Because the pelvis is tilted, the spine must curve in order to allow the person to hold their head upright. The result is the distinctive "S"-shaped curve of the spine known as scoliosis. Here we see how one malfunctioning part can throw the entire body out of whack and gain a better sense of why Paul was so concerned about each part working properly.

Paul understood that if we are to move toward spiritual maturity and fulfilling our calling as witnesses of the new humanity created through Christ's death and resurrection, it will only happen as each member of the body plays its part and as each person exercises his or her own unique gifts for the benefit of the whole. There are no insignificant members of the church. There are no redundant parts in Christ's body. Each and every person has an essential role to play from the very old to the very young, in either age or faith. In practice we deny this reality, on the one hand, by sequestering the young in age and faith by treating them as religious consumers without responsibilities who must be continually entertained and, on the other, by putting the elderly out to pasture in places where they are out of sight and out of mind. These senseless amputations are crippling our churches.

Addressing these issues will strengthen the church, but it will not lead to the development of a church with an Arnold Schwarzenegger-like physique. Like Jacob following his wrestling match with the angel of the LORD, the church will always walk with a limp (Gen 32:22–32). This fragility is a gift and attempts to find the perfect body are actually idolatrous. From my kinesiology background, I know that the bodies which appear to be the strongest are actually often the weakest. Professional body builders, for instance, are at their weakest on the day of competition, because in order to achieve the lean, "cut" look so coveted by the judges they must both starve and dehydrate themselves. Ironically the hulking physical specimens on display on the stage are hardly functional bodies at all. On the other hand, from my pastoral and theological background I know that the weakest appearing bodies are often actually the strongest, for they have nothing else to rely on than the grace and provision of God.

So the church must continue to limp joyfully on its way in the power of the Holy Spirit, "until we all reach unity in the faith and in the knowledge of the Son of God and become mature, attaining to the whole measure of the fullness of Christ" (Eph 4:13). The word "until" signals to us that there is no retirement from ministry. The walking does not end until we reach our goal, or perhaps, better stated, until the goal reaches us. The New Testament commentator Markus Barth has helpfully highlighted this dimension of the church's pilgrimage in his translation of verse thirteen.[19] Barth notes that the phrase translated "until we all reach" in the NIV was also sometimes used in the Ancient Near East to speak of festive processions and therefore could be translated as "until we all come to meet." There were at least two particular types of festive processions that Paul would have been familiar with. One was the ritual of a village going out to welcome an approaching king or important dignitary. We catch a glimpse of this tradition in the accounts in the Gospels of Jesus' triumphal entry into Jerusalem. The other festive procession that Paul would have known about was the custom of the bridal party going out to welcome the approaching bridegroom on the day of a wedding. Either image would be appropriate in our context in Ephesians. This interpretation is further supported by the second clause of the verse which the NIV translates as "become mature," but is quite literally translated as "the perfect man." The image, then, would be that of the church joyfully marching forward into the future on the way to meet its Lord, who in turn is on his way to meet his church.[20] You'll have to decide among yourselves in your Ephesians class whether you think Barth is exegetically convincing at this point. However, this image of Christ the King coming to meet his pilgrim people, or the bridegroom coming to join with the bride for the wedding banquet, is not a bad one to have before our eyes as the Christian year comes to an end this weekend with Christ the King Sunday and as we enter into the season of Advent in the weeks that follow. What a gift it is to

19. Barth, *Ephesians*, 485–86.
20. Ibid., 484–96.

know that as the church goes limping on its way, in humility and gentleness, with patience, building one another up in love, Christ the King is on his way to meet us. What grace it is to be assured that the body of Christ will ultimately reach its goal and come to full maturity when it stands face to face with its living head. Even now the bridegroom calls out to his bride, saying, "Yes, I am coming soon" (Rev 22:20). As his advent draws near, may we, filled with the one hope of our calling, add our voices to the great chorus of the saints who cry out in unity, "Maranatha! Come, Lord Jesus, come!"

24

Producing Professional Pastors

Tyndale Seminary In-Ministry Program Chapel

Toronto, Ontario

Wednesday, February 19, 2014

Ephesians 1:15–23; 2 Kings 6:8–23

I n the final volume of his compelling series of "conversations" in spiritual theology, entitled *Practice Resurrection*, Eugene Peterson recounts the story of how his friends Robert and Anne set out in search of Mount Monadnock.[1] Robert and Anne had lived in New England for many years. On countless occasions they had driven through an intersection where there stood a sign directing travelers to Mount Monadnock. Robert was familiar with the name of the mountain from a poem by Emerson, but over the course of all the years they had passed through, they had never followed the sign to the mountain. One day, after passing by the sign, on an impulse Robert turned to Anne and said, "Isn't it about time we saw this famous mountain for ourselves?" He returned to the intersection and turned onto the road. For miles and miles, they drove. They passed many signs inscribed with the name of Monadnock, yet a glimpse of the mountain was not forthcoming. Finally, they pulled over to consult their map and turned back. Their return-trip has been encapsulated in the final words of a poem Robert wrote while reflecting upon the entire experience:

> we look—trees, a flash of clearing, purple rock—
>
> but we are, it seems, too close to see it:
>
> It is here. We are on it. It is under us.[2]

1. Peterson, *Practice Resurrection*, 84–85.
2. Siegel, "Looking for Mt. Monadnock," in *Waters Under the Earth*, 70, quoted in

The poem stands as a fitting introduction to our passage from the letter to the Ephesians. In the verses leading up to our passage, Paul has described the Mount Monadnock-reality upon which the Ephesians stand. They have been inscribed into the story of the God of Israel, immersed within the deep reality of the workings and ways of the triune God. The seven strong verbs of the opening verses of Ephesians illuminate the darkened terrain like volleys bursting from a Roman candle into the evening sky. God blessed. God chose. God destined. God bestowed. God lavished. God made known. God gathers up.[3] Paul then transitions from blessing God to interceding for his friends in Ephesus. He prays that the great work of salvation that God has worked for them—quite apart from them—would also be worked within them. Paul prays that the Ephesians would be able to more fully appropriate the reality of the gift that is already theirs in Christ Jesus. In a sense, his desire is that they would exchange their *Roots* sweaters and mittens, along with their spot on the couch in front of the TV, for a stick and a helmet and their rightful place on the ice at Sochi.[4] Please note, Paul is not praying that the Ephesians would receive a second blessing, as if in some way what God had accomplished for them in Christ was somehow deficient or incomplete. Rather Paul is praying that they would come to an awareness of the oceans of grace in which they are, in fact, swimming.

From the content of Paul's prayer we see that, for this to occur, what is required is nothing less than the sanctification of the imagination. This sanctification of the imagination is not simply the equivalent of a spring cleaning of the mind, but is more along the lines of a major home renovation. Powerful pneumatic tools are needed for the type of demolition and reconstruction that Paul has in view. There are load-bearing walls that must come down: our modern tendency to look upon the world as a closed causal system; our extreme anthropocentrism and egocentricity; our infatuation with autonomy; our attempts to compartmentalize and divide up life, times, places, and people; and our conceptions of what it means to be a success and to lead a good life. All of these walls must come down. The structures of our imaginations must first be pneumatically razed and only then rebuilt by the Spirit upon the foundation which is Christ.

This emphasis upon the renovation of the imagination seems to be a recurring theme in Paul's letters. He intercedes for the Colossians asking

---

Peterson, *Practice Resurrection*, 84–85.

3. Peterson shapes his discussion of Ephesians 1:3–14 around these seven "verbal rockets" (*Practice Resurrection*, 56–67).

4. This sermon was preached while the 2014 Winter Olympics from Sochi were underway. *Roots* was the official outfitter of the Canadian Olympic team. The Olympic ice hockey tournament, in particular, always seems to capture the attention of Canadians.

that God would fill them "with the knowledge of his will through all the wisdom and understanding that the Spirit gives" (1:9). For the Philippians, he prays that their "love may abound more and more in knowledge and depth of insight" (1:9). He instructs the Romans, at the great turning point of his magisterial letter with the words, "Do not conform to the pattern of this world, but be transformed by the renewing of your mind" (12:2). And, of course, later in the letter to the Ephesians, Paul prays that the Ephesians "may have power, together with all the Lord's holy people, to grasp how wide and long and high and deep is the love of Christ, and to know this love that surpasses knowledge—that you may be filled to the measure of all the fullness of God" (3:18–19). Like his desire for all the congregations he has planted and plans to visit, Paul desires that the Ephesians would be immersed in the transformative truth of God so that they are freed to inhabit the real world. That is, the world that is constituted by the effusive, energetic presence of the power of God which raised Jesus Christ from the dead and seated him at the right hand of the Father in the heavenly realms.

Paul rightly recognizes that the ability to see and inhabit the world in light of the resurrection requires the continuing illumination of the Holy Spirit. Hence, Paul prays for the Ephesians that the eyes of their hearts may be enlightened. This expression can cause us some confusion, as our understanding of the human person differs somewhat from the anthropology of the biblical authors. For example, consider the commercial high-holiday that fell on this past Friday—Valentine's Day. The heart is synonymous with Valentine's Day. In the days leading up to and including Valentine's Day, hearts have been ubiquitous. Children exchange heart-shaped Valentines. Hallmark plasters hearts all over the covers of their greeting cards. Images of hearts are festooned upon lingerie and boxer-shorts, and chocolates and cinnamon candies are molded into forms that we are meant to interpret as hearts. Although there are perhaps slightly different nuances connected to the heart in each of these contexts, it is clear that the heart is associated with feelings of affection and strong emotional attachment. However, in biblical anthropology the seat of strong emotion is not so much the heart, as it is the bowels.[5] (That being said, I've yet to find a Valentine's Day card that says, "You move my bowels!") In biblical thought, the heart represents the whole inward self, encompassing not only the emotions, but also the will and the intellect.[6] This is apparent in our passage this afternoon, where we see that

5. Helmut Köster, "σπλάγχνον, σπλαγχνίζομαι, εὔσπλαγχνος, πολύσπλαγχνος, ἄσπλαγχνος," in Kittel and Freidrich, *Theological Dictionary of the New Testament*, 7:548–59.

6. Johannes Behm, "καρδία, καρδιογνώστης, σκληροκαρδία," in *Theological Dictionary of the New Testament*, Kittel and Freidrich, 3:605–14.

the enlightening of the eyes of the heart is connected with knowing the hope to which God has called his people. For hope, as one biblical commentator has rightly observed, is not an "evanescent emotion," but a steadfast "conviction founded upon God's fidelity."[7]

It is God's fidelity, the faithfulness he has demonstrated in raising Jesus Christ from the dead, that constitutes the real world. It is for this reason that Paul is intensely concerned with cultivating what could be called "bifocal vision" among the Christians in Ephesus.[8] A recent popular representation of this type of bifocal vision can be observed in Guillermo Del Torro's 2006 Academy Award-nominated film *Pan's Labyrinth*. The movie, set in the time of the Spanish civil war, begins as a young fairy-tale-loving girl, named Ofelia, and her pregnant mother make their way to their new home in the country. When they are forced to pull over on account of her mother's nausea, Ofelia discovers a gargoyle-like statue on the roadside that is missing an eye. Ofelia quickly discovers the missing eye and returns it to its place. Having done so, she immediately encounters a gangly insect, which she soon discerns to be a fairy. The fairy introduces her to a magical domain filled with incredible creatures that remain invisible to the adults who surround her. As the story progresses the "fantasy" world and the "real" world increasingly come in contact and overlap with one another, but only Ofelia has the "bifocal vision" necessary to see their intersection.

In a similar way, Paul is interested in cultivating a type of "bifocal vision" within the congregation in Ephesus. He desperately wants his people to recognize that they find themselves on the front lines of an apocalyptic battle, locked in a life-and-death struggle with cosmic forces and powers that have a very real impact on the life of people in this world. Speaking in contemporary terms we might attempt to translate these things with such terms as the Market, the State, the Mall, the Man, or racism, sexism, consumerism, or fashion, sport, and technology.[9] Though these cosmic powers throw hapless human beings to and fro, the good news of the Gospel is that Christ has triumphed over them. He has been enthroned above them all, at the right hand of God in the heavenly places, far above all rule and authority

---

7. Fowl, *Ephesians*, 58.

8. The term "bifocal vision" was coined by the New Testament scholar J. Louis Martyn to describe Paul's understanding of the new way of seeing that is brought into existence through the epistemological crisis occasioned by the apocalyptic advent of Jesus Christ in the midst of the passing evil age. Martyn, *Theological Issues*, 89–110, 279–97.

9. William Stringfellow attempts to transpose the language of "principalities and powers" into contemporary language by providing an evocative and extensive litany in *Ethic for Christians*, 78.

and power and dominion, and above every name that is named, not only in this age, but also in the age to come. However much these anti-God forces rage and conspire against God's anointed, they will not prevail.

This, however, is by no means obvious. Nor is it available to immediate empirical verification. Globally speaking, the twentieth century witnessed unprecedented levels of Christian persecution. It has been estimated that half of all Christian martyrs were killed in the twentieth century alone. This trend, which shows little sign of abating in the twenty-first century, led Pope John Paul II to observe that we live in "a new age of martyrs."[10] Redirecting our gaze to our more immediate context in Canada, we see that where churches are not being cut down by the sword, they are largely succumbing to irrelevancy—ironically, often as the result of a long history of attempting to be culturally relevant. The eyes of our hearts must be enlightened if we are, through the haze of Christian persecution and ecclesial apostasy, to catch a glimpse of Jesus Christ risen from the dead and seated at the right hand of the Father, far above all rule and authority and power and dominion (Eph 1:20–21).

We need "bifocal vision" like that given to Elisha the prophet, who, when surrounded by the horses and chariots of the King of Aram, boldly proclaimed, "Don't be afraid. Those who are with us are more than those who are with them" (2 Kings 6:16). Or like John the elder, who, while languishing in exile on the island of Patmos suffering under the weight of the imperial gauntlet, was allowed to peer into the true nature of things and beheld the slain Lamb upon the throne (Rev 5). When the eyes of our hearts are enlightened we are able to peer through the surface level of things in the recognition that in God's economy those "who bear crosses are working with the grain of the universe."[11] Such Spirit-enabled vision also allows us to see that the theologically illiterate, morally inept, prayerfully incompetent, pastorally exasperating, rag-tag group of nobodies assembled on a Sunday morning and entrusted to our care *is* the body of Christ—the fullness of him who fills everything in every way. This is crucial for pastors and other Christian leaders, for apart from the recognition that this community called church is taken up within the operations of the Trinity, you will inevitably be driven to either distraction or downright despair.[12]

Returning to our text, Paul's prayer is that a Spirit-enabled vision would be cultivated among God's people that would allow them to recognize that

10. Dolan, "Address to the USCCB General Assembly."

11. Yoder, "Armaments and Eschatology," 58.

12. The phrase "operations of the Trinity" is frequently employed by Eugene Peterson in his five volume spiritual theology. See, for example, *Practice Resurrection*, 47.

all of reality has been taken up in the Son unto the glory of God the Father. Notice though, that Paul isn't just hoping that the Spirit would "zap" the Ephesians in a transcendent moment of otherworldly illumination. Paul prays that the Spirit would help the Ephesians to see things as they truly are, but he shares the words of his prayer with them, so that those words may become a tool in the hands of the Spirit in forming their imagination. Paul recognizes that although the Spirit blows where it pleases, the Spirit doesn't act ethereally. Word and Spirit go together. The Word travels on the breath of the Spirit and the sword of the Spirit is the Word. Just as in the beginning God created the heavens and the earth through his Word and Spirit, Paul hopes that a new world will be fashioned in the life of the community at Ephesus as the Holy Spirit uses the words of his letter to attune the community's attention to the presence of the Living Word.

The theological ethicist Stanley Hauerwas was a central figure in my doctoral dissertation. Hauerwas likes to say that "you can only act in the world that you can see, but you must be taught to see by learning to say."[13] In making such a claim, Hauerwas is drawing upon the work of, among others, the philosophers Ludwig Wittgenstein and Iris Murdoch. But long before Hauerwas made his claim, or even before Wittgenstein or Murdoch set pen to paper, the apostle Paul seemed to have recognized this reality. In fact, I think we could say that the entire letter to the Ephesians is a type of extended exercise in speech training. For it is only through learning to properly describe reality with the apostle Paul that the Ephesians are freed to faithfully inhabit the world as it truly is. In a similar way, you can look upon your time here in the In-Ministry program at Tyndale as an extended program of speech therapy. If you'd prefer a slightly different metaphor, you could think of it as an apprenticeship in the art of using words. This is particularly relevant to the work that we will be doing together in systematic theology. Theology, according to the delightful definition of John Howard Yoder, is nothing other than "working with words in the light of faith."[14] There is a good chance that the type of word work that you are doing here with your cohort will end up making you highly dysfunctional in your various life and ministry contexts. In fact, if history is any guide, some of you may discover this long before you walk across the stage at commencement to receive your diploma. In a Canadian church that has largely been operating under the presumption that God is absent from the scene and has therefore based its expectations for pastoral leaders around the models of high-powered business executives and reassuring therapeutic counsellors,

13. Hauerwas, *Hauerwas Reader*, 611.
14. Yoder, *Preface to Theology*, 41.

leaders whose language has been tempered in the furnace of the Gospel are going to have difficulty being understood. Don't get me wrong, our goal, as your professors, teachers, and mentors is to make you good professional pastors and Christian leaders, if, of course, you remember that at the root of the word professional is the verb "to profess." Pastors are to be professionals, in that they are called to profess Christ crucified and risen, and to bring all of their life and ministry into alignment with that profession. Our work as your teachers is about giving you the linguistic tools you need to both recognize the reality of the world in Jesus Christ and to evaluate your ministry in the light of the Gospel. For it is our hope that over your time here with us, you will be formed to be good professionals, those who in the power of the Holy Spirit profess Christ crucified and risen, unto the glory of God the Father. All of pastoral ministry is rooted in this profession, which also means that pastoral ministry is, at its heart, word-work. It may seem rather underwhelming to think that the only thing you'll take with you when you leave this place in two or three years is a fancy piece of paper and a Gospel-shaped facility with words, but please remember that when it comes to the works and ways of God, words do, in fact, make the world. The Holy Spirit delights to use the profession of men and women like yourselves to bring his children into the light of the new day that has dawned in the resurrection of Christ.

In the third year seminar course, we will study the lives of six twentieth century Christian leaders whose formation in the language of prayer and the Scriptures prepared them to lead lives of bold "professional" service in the name of the triune God. One of these figures, the South African bishop Desmond Tutu, found himself thrust by the Spirit into the role of pastor to a nation. For close to twenty years, Tutu stood as the most consistent and outspoken critic of the oppressive system of racial discrimination which plagued South Africa, known as apartheid. One of the reasons that Tutu's voice was so distinctive was that the ruling regime ruthlessly eliminated many of the dissenting voices through imprisonment, as in the case of Nelson Mandela who spent twenty-seven years under lock and key. In other cases, the ruling powers simply made their opponents disappear without a trace. However, due to the historic respect that South Africans held for the church, the regime was unwilling to take action against the outspoken bishop. Tutu recognized that the struggle of black Africans was not against the whites, but rather against a horrendous system of oppression that dehumanized both victim and victimizer alike. He recognized that the only weapons that could be employed in such a spiritual struggle were the weapons of the Spirit: prayer, proclamation, and perseverance. On one occasion, a political protest was cancelled by the government, so Tutu assembled the people in St. George's Cathedral in Cape Town and held a service of worship.[15] As the people joined together in prayer and praise, hundreds of police officers amassed around the outside of the Cathedral. Some of the police officers even made their way into the Cathedral and lined the walls, frantically writing down everything that the Archbishop was doing and saying. At one point, the little bishop in his long flowing robes turned and, pointing at the police officers lining the walls of the sanctuary, proclaimed, "You are powerful. You are very powerful, but you are not gods and I serve a God who cannot be mocked." Then he flashed a broad smile and said, "So, since you've already lost, I invite you today to come and join the winning side!" These are the words and actions of one whose imagination has been captured by the profession of the apostles, that in the death and resurrection of Jesus Christ, we have witnessed the beginning of the end. In being so captured, Tutu has himself become a true professional.

So let us thank God that he raises up professionals for his church like Bishop Tutu, Eugene Peterson, Stanley Hauerwas, John of Patmos, Elisha the prophet, the apostle Paul, and men and women like yourselves. For without those who boldly profess the name of Jesus Christ, we would be like travelers in search of Mount Monandnock. Without pastors who are true professionals, we would stand in perennial danger of remaining oblivious to the gloriously thick presence of the one in whom we live and move and have our being. Thank God, he never leaves his church without faithful witnesses whose eloquence is utilized by the Holy Spirit to enlighten the eyes of our hearts so that we may perceive the firm, Mount Monadnock-like foundation on which we stand. "It is here. We are on it. It is under us."[16] Thanks be to God!

15. I cannot recall where I first heard this story, but a similar recounting of the incident is found in Wallis, *God's Politics*, 347–48.

16. Siegel, "Looking for Mt. Monadnock," in *Waters Under the Earth*, 70.

Works Cited

Aquinas, Thomas. *Summa Theologica*. Translated by Fathers of the English Dominican Province. Claremont: Coyote Canyon, 2010. Kindle.

Arndt, W.F. *The Gospel According to St. Luke*. St. Louis: Concordia, 1956.

Assayas, Michka. *Bono: In Conversation with Michka Assayas*. New York: Riverhead, 2005.

Associated Press. "Shooter's Wife Thanks Amish Community." *Washington Post*. Saturday, October 14, 2004. http://www.washingtonpost.com/wp-dyn/content/article/2006/10/14/AR2006101400510.html.

Augustine. *Confessions*. Translated by F.J. Sheed. New York: Sheed & Ward, 1943.

———. *Expositions on the Book of Psalms*. Vol. 8 of *The Nicene and Post-Nicene Fathers*, ed. Philip Schaff. 1886–1889. Reprint, Grand Rapids: Eerdmans, 1989.

Bailey, Kenneth E. *The Cross and the Prodigal: The 15th Chapter of Luke, Seen Through the Eyes of Middle Eastern Peasants*. St. Louis: Concordia, 1973.

———. *Poet and Peasant*. Grand Rapids: Eerdmans, 1976.

Barth, Karl. *Church Dogmatics*. Edited by Geoffrey W. Bromiley and T.F. Torrance. 4 vols. London: T & T Clark, 2004.

———. *Fragments Grave and Gay*. Translated by Eric Mosbacher. London: Collins, 1971.

———. *The Humanity of God*. Translated by Thomas Wieser. Richmond: John Knox, 1966.

———. *The Word of God and the Word of Man*. Translated by Douglas Horton. New York: Harper & Row, 1957.

Barth, Markus. *The Broken Wall: A Study of the Epistle to the Ephesians*. Vancouver: Regent College, 2002.

———. *Ephesians 4–6*. Anchor Bible 34A. Garden City: Doubleday, 1974.

Barth, Markus and Helmut Blanke. *Colossians*. Translated by Astrid B. Beck. Anchor Bible 34B. New York: Doubleday, 1994.

Bede. *Commentary on the Acts of the Apostles*. Cistercian Studies. Kalamazoo: Cistercian, 1973.

Benedict XVI. *Jesus of Nazareth: The Infancy Narratives*. New York: Image, 2012.

Bethge, Eberhard. *Dietrich Bonhoeffer: Theologian, Christian, Man for his Times*. Rev. ed. Revised and edited by Victoria J. Barnett. Minneapolis: Fortress, 2000.

Betz, Hans Dieter. *Galatians*. Hermeneia. Philadelphia: Fortress, 1979.

Blaising, Craig A. and Carmen S. Hardin, eds. *Psalms 1–50*. Vol. 7 of *Ancient Christian Commentary on Scripture*. Downers Grove: InterVarsity, 2008.

Bondy, Filip. "British Runner is a Hero Even without a Medal." *New York Times.* August 5, 1992. http://www.nytimes.com/1992/08/05/sports/barcelona-track-field-british-runner-is-a-hero-even-without-a-medal.html.

Bonhoeffer, Dietrich. *Berlin: 1932–1933.* Edited by Larry L. Rasmussen. Translated by Isabel Best and David Higgins. Vol. 12 of *Dietrich Bonhoeffer Works.* Minneapolis: Fortress, 2009.

———. *Christ the Center.* Translated by Edwin H. Robertson. San Francisco: HarperSanFrancisco, 1978.

———. *Discipleship.* Edited by Geffrey B. Kelly and John D. Godsey. Translated by Barbara Green and Reinhard Krauss. Vol. 4 of *Dietrich Bonhoeffer Works.* Minneapolis: Fortress, 2001.

———. *Ethics.* Edited by Clifford J. Green. Translated by Reinhard Krauss et al. Vol. 6 of *Dietrich Bonhoeffer Works.* Minneapolis: Fortress, 2005.

———. *Letters and Papers from Prison.* Enl. ed. Edited by Eberhard Bethge. London: SCM, 1971.

———. *Letters and Papers from Prison.* Enl. ed. Edited by Eberhard Bethge. New York: Touchstone, 1997.

———. *Letters and Papers from Prison.* Edited by John W. de Gruchy. Translated by Isabel Best et al. Vol. 8 of *Dietrich Bonhoeffer Works.* Minneapolis: Fortress, 2009.

———. *Life Together and Prayerbook of the Bible.* Edited by Geffrey B. Kelly. Translated by Daniel W. Bloesch and James H. Burtness. Vol. 5 of *Dietrich Bonhoeffer Works.* Minneapolis: Fortress, 1996.

———. *London: 1933–1935.* Edited by Keith W. Clements. Translated by Isabel Best. Vol. 13 of *Dietrich Bonhoeffer Works.* Minneapolis: Fortress, 2007.

———. *Sanctorum Communio: A Theological Study of the Sociology of the Church.* Edited by Clifford J. Green. Translated by Reinhard Krauss and Nancy Lukens. Vol. 1 of *Dietrich Bonhoeffer Works.* Minneapolis: Fortress, 1998.

———. *Theological Education at Finkenwalde: 1935–1937.* Edited by H. Gaylon Barker and Mark S. Brocker. Translated by Douglas W. Stott. Vol. 14 of *Dietrich Bonhoeffer Works.* Minneapolis: Fortress, 2013.

———. *Theological Education Underground: 1937–1940.* Edited by Victoria J. Barnett. Translated by Victoria J. Barnett et al. Vol. 15 of *Dietrich Bonhoeffer Works.* Minneapolis: Fortress, 2012.

Brown, Raymond E. *An Adult Christ at Christmas: Essays on the Three Biblical Christmas Stories: Matthew 2 and Luke 2.* Collegeville: Liturgical, 1978.

———. *A Coming Christ in Advent: Essays on the Gospel Narratives Preparing for the Birth of Jesus: Matthew 1 and Luke 1.* Collegeville: Liturgical, 1988.

———. *A Crucified Christ in Holy Week: Essays on the Four Gospel Passion Narratives.* Collegeville: Liturgical, 1986.

———. *The Gospel According to John (XIII–XXI).* Anchor Bible 29A. Garden City: Doubleday, 1970.

———. *A Once-and-Coming Spirit at Pentecost.* Collegeville: Liturgical, 1994.

Brueggemann, Walter. *Awed to Heaven, Rooted in Earth: Prayers of Walter Brueggemann.* Edited by Edwin Searcy. Minneapolis: Fortress, 2003.

———. *Genesis.* Interpretation. Atlanta: John Knox, 1982.

Bushnell, Horace. *Building Eras in Religion.* Vol. 3 of *Literary Varieties.* 1881. Reprint, New York: Charles Scribner's Sons, 1910.

Calvin, John. *Institutes of the Christian Religion*. Translated by Ford Lewis Battles. 2 vols. Louisville: Westminster John Knox, 2006.

Canadian Press. "Canada's Jedi Knights Not as Much of a Religious Force." *CBC News*. May 8, 2013. http://www.cbc.ca/news/canada/canada-s-jedi-knights-not-as-much-of-a-religious-force-1.1321650.

Capon, Robert Farrar. *Kingdom, Grace, Judgement: Paradox, Outrage and Vindication in the Parables of Jesus*. Grand Rapids: Eerdmans, 2002.

Carlson, Kathryn Blaze. "Organized Religion on the Decline? Growing Number of Canadians 'Spiritual but not Religious.'" *National Post*. December 21, 2012. http://news.nationalpost.com/2012/12/21/organized-religion-on-the-decline-growing-number-of-canadians-spiritual-but-not-religious/.

Carson, D.A. *The Gospel According to John*. Pillar New Testament Commentary. Grand Rapids: Eerdmans, 1991.

Carter, Jimmy. *Public Papers of the Presidents of the United States, Jimmy Carter, 1979*. Best Books, 1980. https://books.google.ca/books?id=XljVAwAAQBAJ&dq=jimmy+carter+public+papers+1979&source=gbs_navlinks_s.

Catechism of the Catholic Church. http://www.vatican.va/archive/ccc_css/archive/catechism/p3s1c1a8.htm.

Chattaway, Peter T. "The Chronicles of Atheism." *Christianity Today* 51/12 (Dec. 2007) 36–39.

Childs, Brevard S. *The Book of Exodus: A Critical Theological Commentary*. Old Testament Library. Louisville: Westminster, 1976.

Church of England. "The Order for Morning Prayer." The Church of England. https://www.churchofengland.org/prayer-worship/worship/book-of-common-prayer/the-order-for-morning-prayer.aspx.

Clarkson BIA. "History of Clarkson." Clarkson BIA. http://www.clarksonbia.com/our-history/.

CNNGo staff. "World's 50 Best Foods." CNN International. July 21, 2011. http://travel.cnn.com/explorations/eat/worlds-50-most-delicious-foods-067535.

Coles, Robert. *Dorothy Day: A Radical Devotion*. Boston: Da Capo, 1987.

Craddock, Fred B. *As One Without Authority: Essays on Inductive Preaching*. Enid: Phillips, 1971.

Danker, Frederick William, ed. *A Greek-English Lexicon of the New Testament and Other Christian Literature*. 3d ed. Chicago: University of Chicago Press, 2000.

Demara, Bruce. "Trivago Guy to Get Much Needed Makeover." *Toronto Star*. August 19, 2014. http://www.thestar.com/life/2014/08/19/trivago_guy_to_get_much_needed_makeover.html.

Dickens, Charles. *A Tale of Two Cities*. London: Penguin, 2002.

Dolan, Cardinal Timothy. "Address to the USCCB General Assembly on November 11, 2013." United States Conference of Catholic Bishops. http://www.usccb.org/about/leadership/usccb-general-assembly/2013-november-meeting/farewell-presidential-address-cardinal-dolan.cfm.

Edwards, O.C., Jr. *A History of Preaching*. Nashville: Abingdon, 2004.

Elowsky, Joel C., ed. *John 11–21*. Vol. 4b of *Ancient Christian Commentary on Scripture*. Downers Grove: InterVarsity, 2007.

Emanuel African Methodist Episcopal Church. "'Mother Emanuel' A.M.E. Church History." Emanuel African Methodist Episcopal Church. http://www.emanuelamechurch.org/churchhistory.php.

Episcopal Church. *The Book of Common Prayer and Administration of the Sacraments and Other Rites and Ceremonies of the Church: Together with the Psalter or Psalms of David According to the Use of the Episcopal Church.* New York: Seabury Press, 1979.

Evans, Craig A. and Stanley E. Porter, eds. *Dictionary of New Testament Background.* Downers Grove: InterVarsity, 2000.

Fabricius, Kim. "Boycott Nativity Plays!" *Connexions: The Blog of Richard Hall, a Methodist Minister in Shropshire.* December 11, 2007. http://theconnexion.net/wp/?p=3239#axzz3OYwoOrMd.

Fee, Gordon D. *God's Empowering Presence: The Holy Spirit in the Letters of Paul.* Peabody: Hendrickson, 1994.

Fitzmyer, Joseph A. *The Gospel According to Luke I-IX.* Anchor Bible 28. New York: Doubleday, 1981.

Fleer, David and Dave Bland, eds. *Reclaiming the Imagination: The Exodus as Paradigmatic Narrative for Preaching.* St. Louis: Chalice, 2009.

Fowl, Stephen. *Ephesians: A Commentary.* New Testament Library. Louisville: Westminster John Knox, 2012.

Freedman, David Noel, ed. *The Anchor Bible Dictionary.* 6 vols. New York: Doubleday, 1992.

———. *Psalm 119: The Exaltation of Torah.* Biblical and Judaic Studies 6. Winona Lake: Eisenbrauns, 1999.

Gaebelein, Frank E., ed. *Matthew, Mark, Luke.* Vol. 8 of *Expositor's Bible Commentary.* Grand Rapids: Zondervan, 1984.

Gaventa, Beverly Roberts. *The Acts of the Apostles.* Abingdon New Testament Commentaries. Nashville: Abingdon, 2003.

Gillinov, Marc and Steven Nissen. *Heart 411: The Only Guide to Heart Health You'll Ever Need.* New York: Three Rivers, 2012.

Goldingay, John. *Psalms, Volume 3: Psalms 90-150.* Baker Commentary on the Old Testament Wisdom and Psalms. Grand Rapids: Baker Academic, 2008.

Gorman, Michael J. *Apostle of the Crucified Lord: A Theological Introduction to Paul and His Letters.* Grand Rapids: Eerdmans, 2003.

Green, Joel B. *The Gospel of Luke.* New International Commentary on the New Testament. Grand Rapids: Eerdmans, 1997.

Green, Joel B. et al., eds. *Dictionary of Jesus and the Gospels.* Downers Grove: InterVarsity, 1992.

Harter, Michael, SJ. *Hearts on Fire: Praying with Jesuits.* St. Louis: Institute of Jesuit Sources, 1993.

Hauerwas, Stanley. *Christian Existence Today: Essays on Church, World, and Living in Between.* 1988. Reprint, Grand Rapids: Brazos, 2001.

———. *Cross-Shattered Christ: Meditations on the Seven Last Words.* Grand Rapids: Brazos, 2004.

———. *A Cross-Shattered Church: Reclaiming the Theological Heart of Preaching.* Grand Rapids: Brazos, 2009.

———. *The Hauerwas Reader.* Edited by John Berkman and Michael Cartwright. Durham: Duke University Press, 2001.

———. *The Peaceable Kingdom: A Primer in Christian Ethics.* Notre Dame: University of Notre Dame Press, 1983.

————. *Performing the Faith: Bonhoeffer and the Practice of Nonviolence.* Grand Rapids: Brazos, 2004.

————. *Sanctify Them in the Truth: Holiness Exemplified.* Nashville: Abingdon, 1998.

————. *War and the American Difference: Theological Reflections on Violence and National Identity.* Grand Rapids: Baker Academic, 2011.

Hauerwas, Stanley and Romand Coles. *Christianity, Democracy, and the Radical Ordinary: Conversations between a Radical Democrat and a Christian.* Eugene: Cascade, 2008.

The Heidelberg Catechism: Four Hundredth Anniversary Edition, 1563–1963. Translated by Allen O. Miller and M. Eugene Osterhaven. Philadelphia: United Church, 1963.

Heifetz, Ronald A. *Leadership without Easy Answers.* Cambridge: Belknap, 1994.

Hiatt, Brian. "Hymns for the Future." *Rolling Stone.* March 19, 2009, 50–91. Accessed electronically through the Canadian Reference Centre.

Hooker, Morna D. *The Gospel According to St. Mark.* Black's New Testament Commentaries. 1981. Reprint, London: Continuum, 2001.

Hopper, Tristin. "Man Will Drink Just Beer—No Solid Food—for the 40 Days of Lent." *National Post.* March 25, 2014. http://news.nationalpost.com/2014/03/25/man-will-drink-just-beer-no-solid-food-for-the-40-days-of-lent/.

Horvitz, Leslie Alan and Christopher Catherwood. *Encyclopedia of War Crimes and Genocide.* New York: Infobase, 2009.

Humphrey, William. *The Ordways.* New York: Alfred Knopf, 1965.

Hunter, Marnie. "Does 'Trivago Guy' Need a Makeover?" CNN. August 18, 2014. http://www.cnn.com/2014/08/18/travel/trivago-guy-makeover/.

Izadi, Elahe. "The Powerful Words of Forgiveness Delivered to Dylann Roof by Victims' Relatives." *Washington Post.* June 19, 2015. https://www.washingtonpost.com/news/post-nation/wp/2015/06/19/hate-wont-win-the-powerful-words-delivered-to-dylann-roof-by-victims-relatives/.

Jeffrey, David Lyle. *Luke.* Brazos Theological Commentary on the Bible. Grand Rapids: Brazos, 2012.

Jersak, Brad and Michael Hardin, eds. *Stricken by God?: Nonviolent Identification and the Victory of Christ.* Grand Rapids: Eerdmans, 2007.

Kannengiesser, Charles, ed. *Early Christian Spirituality.* Translated by Pamela Bright. Sources of Early Christian Thought. Philadelphia: Fortress Press, 1986.

Keener, Craig S. *The Gospel of John: A Commentary.* 2 vols. Peabody: Hendrickson, 2003.

Kelsey, David H. *Eccentric Existence: A Theological Anthropology.* Louisville: Westminster John Knox, 2009.

Kenneson, Philip D. and James L. Street. *Selling Out the Church: The Dangers of Church Marketing.* Eugene: Cascade, 2003.

Kittel, Gerhard and Gerhard Freidrich, eds. *Theological Dictionary of the New Testament.* Translated by Geoffrey W. Bromiley. 10 vols. Grand Rapids: Eerdmans, 1964–1976.

Knox, John. *The Works of John Knox.* Edited by David Laing. 6 vols. New York: AMS, 1966.

Kraft, Charles H. *Culture, Communication, and Christianity: A Selection of Writings.* Pasadena: William Carey Library, 2001.

Krashinsky, Susan. "Trivago Spokesman to Undergo 'Celebrity' Makeover." *Globe and Mail.* August 28, 2014. http://www.theglobeandmail.com/report-on-business/

industry-news/marketing/trivago-spokesman-to-undergo-celebrity-makeover/article20262338/.

Kraybill, Donald B. et al. *Amish Grace: How Forgiveness Transcended Tragedy.* San Francisco: Jossey-Bass, 2007.

Lausanne Committee for World Evangelization. "Lausanne Occasional Paper 1—The Pasadena Consultation: Homogenous Unit Principle." 1978. http://www.lausanne.org/content/lop/lop-1.

Leopold, Todd. "'Trivago Guy' Gets a New Look." CNN. November 4, 2014. http://www.cnn.com/2014/11/04/travel/trivago-guy-new-look/index.html.

Lewis, C.S. *A Grief Observed.* New York: Bantam, 1976.

———. *Surprised by Joy: The Shape of My Early Life.* New York: Harcourt, 1955.

Lischer, Richard, ed. *The Company of Preachers: Wisdom on Preaching, Augustine to the Present.* Grand Rapids: Eerdmans, 2002.

Longenecker, Richard N., ed. *The Challenge of Jesus' Parables.* Grand Rapids: Eerdmans, 2000.

Longman, Tremper, III. *How to Read Exodus.* Downers Grove: IVP Academic, 2009.

Luther, Martin. *Career of the Reformer: I.* Edited by Harold J. Grimm. Vol. 31 of *Luther's Works.* Philadelphia: Fortress, 1957.

———. *The Christian in Society I.* Edited by James Atkinson. Vol. 44 of *Luther's Works.* Philadelphia: Fortress, 1966.

———. *D. Martin Luthers Werke: Kritische Gesamtausgabe.* 136 vols. Weimar: Hermann Böhlau, 1883–2009.

———. *Martin Luther's Basic Theological Writings.* Edited by Timothy F. Lull. Minneapolis: Fortress, 1989.

MacDonald, George. *Unspoken Sermons: Third Series.* Grand Rapids: Christian Classics Ethereal Library. Adobe PDF eBook.

Maček, Ivana. *Sarajevo Under Siege: Anthropology in Wartime.* Philadelphia: University of Pennsylvania Press, 2009.

Maclaren, Alexander. *Expositions of Holy Scripture: Luke.* Grand Rapids: Christian Classics Ethereal Library. Adobe PDF ebook.

Mangina, Joseph L. *Karl Barth: Theologian of Christian Witness.* Louisville: Westminster John Knox, 2004.

Marsh, Charles and John Perkins. *Welcoming Justice: God's Movement Toward Beloved Community.* Downers Grove: InterVarsity, 2009.

Martin, Francis and Evan Smith, eds. *Acts.* Vol. 5 of *Ancient Christian Commentary on Scripture.* Downers Grove: InterVarsity, 2006.

Martyn, J. Louis. *Galatians.* Anchor Bible 33A. New York: Doubleday, 1997.

———. *Theological Issues in the Letters of Paul.* Nashville: Abingdon, 1997.

Matera, Frank J. *II Corinthians: A Commentary.* New Testament Library. Louisville: Westminster John Knox, 2003.

———. *Passion Narratives and Gospel Theologies: Interpreting the Synoptics through Their Passion Stories.* 1986. Reprint, Eugene: Wipf and Stock, 2001.

McClendon, James Wm., Jr. *Biography as Theology: How Life Stories Can Remake Today's Theology.* 1974. Reprint, Eugene: Wipf & Stock, 2002.

McKnight, Scot. *A New Vision for Israel: The Teachings of Jesus in National Context.* Grand Rapids: Eerdmans, 1999.

Mieder, Wolfgang. *"Making a Way Out of No Way": Martin Luther King's Sermonic Proverbial Rhetoric.* New York: Peter Lang, 2010.

Milbank, John. *Being Reconciled: Ontology and Pardon*. London: Routledge, 2003.

Myers, Ched. *Binding the Strong Man: A Political Reading of Mark's Story of Jesus*. Maryknoll: Orbis, 1988.

Neuhaus, Richard John. *Death on a Friday Afternoon: Meditations on the Last Words of Jesus from the Cross*. New York: Basic, 2000.

Newbigin, Lesslie. *Foolishness to the Greeks: The Gospel and Western Culture*. Grand Rapids: Eerdmans, 1986.

———. *The Light Has Come: An Exposition of the Fourth Gospel*. Grand Rapids: Eerdmans, 1982.

Nouwen, Henri J.M. *Life of the Beloved: Spiritual Living in a Secular World*. New York: Crossroad, 1992.

———. *The Return of the Prodigal Son: A Story of Homecoming*. New York: Image, 1992.

Oberman, Heiko A. *Luther: Man between God and the Devil*. Translated by Eileen Walliser-Schwarzbart. New Haven: Yale University Press, 1989.

Pelikan, Jaroslav. *Acts*. Brazos Theological Commentary on the Bible. Grand Rapids: Brazos, 2005.

Perkins, John M. *Let Justice Roll Down: John Perkins Tells His Own Story*. Glendale: Regal, 1976.

———. "A Quiet Revolution." Lecture, Seattle Pacific University, Seattle, April 5, 1978. Audio recording accessed on iTunesU.

———. *With Justice for All: A Strategy for Community Development*. Rev. ed. Ventura: Regal, 2007.

Peterson, Eugene H. *A Long Obedience in the Same Direction: Discipleship in an Instant Society*. Downers Grove: InterVarsity, 1980.

———. *Practice Resurrection: A Conversation on Growing Up in Christ*. Grand Rapids: Eerdmans, 2010.

Propp, William H.C. *Exodus 1–18*. Anchor Bible 2. New York: Doubleday, 1999.

Purves, Andrew. *Reconstructing Pastoral Theology: A Christological Foundation*. Louisville: Westminster John Knox, 2004.

Ravitz, Jessica. "After Confederate Flag Comes Down, Charleston Church Starts New Chapter." CNN. July 22, 2015. http://www.cnn.com/2015/07/12/us/charleston-south-carolina-emanuel-ame-church-new-chapter/.

Robinson, Anthony B. and Robert W. Wall. *Called to Be Church: The Book of Acts for a New Day*. Grand Rapids: Eerdmans, 2006.

Rogers, Pat. *The Alexander Pope Encyclopedia*. Westport: Greenwood, 2004.

Ruth, John L. *Forgiveness: A Legacy of the West Nickel Mines Amish School*. Scottdale: Herald, 2007.

Rutledge, Fleming. "A Norman Rockwell Scene at the Door of Mother Emanuel AME Church, Only it's not Posed." *Generous Orthodoxy*. June 29, 2015. http://tips. generousorthodoxy.org/2015/06/a-little-girl-at-door-of-ame-church-in.html.

———. *The Undoing of Death: Sermons for Holy Week and Easter*. Grand Rapids: Eerdmans, 2002.

Scharen, Christian. *One Step Closer: Why U2 Matters to Those Seeking God*. Grand Rapids: Brazos, 2006.

Schlier, Heinrich. *Der Brief an die Epheser: ein Kommentar*. 2d ed. Düsseldorf: Patmos, 1958.

Seitz, Christopher B. *Colossians.* Brazos Theological Commentary on the Bible. Grand Rapids: Brazos, 2014.

Senior, Donald. *Matthew.* Abingdon New Testament Commentaries. Nashville: Abingdon, 1998.

Shakespeare, William. *Hamlet.* Edited by Shane Weller. New York: Dover Publications, 1992.

Shepherd, Victor. *Our Evangelical Faith.* Toronto: Clements, 2006.

Siegel, Robert. *The Waters Under the Earth.* Moscow, ID: Canon Press, 2003.

Spurgeon, Charles Haddon. *Spurgeon's Sermons.* 1871. Reprint, Grand Rapids: Christian Classics Ethereal Library. Adobe PDF ebook.

Stone, Daniel. "NEWSWEEK Poll: Americans' Religious Beliefs." *Newsweek.* June 4, 2009. http://www.newsweek.com/newsweek-poll-americans-religious-beliefs-77349.

Stott, John R.W. *The Message of Acts: The Spirit, the Church and the World.* Bible Speaks Today. Downers Grove: InterVarsity, 1990.

———. *The Message of Ephesians: God's New Society.* Bible Speaks Today. Downers Grove: InterVarsity, 1979.

Stringfellow, William. *An Ethic for Christians and Other Aliens in a Strange Land.* Eugene: Wipf & Stock, 2004.

Swanson, Ana. "What the Aftermath of the Charleston Shooting Looked Like Through the Eyes of a Little Girl." *Washington Post.* June 26, 2015. https://www.washingtonpost.com/news/wonk/wp/2015/06/26/what-the-charleston-shootings-looked-like-through-the-eyes-of-a-4-year-old-girl-from-the-bronx/.

Vanier, Jean. *Becoming Human.* Toronto: Anansi, 1998.

———. *Drawn into the Mystery of Jesus through the Gospel of John.* Ottawa: Novalis, 2004.

Volf, Miroslav. *Free of Charge: Giving and Forgiving in a Culture Stripped of Grace.* Grand Rapids: Zondervan, 2005.

Wallis, Jim. *God's Politics: Why the Right Gets It Wrong and the Left Doesn't Get It.* San Francisco: HarperSanFrancisco, 2005.

Waltke, Bruce K. with Cathi J. Fredricks. *Genesis: A Commentary.* Grand Rapids: Zondervan, 2001.

Webber, Robert E., ed. *The Services of the Christian Year.* Vol. 5 of *The Complete Library of Christian Worship.* Peabody: Hendrickson, 1993.

———. *Worship is a Verb: Eight Principles for Transforming Worship.* 2d ed. Peabody: Hendrickson, 1996.

Weiser, Artur. *The Psalms.* Philadelphia: Westminster, 1962.

Wells, Samuel. *Improvisation: The Drama of Christian Ethics.* Grand Rapids: Brazos, 2004.

———. *Power and Passion: Six Characters in Search of Resurrection.* Grand Rapids: Zondervan, 2007.

Willimon, William H. *Acts.* Interpretation. Atlanta: John Knox, 1988.

Witherington, Ben, III. *The Acts of the Apostles: A Socio-Rhetorical Commentary.* Grand Rapids: Eerdmans, 1998.

———. *Conflict and Community in Corinth: A Socio-Rhetorical Commentary on 1 and 2 Corinthians.* Grand Rapids: Eerdmans, 1995.

———. *The Gospel of Mark: A Socio-Rhetorical Commentary.* Grand Rapids: Eerdmans, 2001.

Wood, Ralph C. "God's Repentance-Enabling Forgiveness." *Christian Reflection* (Sept. 2001) 64–70.

———. *Preaching and Professing: Sermons by a Teacher Seeking to Proclaim the Gospel.* Grand Rapids: Eerdmans, 2009.

Wright, Tom. *John for Everyone, Part Two: Chapters 11–21.* Louisville: Westminster John Knox, 2004.

Yoder, John Howard. "Armaments and Eschatology." *Studies in Christian Ethics* 1/1 (1988) 43–61.

———. *Body Politics: Five Practices of the Christian Community Before the Watching World.* Scottdale: Herald, 2001.

———. *Preface to Theology: Christology and Theological Method.* Grand Rapids: Brazos Press, 2002.

Yoder Neufeld, Thomas R., *Ephesians.* Believers Church Bible Commentary. Scottdale: Herald, 2002.

Young, Frances and David F. Ford. *Meaning and Truth in 2 Corinthians.* London: SPCK, 1987.

CPSIA information can be obtained
at www.ICGtesting.com
Printed in the USA
LVOW10s2330020318
568565LV00006B/37/P